Advance Praise for

The Lion's Roar of a Yogi-Poet

"*The Lion's Roar of a Yogi-Poet* includes Khenpo Migmar Tseten's discourse on *The Great Song of Experience* by Jetsun Rinpoche Dragpa Gyaltsen alongside a complete translation of the doha as well as *The Praise to Jetsun Rinpoche* by Sakya Pandita. Jetsun Rinpoche shares his experiences of view, meditation, conduct, and result with their deviations to help yogis practice more holy Dharma and abandon the eight worldly dharmas. Khenpo elucidates Jetsun Rinpoche's yogic teachings and practices for contemporary practitioners."
—His Eminence Thartse Kunga Rinpoche

"*The Great Song of Experience* is delivered straight from the heart of the great Sakya forebear Jetsun Drakpa Gyaltsen. Expressing his innermost, inexpressible experience in a loud and clear manner with striking and courageous words, it is like a fearless lion's roar. Being a poet, the author sings his song in beautiful expressions that touch the heart. Being a yogi, his words are not only poetically refined but transmit mind's ultimate reality—the Buddha within. Thus, this masterpiece of timeless wisdom, skillfully enhanced by Khenpo Migmar Tseten's contemporary commentary, is a treasure to be kept close to every practitioner's heart."
—Karl Brunnhölzl, author and translator, *Sounds of Innate Freedom: The Indian Texts of Mahāmudrā*

The Lion's Roar of a Yogi-Poet

The Great Song of Experience of Jetsun Dragpa Gyaltsen

༄། །ཉམས་དབྱངས་ཆེན་མོ་བཞུགས། །

Discourse by

Khenpo Migmar Tseten

Wisdom

Wisdom Publications
132 Perry Street
New York, NY 10014 USA
wisdomexperience.org

Library of Congress Cataloging-in-Publication Data
Names: Tseten, Migmar, author. |
Grags-pa-rgyal-mtshan, 1147–1216. Nyams dbyangs chen mo bzhugs so. English. |
Grags-pa-rgyal-mtshan, 1147–1216. Nyams dbyangs chen mo bzhugs so.
Title: The lion's roar of a yogi-poet: the Great Song of Jetsun Dragpa Gyaltsen / discourse by Khenpo Migmar Tseten.
Other titles: Nyams dbyangs chen mo bzhugs so
Description: First edition. | New York: Wisdom Publications, 2024. | Includes index.
Identifiers: LCCN 2023052479 (print) | LCCN 2023052480 (ebook) |
ISBN 9781614298960 (paperback) | ISBN 9781614299097 (ebook)
Subjects: LCSH: Spiritual life—Buddhism. |
Grags-pa-rgyal-mtshan, 1147–1216. Nyams dbyangs chen mo bzhugs so. |
Didactic poetry, Tibetan. | Sa-skya-pa (Sect)—Doctrines.
Classification: LCC BQ5640 .T74 2024 (print) | LCC BQ5640 (ebook) |
DDC 294.3/44—dc23/eng/20240109
LC record available at https://lccn.loc.gov/2023052479
LC ebook record available at https://lccn.loc.gov/2023052480

ISBN 978-1-61429-896-0 ebook ISBN 978-1-61429-909-7

28 27 26 25 24
5 4 3 2 1

Cover design by Marc Whitaker. Interior design by James D. Skatges.

Printed on acid-free paper that meets the guidelines for permanence and durability of the Production Guidelines for Book Longevity of the Council on Library Resources.

Printed in Canada.

The merit of this book is dedicated to the long lives of
H. H. the Dalai Lama and H. H. the Sakya Trichen.

Contents

འབྲེལ་བའི་སྒྲོ་ནས་མི་བསྟོད་དེ།
བཀའ་དྲིན་སྒྲོ་ནས་ཅེས་མ་བསྟོད།
གལ་ཏེ་ཕྱོགས་སུ་ལྷུང་ཉིད་ན།
བསྟོད་པར་གྱུར་ཀྱང་སྨད་པའི་གནས།

དུ་བས་མེ་བཞིན་རྣམ་ཐར་ལས།
ནང་གི་ཡོན་ཏན་ལེགས་བརྟགས་ཏེ།
གྲགས་པ་རྒྱལ་མཚན་ལ་བསྟོད་པ།
འདི་འདྲ་ཁོ་ནས་བསྟོད་ལགས་གྲང།

I am praising [Jetsun Dragpa Gyalsten] neither because we
are related
nor because of his kindness;
if there is bias,
even praising can become degrading.

Like inferring fire from smoke,
this praise to Dragpa Gyaltsen
is praise composed solely by
investigating (his) inner qualities as found in his
hagiography.

—Sakya Pandita, *Praise to Jetsun Rinpoche Dragpa Gyaltsen*

Preface

These discourses on Jetsun Rinpoche Dragpa Gyaltsen's *Great Song of Experience* (*Nyams dbyangs chen mo*) were given over the course of several months by Khenpo Migmar Tseten at the Sakya Institute in Cambridge, Massachusetts. The classes were then transcribed and adapted to book form.

In the interest of making this work widely available to fellow yogis, and to preserve the spontaneous nature of these teachings, we have chosen to leave the transcriptions much as they were. For this reason, the book remains conversational and informal in nature.

It is our hope that the following pages offer a window into the awakened state of a highly realized meditation master, and that the profound words of this song inspire you in your own practice. May all sentient beings everywhere experience peace.

Introduction

Jetsun Rinpoche roars like a lion, warning practitioners to abandon the eight worldly dharmas[1] and practice the purer holy Dharma; he warns us that practitioners can become more worldly, sectarian, biased, and intellectual by identifying themselves with the different schools of philosophy, or any group or tradition.

Jetsun Rinpoche Dragpa Gyaltsen (1147–1216), the third of the three lay patriarchs of the Sakya tradition of Tibetan Buddhism, was born in the fire rabbit year to Sachen Kunga Nyingpo and Jomo Machik Ödrön. As a young child Jetsun Rinpoche delighted in solitude, was free from mundane desires, was diligent in practicing virtuous qualities, and was free from childish conduct.

His principal gurus were his father, Sachen, and his elder brother, Master Sönam Tsemo. He received many teachings of the Tripitaka—the Vinaya, Abhidharma, and Sutra, or the "three baskets" of the Buddhist canon—and the four classes of tantras from numerous Tibetan, Indian, and Nepalese masters, such as Nyen Tsuktor Gyalpo, Shang Tsultrim Drak, Nyak Wanggyal, Jayasena, the translator Palchok Dangpo Dorjé, and the yogi Avadhutipa.

Jetsun Rinpoche was never separate from the *samadhi* of the two stages of generation and completion, even in the midst of his daily

---

1. The eight worldly dharmas (Skt. *aṣṭalokadharma*; Tib. *'jig rten chos brgyad*) are traditionally presented as a set of four pairs: pleasure-pain, gain-loss, praise-blame, and esteem-contempt.

activities. When he went to give teachings, for instance, he meditated on Hevajra, and when he settled on his throne, he concluded his practice up to the seal of the lord of his buddha family. The general offerings he made represented the daily torma offerings of post-generation and completion practice. The Dharma teaching he did substituted for the mantra repetitions. And when he left to return to his residence, he meditated on Chakrasamvara. In one twenty-four-hour day, Jetsun Rinpoche meditated on seventy different deity mandalas.

Jetsun Rinpoche began teaching at eleven years of age, and after his father passed away, he taught Chandragomin's *Twenty Verses on the Bodhisattva Vows* and the extensive Hevajra sadhana, to the astonishment of all.

Jetsun Rinpoche Dragpa Gyaltsen was fully conversant in all aspects of Buddhist learning as well as outer sciences like medicine and grammar, but for the most part his writings focused on the Vajrayana systems he received from his father and other teachers. These writings consist of commentaries on tantras, sadhanas, and initiation rituals from the Hevajra system and the Chakrasamavara system, including Vajrayogini. He was also a highly skilled physician, composing the medical compendium called *The Royal Treasure of Healing Analysis*,[2] which Tibetan physicians still consult in the modern era.

Through explanation, debate, and composition, Jetsun Rinpoche spread Buddhism, and in particular, he liberated many fortunate beings through the *lamdre*, or path and result, and other tantric teachings. In this way, Jetsun Rinpoche benefited limitless sentient beings throughout his seventy years. He passed away in the fire rat year.

His main students were his nephews Sakya Pandita and Zangtsa. Further, he had eight disciples to whom he bestowed the last name "Dragpa" and four disciples who held the teaching of Vajrapanjara. He had four great vidyadhara[3] disciples, as well as many others.

2. *Gso dpyad rgyal po'i dkor mdzod*.

3. The Tibetan, *rigdzin* (རིག་པ་འཛིན་པ, *rig pa 'dzin pa*), means "holder of rigpa."

I have chosen to give discourse on Jetsun Rinpoche Dragpa Gyaltsen's *Great Song of Experience* because it covers the view, meditation, conduct, and result based on the complete teachings and practices of Buddha's three trainings of wisdom, discipline, and meditation. All the Buddha's sutras and tantras are included in these three trainings. The trainings of wisdom are related to the view, the trainings of meditation are related to the meditation practice, and the trainings of discipline are related to the conduct. The result, buddhahood, is achieved with the perfection of the view, conduct, and meditation through those trainings.

When Rinpoche says, "If there is no proliferation, that is the view," he refers to all of our philosophical studies of Vaibhashika,[4] Sautrantika,[5] Chittamatra,[6] and Madhyamaka[7] in the trainings of wisdom. While we are establishing the right view at the base, if the conclusions of the different philosophical schools fall into any extremes, they may become part of the proliferation—then, we do not have the right view.

When Rinpoche says, "If there is no distraction, that is meditation," he refers to all of our meditation practices of *shamatha*, or concentration; *vipashyana*, or insight; *tonglen*, or giving and taking; *bodhichitta*; and daily *sadhana* practices of tantra, including Mahamudra and Dzogchen.[8] While we are establishing the right meditation at the base, if those meditations have any distractions, then we do not have the right meditation.

When Rinpoche says, "If activity is abandoned, that is conduct," he refers to all of our vows of Hinayana, Mahayana, and Vajrayana

4. Vaibhashika (*bye brag smra ba*) is a Buddhist Abhidharma tradition, a subgroup of the larger Sarvastivadin school.

5. Sautrantika (*mdo sde pa*) is also a Sarvastivadin philosophical school; however, it's distinct from the Vaibhashika in its rejection of Abhidharma.

6. Chittamatra (*sems tsam*) is the Buddhist philosophical tradition emphasizing the ultimate reality of mind.

7. Madhyamaka (*dbu ma*) is the Buddhist philosophical tradition emphasizing the freedom from extremes.

8. Dzogchen, or Atiyoga, is the highest teaching of the Nyingma school of Tibetan Buddhism.

disciplines. While we are establishing the right conduct at the base, if activities opposite to those conducts are not abandoned, then we do not have the right conduct.

When Rinpoche says, "If mind itself is comprehended, that is the result," he refers to realizing the nature of the mind. While we are establishing buddhahood, if the nature of the mind is not comprehended, then we do not have the right result.

After establishing the view, meditation, conduct, and result at the base and in the middle, the yogi practices view, meditation, and conduct focusing on the result—buddhahood. The yogi uses the view as the guide of the mind to examine if their mind has the existence or nonexistence of permanence and annihilation. The yogi uses the meditation as the path of the mind to examine if their mind has the existence or nonexistence of distraction. The yogi uses the conduct as the friend of the mind to examine if their mind has existence or nonexistence of misconduct. The yogi uses the result as the host of the mind to examine if their mind has the existence or nonexistence of the ability to endure hardships with patience without reacting to hope and fear.

Ultimately, at the result level, the yogi's perfect view is blissful and amazing because, as Rinpoche tells us, biased opinions do not exist. Perfect meditation is blissful and amazing because sluggishness and agitation do not exist. Perfect conduct is blissful and amazing because acceptance and rejection do not exist. Perfect result is blissful and amazing because hope and fear do not exist.

Acknowledgments

I wanted to acknowledge the following for their help, without which I would not be able to bring out this book:

His Eminence Thartse Kunga Rinpoche
David Talamas
Dr. Raga Markely
Malcolm Smith

Heidi Kaiter
Judith Wright
Meg Hutchinson
Olivia Smith
Kevan Gale
Tenzin Tharchin
Sonam Choedon
Pasang Lhamo
Tenzin Nankey
Tenzin Dadon
James Wilton, Ropes & Gray LLP
Professor Klaus-Dieter Mathes
Karl Brunnhölzl
Laura Cunningham
Chris Hiebert
Daniel Aitken
Ben Gleason
And others from Wisdom Publications

I

Homage

Namo gurubhadraya.

THIS OPENING LINE INDICATES that Jetsun Rinpoche is a great Vajrayana practitioner. Rinpoche is paying homage to *gurubhadraya*, the "excellent guru"—who, in Vajrayana Buddhism, is considered even more important than the Buddha.

Within Buddhism we have three main traditions: Theravada, Mahayana, and Vajrayana (or Tantrayana). In Theravada and Mahayana, the teacher is referred to as a guide or "spiritual friend," but the term "guru" is not used. But in Vajrayana practice, the guru is extremely important. Without a guru, we cannot receive any initiations or instructions. Without a guru, we cannot be connected to an unbroken lineage of teachers. Without a guru, we cannot receive transmission of the most sacred mantras and practices. In order to access the transformative tantric essence of the Buddha's teachings, we must be connected with an authentic guru. That is why in Vajrayana practice we have four objects of refuge—we take refuge in the Guru, Buddha, Dharma, and Sangha.

In Vajrayana empowerment rituals, the guru introduces you to the true nature of your own mind, to your buddha nature. Through receiving empowerment, you are introduced to the Buddha's body, speech, and mind, and you become qualified to practice a particular kind of deity meditation, called a *sadhana*. For example, if you receive a Vajrayogini empowerment and instruction, you will then become qualified to practice the Vajrayogini sadhana, including eleven yogas. Without transmission and instruction from a guru, it would not be beneficial to practice a sadhana. That is why these teachings have remained closely guarded through the centuries. There is even a danger that the tantric teachings will be grossly misunderstood; without the empowerment and guidance of a qualified guru, they can even be harmful.

To the gurus and personal deities residing inseparably,
who join all qualities to the mindstream,

The guru is like a spiritual parent who helps us to be born into our spiritual lives. They join us to the lineage of the Buddha. In the beginning, we rely on the *relative guru*, our Buddhist tantric teacher. Early in our preliminary practices, we may think of the Guru, Buddha, Dharma, and Sangha in a dualistic way—as *external* refuge objects. But after initiation and extensive practice, the guru becomes the mirror in which we begin to recognize the ultimate nature of our own minds. Eventually, the dualism begins to dissolve: we see the ultimate Guru, Buddha, Dharma, and Sangha *within* us as the nature of our own mind.

It is through the guru's blessings, and through the initiation, instruction, and sadhana practice, that all of these positive qualities are cultivated in the mind. In this way we "join all qualities to the mindstream." If we have a very strong karmic connection with our guru, we may even glimpse the true nature of our mind instantaneously upon meeting them. We can read many biographies of disciples who see their guru and immediately realize clarity in their minds. If there is a strong karmic connection, the disciple can awaken to their true nature in this lifetime very quickly.

I prostrate with pure body, speech, and mind;

In the beginning, doing prostrations can be very physically, verbally, and mentally challenging— especially if we do not understand the practice. Many Western students say that when they first try prostrations, they feel very uncomfortable; they feel that they are being too submissive, especially when bowing to a Buddhist teacher. The ego can feel very rebellious!

Prostrating can be especially hard in a culture where individualism is valued and where asserting the ego is associated with confidence and success. Due to this societal conditioning, it is very challenging to show humility or to appear subservient. It can feel very frightening to let go of that ego; it may even feel life-threatening. We may feel that without ego we will not survive.

In Buddhism we learn to surrender that ego, to offer that ego to all the refuge objects. If we cannot loosen our grasp, then it will be very difficult to learn anything spiritually. The ego is excellent at collecting and storing knowledge—the ego excels in academia. But there is a risk that we may become so filled with information that there is no space to receive any blessings or spiritual realization.

When we are ego-driven, everything we consume only fuels the ego. With such an outlook, we are never satiated; we are always chasing greater knowledge. We may acquire so much information—but we use that to inflate the ego even more! We use our knowledge to publish papers, to impress our colleagues, or to improve our wealth and social status, but we do not make space for inner cultivation and growth.

For the Buddhist practitioner with correct motivation, all study and practice become antidotes to the ego. When Rinpoche says, "I prostrate with pure body, speech, and mind," these prostrations are arising from ultimate awareness, from the purity of his own inner buddha nature. It is only through surrendering our ego that we can offer true prostrations.

Some students may do a hundred thousand prostrations in their *ngöndro*[9] practice and become very proud of their accomplishment. If your prostrations are making your ego stronger and you are boasting of your progress to everyone, then you are not prostrating with correct motivation. On the other hand, with correct motivation and understanding, the practice will become very effective in purifying your ego.

Jetsun Rinpoche is doing prostrations "with pure body, speech, and mind," so he is doing a perfect prostration to the guru. It's interesting to note that his main guru was his own father, Sachen Kunga Nyingpo (1092–1158). Jetsun Rinpoche was also related to Sakya Pandita (1182–1251), who was the fourth founding Sakya master; Rinpoche was Sakya Pandita's uncle and served as his main guru.

The better we know someone, the harder it may be to view them as the guru. Family relationships can be especially challenging. There was a very famous Indian teacher who was renowned internationally. An interviewer once asked him, "You are so highly respected; how do your wife and children treat you?" The man said, "Oh, they don't think I'm special at all!"

Sakya Pandita was a great scholar; he knew Sanskrit from an early age, and he was an esteemed *pandita* who introduced the ten subjects of classical Indian learning in Tibet. However, when Jetsun Rinpoche became ill, Sakya Pandita cared for him throughout his illness with devotion, honoring him as a guru rather than a mere uncle, and it is said that from that point onward, Sakya Pandita's spiritual realization increased significantly.

The human mind is conditioned with all these habitual patterns and judgments. This individual conditioning and karma determine what kind of value we place on any object. Such judgments are all in our minds and not based on any ultimate reality. One person's treasure may be completely insignificant to someone else. The more value we place

9. Tib. *sngon 'gro*; a set of preliminary practices used to prepare and purify a practitioner for Vajrayana practice.

on something, the more power it has for us. If we have faith in a guru, that connection can be profoundly transformative.

The value we place on something can change dramatically. We see this in relationships, for instance, all the time. When someone is in love, they place so much value on their partner. But if the relationship falls apart, they may have so much aversion to that person they once loved. They may even say terrible things about that person. These changing attitudes and emotions impact the value we place on everything in our lives.

Vajrayana empowerment rituals may seem very strange and illogical to us at first. We may ask, "How can an initiation practice change how we view the guru, and how we view ourselves? What is the purpose of seeing ourselves and the guru in the form of buddhas or deities? Why do we have to suddenly venerate a person who used to seem very ordinary to us?"

The purpose of these practices is to purify the mind and to alter our underlying attitudes. The purer our vision becomes, the more we will perceive the goodness and purity in the world around us. Changing ourselves is very uncomfortable, and we often resist it. It is much easier to project all our negative emotions onto those around us. But the more we transform ourselves, the more we will notice a change in how we perceive other people.

When we project value onto a spiritual object, it has so much power to transform us and to bestow blessings. When Jetsun Rinpoche prostrates "with pure body, speech, and mind," there is no longer any ego involved. He is doing prostrations out of ultimate wisdom. It is only when we give up the ego and pride that we can do a completely pure prostration with body, speech, and mind.

I make an offering free from both grasper and grasped;

In our ordinary lives we are always giving things to others. But if we are really honest with ourselves, have we truly given? Is our motivation pure? Are we actually expecting something in return? We often give with the expectation of receiving something. Maybe we want love, security, recognition, health, or acceptance. Maybe we give to feel good about ourselves. Or maybe we feel forced to give due to societal expectations.

In order to truly give a gift to someone, we must do so selflessly and without any expectations. Even when we make offerings to the Buddha, we may be expecting something in return. For instance, it is common to go to a temple and make shrine offerings when we are sick or frightened. Although we are offering gifts to the Buddha, we are still hoping for healing or blessings in return.

Even when we are giving charitable donations, we often choose causes or people that we are attached to in some way. There can be mixed emotions even when the cause we are supporting is very good. Maybe we are hoping to have our names listed as donors. Maybe we are hoping to receive praise from others for being charitable. Maybe we are invested in a certain outcome. We may be very generous but there is still some attachment involved. It's very hard to give selflessly.

From a spiritual perspective, there is more merit in making offerings to the Buddha than to a human being, even if we do so with some self-clinging and grasping. It can help to free us. It can help us to see that ultimately there is no gift, no giver, and no receiver. The Buddha doesn't need our shrine offerings! The Buddha doesn't need lights and incense and flowers! The more selflessly we give, the more transformative it will be. If we can give "free from both grasper and grasped," we are offering from a place of perfect compassion and wisdom.

We can see from these lines that Jetsun Rinpoche has a very high level of realization of wisdom based on understanding emptiness. When he makes an offering, the offering is not based on any object. There is no gift, no giver, and no receiver. He has realized the empty nature of all objects. This is the ultimate offering, the perfection of giving.

The highest form of offering arises from emptiness. That's why we recite the emptiness mantra first in our practice—to purify all of the offerings into emptiness. Out of that emptiness, we are then able to generate an offering free from both grasper and grasped. When something is free from the offerer, free from the receiver, and free from the offering itself, we are able to make a perfect offering through seeing the underlying empty nature of the offering, the offerer, and the receiver. It is with this purity that Jetsun Rinpoche is making an offering to his guru.

I offer praise with my mind, beyond the activity of speech, free from proliferation;

We are accustomed to offering ordinary praise in our lives. We are taught to compliment people, to be courteous, to say nice things. If we work in the hospitality industry or in marketing, we are trained to be extremely polite and flattering to people even if they are rude. Salespeople are very nice when they are promoting their products, but they are complimentary in order to gain something for themselves or for their company. Ordinary praise is complicated and there are often ulterior motives. When someone is praising you a lot, that's not always a good thing. They may want something from you. Their praise may have much more to do with their own ego and expectations.

Jetsun Rinpoche praises his guru with pure mind. He doesn't even need words. He praises his master without any mixed emotions or self-clinging. When we have that pure mind and our hearts are filled with faith, then that is the best praise we can offer to the guru and to the Buddha. Words are expressions of proliferation of our ordinary concepts in the impure mind.

I make a confession untouched by the sins of the three times;

Jetsun Rinpoche's confession is also arising from a pure mind. With such a mind, even actions that appear to be immoral are not considered sin (*dikpa*; *sdig pa*). With a pure mind, even if you walk on an insect and kill it, it is not considered killing because you are not acting out of anger, desire, or ignorance.

If we read stories about the lives of the eighty-four mahasiddhas, the great Indian tantric masters, we can see that they did many things that appear immoral to us. Some mahasiddhas went fishing. Some mahasiddhas, like Virupa, are described as drinking alcohol. But was Virupa actually intoxicated? Were the mahasiddhas actually killing fish? This can seem very paradoxical, but from a pure mind, these actions have different significance.

If your mind has realized emptiness, and if you have that perfect wisdom and compassion, then even actions that appear immoral are not necessarily sinful. On the other hand, if we are not at Rinpoche's level of realization, we sin today, make a confession tomorrow, and then sin again the next day! Why are we trapped in that cycle? It is because we haven't realized that pure mind yet. We are still motivated by the negative emotions of desire, anger, and ignorance. We are still caught in addictive patterns. We repeat these negative cycles again and again. But when we have that pure mind, then we can even cut through dualistic thinking.

The actions of the mahasiddhas may seem very erratic and strange to us. There is a term, "crazy wisdom," that refers to this type of behavior. We can think of it almost like they are magicians; the mahasiddhas can create many illusions. Virupa may spend all night drinking, yet he may never become intoxicated. Great teachers may do very unusual things to cut through the dualistic thinking of their students.

I go for refuge without an object, free from fear;

We begin our Buddhist practice by taking refuge in the outer objects of the guru, Buddha, Dharma, and Sangha. We often seek refuge due to our own suffering, or fear, or loneliness. We may go for refuge because we want help, we want protection, we want peace. We are like frightened children who turn to God or to the Buddha for comfort.

However, in order to completely free ourselves, we have to become independent. The only way to become independent is to dissolve those refuge objects into light in our minds. With that dissolution practice we can begin to realize that the refuge objects are no longer outer objects; they are the true nature of our own mind. Ultimately, there are no objects of refuge. The perfect refuge is when you realize that the true nature of the mind is the guru, the Buddha, the Dharma, and the

Sangha. In that independence, there is no longer any fear. That is the true refuge Jetsun Rinpoche is referring to.

I generate limitless *bodhichitta* without objects,

In the Mahayana and Vajrayana traditions, we generate *bodhichitta* by taking the bodhisattva vows. We vow to achieve buddhahood for the sake of all sentient beings. At the time we take these vows, they are merely an aspiration, a prayer or wish that we have generated in the mind. It is not enough to simply generate the aspiration, though. To achieve buddhahood, we need to cultivate bodhichitta through our spiritual practice.

Bodhichitta is cultivated through generating compassion and loving-kindness, and through practicing the six perfections. The six perfections, or *paramitas*, include the cultivation of generosity, discipline, patience, diligence, meditative concentration, and wisdom. As our loving-kindness and compassion become more extensive through our practice, we will want to help all sentient beings, even our enemies.

When we first take bodhisattva vows, the aspiration is not objectless. We have an ordinary mind generating the aspiration; we have the object of our aspiration, which is all sentient beings; and we also have a result, which is buddhahood. So this initial aspiration has a subject, an object, and an aspirational result.

There are two forms of relative bodhichitta: "wishing bodhichitta" and "entering bodhichitta." They are relative because they still have an object. If a practitioner has practiced and realized the six perfections, then there can be bodhichitta without an object—there can be *ultimate* bodhichitta.

the nature of which is the space-like *dharmata*;[10]

---

10. *Dharmata* (*chos nyid*) refers to the ultimate nature of dharmas, freedom from extremes.

The nature of ultimate bodhichitta is the union of wisdom and emptiness. Its nature is called *dharmata*, which is like space, the emptiness of all phenomena. When we have such a realization of wisdom and emptiness based on the practices of wishing and entering bodhichitta, then we will experience the ultimate bodhichitta. Ultimate bodhichitta is the realization of the true nature of our own minds and of other phenomena. We realize the truth of emptiness and we go beyond the dualism of subject and object. When Rinpoche says "limitless bodhichitta without objects," it refers to the wisdom of the ultimate bodhichitta that is free from all dualism.

I dedicate the root of virtue not gathered to enlightenment;

In that ultimate perfection, "the root of virtue not gathered" is dedicated to enlightenment. In that ultimate perfection, there is nothing to accumulate; there is no merit in the ultimate dedication, which is free from the three wheels of practitioner, practice, and objects. There is nothing to gather because, in that ultimate state, the accumulator and accumulation[11] have become one. Such dualisms have been transcended in the ultimate state. Therefore, the virtue that arises from emptiness cannot be gathered. It is this kind of perfect virtue—rooted in wisdom and emptiness—that Jetsun Rinpoche is dedicating to enlightenment.

Please accept this mandala of empty phenomena
and bestow blessings upon me, the fortunate one.

From an ordinary perspective, when we make a mandala offering in our practice, we have a subject, an object, and all of these ritual components that act as means. The universe is the object; we, the spiritual practitioners making that offering, are the subject; and we are using physical materials like rice or jewels as a means to represent those offerings. From an ultimate perspective, with the level of spiritual realization that

11. The accumulations of wisdom and merit.

Rinpoche has, it is possible to generate and offer a mandala with complete awareness of the empty nature of that offering. At that stage, there is no one making the offering and there are no physical ingredients—no jewels, no rice, no silver mandala set. We are not separate from the universe. There is no longer a subject nor an object. The ultimate mandala offering arises out of emptiness. It is with such an ultimate offering to the guru and to the deities that Rinpoche is requesting blessings.

In these initial lines, Rinpoche makes the ultimate prostration, offering, praise, confession, bodhichitta, dedication, and mandala offering right at the beginning of the *doha* in order to accumulate wisdom. These are also called *tathata mahamudra* offerings, which are beyond the perception of the three wheels of practitioner, practice, and objects.

2

View, Meditation, Conduct, and Result

When only the view is established,
it has been said by the buddhas
"All views of emptiness are a source of faults."
Therefore, the view cannot be viewed.

In order to have a philosophical view or belief system, there must be someone *doing* the viewing and reaching those conclusions. There needs to be a perceiver who is establishing that view. In Sanskrit, view is called *darshana*. Darshana often carries the sense of ordinary eyesight, but it can also mean "philosophical view." Rinpoche is reminding us what the buddhas have said: that all the philosophical conclusions of emptiness, due to their dualistic nature, are sources of faults.

Establishing a view means there is still a subject doing the viewing and an object to be viewed and established. Philosophical conclusions do not represent the experience of the awakened state. In the awakened state there is only wisdom and emptiness. There is nothing to discuss, no philosophical tenets to establish, no arguments to make, and nothing to conclude. Even by saying we have "realized a view," we are already falling into the extremes of dualism. All philosophical views are really only a *reference* to something. The *experience* of emptiness cannot be described; it cannot be "viewed" in the ultimate sense. That is what Rinpoche means when he says, "The view cannot be viewed."

Within Buddhism there are so many different philosophical schools. There are many scholarly debates, even regarding views on emptiness. However, without any direct spiritual realization, all of these discussions are merely mental exercises. Indeed, such debates and discussions often *increase* our grasping to ideas and mental concepts. Instead of helping to liberate us, we may become more and more attached to our own opinions and belief systems. That is why the Buddha said, "All views of emptiness are a source of faults."

Even if we have a very profound understanding, if we become attached to that understanding and think that it is the only correct view, then automatically it becomes a wrong view because of that attachment. We can think of all of the philosophical conclusions in Buddhism as a staircase that can help us to go beyond conceptual thinking. But if we become attached to the staircase, or if we say, "this step is the only correct step," then we will just be stuck talking about the staircase and we will never experience any wisdom or liberation.

For one with wisdom, there is no view;

For the meditator who has a perfection of wisdom (*prajna paramita*) free from the three wheels of view, viewer, and viewing, there is no need for a view at all. All of the mental concepts that have helped us to progress in our practice, all of the philosophical debates that have helped us train our minds, are no longer relevant. Once we have a direct realization of wisdom and emptiness, then we have gone beyond the view. We don't need the staircase anymore. That experience is within us, and there is no outer object, no mental construct, no longer any distinction between subject and object.

for one with sharp intelligence, it is beyond words;

We use words to refer to meaning, but for those who are highly intelligent with the perfection of wisdom, they can realize the meaning through direct experience without relying on language. As long as we are using words to describe spiritual experiences, then we are still not conveying the ultimate truth. Words are merely the expression of thoughts. The truth is beyond all concepts and beyond all words. It is indescribable. When the mind has gone beyond all mental constructs, we cannot express the truth of that wisdom with language.

for one with diligence, nothing is to be meditated on;

A highly realized yogi who has the perfection of diligence (*virya paramita*) no longer needs to be diligent in their practice; every moment is full of the awareness of emptiness. For those who have not yet realized that wisdom, there is still a need to rely on relative diligence in order to be disciplined in their daily meditation practices. At the relative level, there is still a need for effort. Effort and enthusiasm for practice are necessary when our diligence is not yet perfected.

For the ordinary practitioner, there are some days when we feel like doing spiritual practice, and there are other days when we may feel tired or lazy. As a result, we need diligence to encourage us to maintain our daily meditation. Diligence is the antidote to laziness and distraction. But for someone like Rinpoche, who has realized wisdom at that ultimate level, there is no longer any effort involved. They are living every moment with that ultimate awareness, without any laziness or distraction.

for one with faith, there is no cause and result;

Early in our spiritual practice it can be very challenging to maintain faith. Our faith may fluctuate and be easily shaken by outer circumstances. When our faith is shaky we can strengthen it by understanding how the law of karma works. We can reflect on how negative actions result in suffering. We can observe how good actions result in happiness. The more that we understand this law of cause and result, the more stable our faith will become.

Faith and karma are interdependent. Buddhist teachings say that cultivating faith in the law of karma is the best way to strengthen our faith. But someone who has the perfection of faith (*shraddha paramita*) always leads a spiritual life free from negative karma and eventually goes beyond karma.

for one with compassion, there are no sentient beings;

In ordinary life, we feel compassion *toward* something or someone. For example, we often feel compassion for a person or for an animal who is suffering. Compassion is cultivated by seeing the suffering of sentient beings. But the perfection of compassion (*karuna paramita*) that arises out of nondual wisdom can be objectless. When compassion is integrated with wisdom it is no longer simply a feeling—it has gone beyond emotion. In that ultimate experience of compassion there is no subject or object.

for the gatherer of the accumulations, there is no buddhahood.

As long as we are focused on accumulating merit and wisdom, then we are thinking of buddhahood as some kind of future goal or destination. We may think of our spiritual practice as a long checklist of things we need to do in order to arrive at buddhahood. It may be surprising to realize that buddhahood is already existing within us right now; it is merely being obscured by our negative karma and emotions. When we have the perfection of accumulations (*sambhara paramita*), we experience our innate buddhahood, which has always been there inside us. There is no need to search elsewhere for buddhahood.

Freedom from extremes is beyond knowledge, expressions, and objects;

All of our relative spiritual expressions and practices are susceptible to falling into one of the four extremes: existence, nonexistence, both, or neither. As we have been discussing, ultimate perfection of wisdom is actually beyond knowledge, beyond words, and beyond all objects. Ultimate wisdom is even beyond mind, so we cannot express it with any kind of mental formation.

Madhyamaka, Chittamatra, and so on
are expressions in words, proliferations.

Jetsun Rinpoche is pointing out again that all the philosophical conclusions about emptiness are ultimately sources of faults. They are merely proliferations and those who become attached to them are prone to falling into the extremes. Whether it is the philosophical schools of the Madhyamaka, the Chittamatra, and so forth, Rinpoche is saying that all expressions of words about the ultimate perfection of wisdom are merely proliferations because ultimate reality cannot be expressed.

Thoughts in the mind are concepts;
the nature[12] is inexpressible and unthinkable.

All views of emptiness that we express with words are comprised of false understanding because they are rooted in mental constructs and thoughts. The nature of emptiness, of ultimate truth, is inexpressible and unthinkable. When something is unthinkable and inexpressible, then whatever is expressed in reference to that experience can only ever be a relative truth.

For as long as views continue to exist,
there will be no liberation from all suffering.
Conceptuality is great ignorance,
[from which] it is said one sinks into the ocean of samsara.

---

12. "Nature" (*rang bzhin*; Skt., *svabhava*) in this context, refers to the nature of reality that is free from extremes.

Jetsun Rinpoche is reiterating that as long as we have philosophical views with which we identify, we will never experience freedom. As long as we have views, we will have attachment to ideas, we will have mental formations, we will fall into the extremes, and we will never experience liberation. All of our concepts are rooted in great ignorance. It is said that ignorance is actually the root cause of all of the defilements in our mind. Because of ignorance, because of misconceptions, the other negative emotions of anger and desire arise, and we sink further into the ocean of suffering of samsara.

Without the mindstream being liberated by hearing,
do not express the view in words.
With scripture, reason, and *upadesha*,
the view is determined, mind is at ease.

Jetsun Rinpoche is warning us that until our mindstream is liberated from defilements through hearing and meditation, we should not express the view in words. At our level of understanding, sometimes these teachings can be very challenging, paradoxical, and maybe even frightening. When a yogi's view is validated by scripture, reason, and *upadesha*—personal instruction by a qualified teacher—they may experience peace and ease without any doubt. There is a saying that the sign of extensive hearing is peace of mind.

When only meditation is practiced
there is no meditation and no meditator.
That meditation, free from extremes, is without an object;
leave aside activities, and practice!

As an antidote to the three root defilements of ignorance, anger, and desire, the Buddha gave the complementary trainings of wisdom, meditation, and discipline. These three trainings are essential to our spiritual practice. The root defilements can only be transformed when we apply the correct antidotes through the cultivation of wisdom, meditation practice, and discipline. In this verse, Jetsun Rinpoche is challenging our ordinary understanding of meditation.

Traditionally, we are introduced to meditation in a gradual way. First, we train in shamatha, concentration meditation, by learning to focus all our attention on a meditation object. Sometimes this object is an image or a sound. Sometimes we are instructed to use our own breath as the focus of awareness. In the Sakya tradition, when we are learning to meditate we often begin our shamatha meditation practice by focusing on an image of a blue flower to calm the mind.

Jetsun Rinpoche is challenging that kind of meditation. He is speaking of a higher level of meditative awareness. Rinpoche is saying that in the perfection of meditation (*dhyana paramita*), there is actually no longer a meditator or a meditation—the subject and object have dissolved. Ultimate meditation goes beyond objects; it transcends all activities and effort.

Such perfected awareness would be very hard for us to achieve early in our meditation practice. At our level, we still need a meditation object to aid in focusing and training the mind. We cannot develop concentration without an object to concentrate on. Even learning to remain aware of our breath from moment to moment can be such a struggle for our wandering minds.

In the early stages of cultivating a meditation practice, we need to have good physical discipline. Even just sitting properly in meditation posture without moving the body or blinking the eyes can take so much effort. Whenever we try to meditate, we can observe that the mind is always distracted. It can be so hard to focus on the image of a blue flower for even a minute. The mind is so rebellious. It is constantly filled with inner chattering and emotions. This is especially true for people who are very mentally curious and active.

When the mind is very active, it can be extremely challenging to count even ten breaths without becoming lost in ideas and feelings. As our meditation practice becomes stronger, our mind becomes less active. We may stabilize our concentration to the point where we can maintain focus on the meditation object, and that will help to settle the mind.

Meditation manuals use the analogy of the flame of a butter lamp. They say that if there is wind blowing, then the flame will flicker and everything will be obscured. Likewise, if there are many mental activities, then the mind will be flickering and full of deceptive shadows. But if the mind is very settled, it is like a butter lamp flame without any wind; it has a clear and illuminating light. That kind of clarity only happens when we have extensive meditation practice.

In the beginning stages of our practice, we can observe how the thoughts are gushing like a rapid stream through the mind. It is difficult for us to find any space between the thoughts. But at Rinpoche's level of experience, he is always in that space. There are no mental activities, no effort, no meditator or meditation, and no objects of meditation. In that state, karma ceases because there is no activity.

All of our karma, and all of our mental restlessness, arises from our mindstream. In ordinary life we usually value thinking. We associate thinking with creative people, successful entrepreneurs, or great scholars. It may be true that having a very active mind can increase your productivity, but does it bring you more peace or happiness?

The deepest peace we can achieve comes through cultivating that space *between* the thoughts. That is where we can find refuge from all of the turbulence of life. The more activity there is around us, the more our mind will react, and the more thoughts we will generate. Thinking tends to have an addictive quality. The mind is always grabbing onto excitement or aversion to activate us. That's why, traditionally, meditators go on retreat; they go to get away from the hustle and bustle of the marketplace in order to create a more conducive environment to slow the mind.

We have a choice: we can live life with a mind that is very active and unfocused, or we can choose to begin training the mind, slowing the rushing river of thoughts and finding refuge and peace. We also have to be realistic because there are so many demands on us in ordinary life. We have to work, we have to care for others, we have to survive all of the pressures and the rapid pace of modern life. We may not even realize how exhausted we are because we have become so habituated to the overstimulation of our senses. We may just drink more coffee to get through the day. We may come home and drink alcohol and watch TV because we think it will be relaxing. But the alcohol will make our minds even less focused, and the TV may generate even more thoughts, even more attachment and aversion.

Meditation provides a profound and restorative rest for the mind. When our meditation practice is strong, we stop creating mental karma, physical karma, and verbal karma—that's why it is so peaceful. There is a saying that the sign of the perfection of meditation is that the mind is liberated from distractions.

With the mind without mind, look into the mind;
if seen, that is not mind itself.

With seeing without seeing, mind itself is seen;
remain undistracted in unseeing mind.

At our level of understanding, there are many contradictions here. These are profound teachings and may seem very paradoxical to us. You may wonder how we could possibly do this. How can the conditional mind investigate the ultimate mind? How can we experience this "mind without mind?"

In the *Heart Sutra* teachings there is a saying: "mind does not exist in the mind; the nature of the mind is clear light." "Mind" here refers to the subtle mind, which is looking into the processes of mind. When the subtle mind sees the nature of the mind, which is clear light, that is not mind *itself*. It is only through pure awareness that we can experience the true nature of the mind. It is only through perfect insight meditation, through remaining undistracted in that pure awareness, that we can experience the union of clarity and emptiness, which is the true nature of mind itself.

If attached, make a connection with clarity;
if scattered, hold with the iron hook of recollection.

Generally, there are two main obstacles to perfect meditation. The first obstacle is related to sleepiness, and the second obstacle is related to excitement. When Jetsun Rinpoche says, "If attached, make a connection with clarity," he's referring to that first obstacle of sluggish sleepy energy where we do not focus or concentrate clearly on the object of meditation. According to Buddhism, sleepiness is part of laziness, which is distracting us from the positive karma generated by meditation.

When Rinpoche says, "if attached," he is referring to the laziness due to attachment to the desirable objects, which distracts us from the object of meditation. When Rinpoche says, "make a connection with clarity," he is referring to the antidotes to laziness—diligence, faith, and so forth—which, when practiced, help to overcome the laziness so that our meditation will continue to develop and improve.

When Rinpoche says, "if scattered," he is referring to the second obstacle of meditation—mental excitement. Due to this excitement, the mind becomes scattered in many different directions and we lose all focus on the meditation object. When Rinpoche says, "hold with the iron hook," he is referring to the antidote to that excitement and how we can hook the mind back to the object of meditation with the help of memory or recollection.

There are many potential missteps along the way. When we have very good concentration meditation, we may have special experiences and sometimes we get attached to those experiences. We may feel very relaxed physically—it is said that at the peak of concentration meditation, the practitioner may feel very supple and very light—and we may get attached to these positive sensations. At the other extreme, in meditative absorption in the formless realm our gross thinking may be reduced and it is possible to fall into a subtle sleep state in which there are no thoughts, but also no clarity. Sometimes we mistake that non-ideation of the absorption state as some kind of a high realization.

Meditation is clarity without concepts.

This is the essence of Jetsun Rinpoche's teaching on meditation. Through meditation, we extend the space between the thoughts in the mental continuum. In perfect meditation, there is only space—ultimate awareness without any conceptual mind. At the relative level, we still use terms like "insight meditation" or "mindfulness," but at the highest level that space between the thoughts is the union of clarity and emptiness. It is in that union of clarity and emptiness that we experience the true nature of the mind.

Without being connected with the nectar of experience,
do not express meditation in words.

Jetsun Rinpoche is recommending that we should first practice and have some direct meditation experience and realization before trying to teach or talk about meditation. As we have discussed, it is not possible to express ultimate awareness with language; how can you express a space beyond thoughts? A direct nonconceptual experience cannot be expressed with words. The realization of clarity and emptiness is indescribable.

Begin with developing compassion and bodhichitta;
at the end, dedicate the merit to enlightenment.

Here, Jetsun Rinpoche is advising how we should structure our practice sessions. There are four parts to a complete meditation practice: refuge, bodhichitta, meditation, and dedication. It is through this structured practice regimen that we integrate our meditation into the path of enlightenment. From a Buddhist perspective, if we just do sitting meditation without taking refuge, it is not considered spiritual practice. It may be therapeutic and relaxing but it is not motivated by refuge, it is not based on renunciation, so it is not considered spiritual practice.

Likewise, if we don't do the bodhichitta practice and cultivate compassion, our meditation will not be considered a *Mahayana* meditation practice. If we do not cultivate the wish to achieve enlightenment for the sake of all sentient beings, then our practice is without correct motivation according to Mahayana and Vajrayana Buddhism. It may become a spiritual practice—we may even go beyond samsara and achieve nirvana—but it will not be a complete practice because it will not be for the benefit of all sentient beings.

Furthermore, if we don't close our meditation with a dedication, then the merit we dedicated toward the result will not be protected from future negative emotions. According to Mahayana and Vajrayana Buddhism, these four elements of practice are necessary to make meditation a complete spiritual practice.

When only conduct is practiced,
view and meditation are experienced.

Here, Jetsun Rinpoche is teaching us how to integrate view and meditation with conduct. Rinpoche has the realization of perfect emptiness and, from that view, from that wisdom, he is experiencing meditation and conduct. This is a completely different order from how it is taught in the Abhidharma texts and in many other teachings. Ordinarily, the order is conduct, meditation, and then view. For those of us who are on the graduated path, we cannot describe the view yet because we do not have any experience of emptiness. In the Abhidharma, it is said that first you have to have the fertile ground of discipline, of conduct. If you do not have discipline you cannot do meditation. If you cannot do meditation, then you cannot experience the view, the ultimate wisdom.

It is only through discipline that our practice will progress. For those of us who have a daily sadhana practice, we understand how much commitment, devotion, and discipline it takes to do that practice day after day. We have to apply our body, speech, and mind to maintain and accomplish that practice. We need discipline in order to meditate even if we are sick, even if the weather is gloomy, even if we are busy or tired. Discipline helps us overcome the many fluctuations of the body, speech, and mind. When we do something again and again, year after year, it may eventually become easier. When such discipline is integrated into our lives, it won't take as much force and effort to do our daily practice.

For very good practitioners, even when they are dying they are able to meditate, as long as they have not been overmedicated with painkillers. This is a real challenge in modern medicine, however, where it is common to give so many drugs to patients who are dying. Sometimes medications are also used to treat existential pain, the acute anxiety some people experience at the end of life. If you have cultivated a strong meditation practice over your lifetime you will not experience as much anxiety and fear and you may be able to practice your sadhana even as you are dying.

Practitioners are also instructed to meditate on their sadhana deity just before going to bed each night in order to practice sleeping yoga. Whether you practice a Tara sadhana, or Chakrasamvara, or Vajrayogini, and so forth, it is said that if you remember the deity as you fall asleep, this will also help prepare you for death. Sleep is like a small death. When you remember the deity as you are falling asleep, your mind may carry that connection throughout the night.

If we apply ourselves to our daily practice in this way, there is a better chance of remembering the deity at the time of death. That is very significant because it will protect the mind from many other things. It will protect the mind throughout the *bardo* stage—the intermediate stage between death and rebirth. It will also influence rebirth if we die with this peaceful mind. Without many years of practice, the mind can be easily disturbed by strong emotions at the time of death.

There are so many challenges that can arise during the dying process. Often family members can become very emotional, and if we have regrets or unfinished business in our lives it may activate many negative emotions. The more discipline we have in our practice, the more wisdom we will cultivate. That wisdom will influence our death and our rebirth.

For someone who has a very high level of intelligence and realization, the path is different. Jetsun Rinpoche starts with wisdom first, and from that, view, meditation, and conduct arise. If you have the right wisdom in the mind, then everything is perfect meditation, everything is perfect conduct, because that view has the power to protect the mind.

Having sealed the appealing things,
perform conduct without accepting and rejecting.

It is only when we have realized the view of emptiness that we can "seal the appealing things" with their own empty nature. When we understand the empty nature of all things, then we can go beyond all attachment and aversion to objects. On the other hand, if we don't have any realization of emptiness, then we have so many emotions arising in relation to apparent objects. We get attracted to pleasant objects and we get disgusted by ugly and disagreeable objects. These emotions arise because we do not have a proper understanding of the view.

When we have a proper understanding of the view, whatever happens in the outside world doesn't impact us emotionally anymore. There is no longer any grasping after agreeable objects nor any aversion felt toward disagreeable objects. There is no longer that push and pull between attachment and aversion that we experience in our ordinary lives.

Normally, our minds are overpowered by these conflicting emotions of attraction and aversion. This creates so much mental and emotional turbulence for us—it is very exhausting! We are always making judgments; we are always running after pleasurable experiences and avoiding unpleasant ones. This fuels such divisive thinking and causes such commotion internally. Not only is there a war *inside* us, but we can see how much havoc is caused *externally* when this plays out on a larger scale between entire political parties or nations.

We know that agreeable objects and experiences will bring us temporary pleasure and happiness. Disagreeable experiences and objects may cause us pain and suffering. As long as we have these reactions and all of these conflicting emotions inside us, we will never experience true peace. Our happiness will be only temporary because everything is always changing. Objects we become attached to will ultimately cause us suffering.

Jetsun Rinpoche is clarifying that the only way to have peace is to "perform conduct without accepting and rejecting." Our physical and verbal conduct is ruled by the emotions in the mind. There needs to be a change in the mind before we can experience true change at the verbal and physical level. If there is a realization of right view in the mind, then that wisdom will change our conduct on all levels. With right view, everything we do is part of our meditation; right conduct is effortless. Highly realized masters no longer need to do any formal practice—every moment is practice, every moment is filled with awareness.

On the other hand, if we do not have the right view, then everything takes effort; everything is a struggle. If we do not have wisdom, then we live in this dualism of right and wrong, good and bad, attractive and repulsive. Someone who has realized the view has gone beyond the concept of right and wrong. They have "sealed the appealing things," protecting themselves from all of this dualistic thinking; objects no longer have any emotional power over them.

We can see that Rinpoche is a highly realized master because he is teaching from the top to the bottom. When we have that highest realization of right view, then everything else we do will arise from that wisdom. We will automatically have right meditation and right conduct. There will no longer be any effort or struggle. This entire mystical song arises from that wisdom view.

Do not throw away such naturally unfabricated conduct by siding with misconduct.

On the other hand, for those of us who have not realized that view, the more naturally we act, the more our weaknesses may arise. We excuse so many emotional behaviors as "just a part of human nature." We think that it is human nature to get angry, to be aggressive, or to have so much desire. Our emotions have developed such strong habitual patterns across lifetimes; we are so used to experiencing these negative emotions, that we think they are inherent in us. The teaching is saying that if we have not realized the right view, then the more natural we act, the more apt we are to engage in misconduct based on habitual patterns.

Do not throw away friendly conduct
by siding with wild behavior.

If we do not have the realization of that wisdom view, then our social lives may increase our bad conduct. We may do many wild things with our friends! We see this especially with young people. When teenagers have a party, they do much more dangerous activities. In the name of socializing and having fun, people often drink and do drugs. If we are intoxicated, we may engage more easily in verbal and physical misconduct and wild behavior. Jetsun Rinpoche is warning us about these dangers.

Do not throw away the conduct of non-grasping one taste
by siding with desire and anger.

When we have the realization of that wisdom view, we become freed from desire and anger, freed from accepting and rejecting. The conduct of "one taste" means that we have gone beyond dualism due to the realization of the wisdom view. There are no good and bad tastes, no pleasurable or unpleasurable characteristics; there is nothing to grasp. If we do not have that right view, we remain in ignorance. There is a saying: "ignorance is bliss!" But along with that ignorance, we always have the other root defilements of desire and anger.

Those who have the right view will go beyond relativity. They will no longer be trapped in samsara. They will not be susceptible to attachment and aversion to objects. Their actions will no longer arise from desire, anger, or ignorance.

Do not throw away the conduct of relaxing without activity
by siding with nonvirtue.

The Buddha responded to circumstances out of wisdom, not out of emotional reactivity. His activities were not fueled by negative emotions and they were not generating karma. He was free from stress. At our level, we often feel very stressed when we are busy. Our actions arise from the defilements and they generate more karma, trapping us in a cycle of activity and reactivity. When we want to relax, we often distract ourselves with movies, video games, vacations, fishing, hunting, gambling, and the like. Jetsun Rinpoche is cautioning us here that the kinds of relaxation that do not arise from right view will fall into nonvirtue.

Many of the activities we do for relaxation actually feed the defilements. We feed our desires by partying, by eating, by consuming. We feed our anger by playing violent video games or watching action films. We feed our ignorance by drinking and doing drugs and getting sleepy and lazy. When we feed the defilements, we may find temporary satisfaction and pleasure—we don't realize that we are actually increasing our addiction to these negative emotions; the more we consume, the more we crave. The more violent games we play, the more we increase our propensity for anger. The more rich foods we eat, the more we crave the next good meal.

We do not recognize that we are only increasing and reinforcing these habitual patterns. We may feel relaxed momentarily—the way that a thirsty person feels relieved when they drink a glass of water—but we are actually sowing the seeds for more craving. It is like drinking salty water; the more we consume, the thirstier we become. That's why our methods of relaxation are not pure: they do not arise from awareness.

Do not throw away the conduct of completely purifying the three wheels
by siding with defiled virtue.

Most of our experiences in life are based on our interactions with the outer world. There are three aspects—or "wheels"—of this interaction at the relative level. If we are giving something, there is a gift, a giver, and a receiver. If we are angry, there is a subject experiencing the anger, an object or enemy we are angry at, and there is the emotion of anger itself. So at the relative level, there are always three components.

How much karma we create and how much emotion we will generate depends on how clearly we understand these three wheels. The more our negative emotions are involved, the more negative the effects will be. The more clarity we have about these wheels, the more perfect the results will be.

Jetsun Rinpoche is cautioning us not only to abandon *obvious* nonvirtue but also at a subtler level, to examine even our virtuous practices. At our level, many of our spiritual practices are still mixed with negative emotions. Maybe our motivation is not pure. Maybe our practice is inconsistent or distracted. This admixture of negative influences means that even our virtuous activities are still, to some degree, defiled, because our mind has not been purified.

"Purifying the three wheels" refers to seeing the empty nature of the giver, the gift, and the receiver. It is only when we see the empty nature of all three wheels—when we see that there is ultimately no gift, no giver, and no receiver—that we can transcend the dualism of virtue and nonvirtue. Rinpoche is saying that the realization of the emptiness of the three wheels is the only way to go beyond all karma of virtue and nonvirtue. That recognition of emptiness is the ultimate conduct.

If we give a gift out of that ultimate wisdom, our giving becomes a perfection. If we practice discipline out of that wisdom, our discipline becomes perfected. Until we are practicing out of that understanding of emptiness, even good actions will remain defiled virtues. Rinpoche is emphasizing that in order to have perfect conduct, we have to go beyond the three wheels.

Do not throw away the conduct without virtue and nonvirtue by siding with neutrality.

Jetsun Rinpoche is referring to the three kinds of karma: virtue, nonvirtue, and neutral karma. At our level, we have not gone beyond karma. All of our thoughts and activities are creating more karma. Many of our daily activities—like sleeping or eating or walking—can be considered neutral karma. The majority of our time is consumed by these neutral activities. These activities may be relaxing, because they don't generate strong emotions. Sleeping can be very relaxing if we are not having bad dreams. But virtuous activities are always better than neutral activities on the spiritual path. Rinpoche is essentially saying, "Don't waste your time in neutrality."

At the least, we must try to transform our nonvirtuous activities into neutral activities. If we have an appointment to go fishing, we could cancel that trip and take a nap instead. That's better than killing fish, even though napping is only a neutral activity. But if we remember the deity when we are napping, if we do some sleep yoga, then even napping can become a virtuous activity. When we sleep in the clear-light nature of the mind, we go beyond the person and the sleep and we transcend virtue, nonvirtue, and neutrality.

3

Do Not Seek Elsewhere for Buddha

Once buddhahood is established,
there are no dharmas aside from mind.
When mind itself is comprehended, *that* is Buddha;
do not seek elsewhere for Buddha.

ONCE WE HAVE COMPLETELY transformed the mind through right view, right meditation, and right conduct, we will have awakened to our inherent buddha nature. As we have discussed, although buddhahood is the result, we should not have a dualistic misconception that buddhahood is somewhere else, some future goal up ahead of us on the spiritual path. Jetsun Rinpoche is helping to clear away that misconception by saying that, actually, all of the conditioned and unconditioned dharmas—all phenomena—are actually already in our mind.

In Buddhism there is no belief in a divine creator. We do not have a God who created the world. According to Buddhism, it's our own mind that creates all of the karma. That individual and collective karma is what manifests our entire experience of the universe. As long as we have a mind, we create the universe and all of conditioned and unconditioned phenomena.

All of our experiences of both the outer phenomenal world and the inner mental world arise from our conditioned mind. As a result, all of our experiences are experienced through the lens of our past karma and emotions. That is how we store information; that is how we remember things.

All the affinity we feel toward objects is based on past karmic connections we have made. We may feel a strong affinity for certain foods, people, or places, and that is all based on some history we have. Maybe someone reminds us of someone else we have loved. Maybe a certain food reminds us of happy childhood memories. Often, we cannot even locate the source of that affinity, because it is not necessarily from this lifetime. All of these past experiences become conditions for future projections. All of that stored information in the mindstream impacts how we experience our current lives.

When Rinpoche says, "there are no dharmas aside from mind," he is saying that anything that is apparent to us arises out of our own karma. Apparent objects are not independently existing. If our minds were completely empty, what would our experience of the phenomenal world be? Without any thoughts or karma, how would apparent objects appear to us? We cannot conceive of this state of clarity and emptiness.

The mind is the creator of the universe as we experience it. But our experience as humans is not universal; through our individual karma and our collective karma, we are conditioned to experience everything through a particular lens. Everything we do is based on thinking, based on emotional reactions, based on conscious and unconscious memories imprinted in our mindstream.

At the highest level of meditation when we stop thinking altogether, our entire experience of the phenomenal world is altered. When we are in that space of clarity and emptiness, our experience of reality is completely changed.

Our experience of ordinary reality can also be altered through drugs, alcohol, or illness. But experiences based on substances or mental imbalances will not help us to see the empty nature of ultimate reality. They may help us realize how conditional our experiences are, but they will not produce any clarity or wisdom.

The teachings are reminding us that our entire outer experience is based on our mental conditioning, that the mind is the creator of our universe. As we have discussed earlier, it is very difficult for the mind to comprehend itself. But once we comprehend the ultimate nature of the mind, we realize buddhahood. We do not need to "seek elsewhere for Buddha"; buddhahood is already present within us.

Jetsun Rinpoche is teaching us here that the mind is the creator of the universe and that mind is the basic foundation (dharma) of phenomena; therefore, all things we do in the mental world are also mind. Mind is sleeping and mind is also awakening. Mind is meditating and mind is also distracted. Mind is forgetting and mind is remembering. The mind has all of these polarities and contradictions. But when the nature of the mind itself is comprehended, then we understand ultimate reality. When the lens through which we experience the phenomenal world is purified, then we will experience the empty nature of all things.

Buddhahood is the result of looking deeply into all of our mental experiences. When the mind completely comprehends itself, when the mind realizes the union of clarity and emptiness, that is the awakened state. We cannot know the true nature of the mind through intellect, through psychology, through accumulated knowledge. Knowing the nature of the mind is about going beyond all of this intellectual grasping. Meditation is the only way to go beyond the mind to see the true nature of the mind itself.

We cannot attain this experience of ultimate reality through thinking. There is no limit to the conceptual world—there are so many mental activities. If we pause for one minute and observe the mind, we can see how many thoughts are rushing through it all the time. Thinking is limitless. Intellectual inquiry will not lead us to the experience of clarity and emptiness.

As I have mentioned, study and training are very helpful early in our spiritual practice. But wisdom that will help us to see the nature of reality is far more important than knowledge that increases our thoughts. That is why Rinpoche reminds us to look within. If we keep looking for buddhahood somewhere else, we will never actually have that experience of ultimate reality.

Please do not throw away the *dharmakaya*[13] possessing two purities,[14]
by siding with the basis.[15]

When the mind transcends itself through meditation, what is it we are transcending? We are transcending all of our karma and defilements to uncover our true nature. That true nature is also known as the *dharmakaya*. When you realize the nature of the mind, then you have simultaneously realized the nature of the universe; they are one and the same. By knowing the empty nature of your mind, you will know the emptiness of all phenomena. That realization is buddhahood.

"Basis" refers to the relative world. In Vajrayana practice, we refer to three stages: base (or foundation), path (or method), and result (buddhahood). Our five aggregates are the base. The five aggregates include form, feeling, ideation, formations, and consciousness. When these five aggregates are brought into our meditation and when there is right conduct and right view, then they become the path. Through

---

13. *Dharmakaya* (*chos sku*) is the result of the wisdom accumulation, the full realization of the ultimate nature of the mind.
14. The "two purities" are the dharmakaya's freedom from the obscuration of defilement and of knowledge.
15. The "basis" (*gzhi*) refers to the cause continuum, which contains all dharmas of samsara and nirvana.

practice we will ultimately realize the result: the awakened state of buddhahood.

Although the nature of the mind is already Buddha, it takes method and practice to realize that nature. If we have not realized our true nature, then we have left buddhahood at the foundational stage; we have not awakened to our inherent nature. That is why Jetsun Rinpoche is warning us not to throw away the dharmakaya in order to side with the basis.

We purify our negative emotions and karma through the methods of right view, right conduct, and right meditation. When the two obscurations are removed, then we see the two purities, we see the buddha nature within us, we experience the result.

Do not grasp the essence of the Buddha
in the *rupakaya*,[16] which appears to those [sentient beings] to be tamed.

The *rupakaya*, or form body, manifests as both *sambhogakaya* and *nirmanakaya* to benefit sentient beings. *Sambhogakaya* refers to the buddhas in the pure realms with all the bodhisattvas. *Nirmanakaya* refers to buddhas like Shakyamuni Buddha who are manifesting in samsara in order to help sentient beings.

The essence of Buddha is the union of wisdom (emptiness) and compassion (clarity). Until we experience wisdom and compassion directly, we relate to Buddha through representations, through images and statues of Buddha. We connect to Buddha through being with a guru and through visualization of the deity in our sadhana practice. This can be very helpful early in our practice as a reminder of that result. But until we realize our own buddha nature, Buddha will still be something outside ourselves. Many practitioners get stuck at that level of practice and

16. *Rupakaya* (*gzugs sku*) is the result of the merit accumulation, physically appearing in buddha realms and in samsara.

remain attached to outer representations of Buddha. This can become an obstacle to the deeper realization of wisdom.

Jetsun Rinpoche is cautioning us to avoid the spiritual trap of becoming attached to outer representations. He is warning us not to try grasping the essence of Buddha through the rupakaya, the form body. Those forms will become obscurations and will block our direct realization of the essence of buddhahood.

I am reminded of a Zen story I heard once: There was a Buddhist nun who had a very beautiful statue of the Buddha. Whenever other people would visit the statue and make offerings, she would be very protective. If they burned incense and candles, she would get so upset if any ash or smoke fell on the statue. She was very possessive and attached to this representation of the Buddha. Even though her goal was to honor the Buddha, in her grasping at the object, her own innate wisdom was obscured.

We are all susceptible to getting attached to outer appearances of the Buddha. That is the main reason why we have all the dissolution practices in our Vajrayana meditation. After generating ourselves in the image of the deity in our daily sadhana practice, we always dissolve that deity back into emptiness. This is so that we do not get attached to these images and forms.

Attachment may be useful as a starting point in our practice. We may feel connected to a teacher, which can inspire our practice. We may feel a sense of peace and happiness when we view a Buddha statue in a beautiful temple. These outer forms can kindle our curiosity and our interest in spiritual practice. But if this interest develops into a habitual pattern of grasping and attachment to these spiritual objects, then our faith will remain very shaky. Our clinging to these objects and teachers will obscure our path to liberation, we will not realize the wisdom essence inside us, and we will not cultivate unshakable faith.

In the basis, there is no Buddha;
do not hope for attainment.

Hope can be a positive force in our lives. If we are feeling vulnerable and afraid, hope may give us strength. If we are suffering, hope can give us courage. But hope can also be an obstacle—especially if it is based on something false. Hope can be shaken when a scandal occurs in a spiritual community. Hope can be shattered when an illness persists in spite of prayers. Hope can be filled with grasping for a desired outcome.

It is for this reason that Buddhist teachings emphasize letting go of both hope and fear. Hope and fear are primary obstacles in our lives and in our spiritual practice—they are based on attachment and aversion. This is why Jetsun Rinpoche cautions, "do not hope for attainment." He is reminding us that in the basis, there is no Buddha.

"Basis" refers to relativity. If we want to achieve buddhahood, we have to go beyond the relative world by purifying the relative base. If we are looking for the emptiness of the cup but we get attached to the cup itself, then we will never see the empty nature of the cup. If we look for the Buddha in the basis—at the relative level—we will never experience the wisdom of buddhahood, leading us to become discouraged. Rinpoche is teaching us to go beyond false hope.

In the ultimate, there are no sentient beings;
do not fear suffering.

Fear can be another major obstacle on the spiritual path. Although we may wish to achieve liberation, we may actually be using our practice to strengthen our ego. Letting go is terrifying. When we hear teachings about emptiness, we may feel quite frightened. We want enlightenment, but we don't actually want to loosen our grasp on our self-image and on our material lives. We may want to practice for the sake of all sentient beings, but we may feel a deep aversion to their suffering. We might cross the street to avoid someone experiencing homelessness or mental illness. We may turn off the news because we cannot bear to hear about the suffering of war or the destruction of the earth due to climate change. We might try to distract ourselves from our own suffering with television, alcohol, drugs, food, or relationships.

Jetsun Rinpoche is reminding us that, in the ultimate wisdom, there are no sentient beings, nothing to grasp onto, nothing to feel aversion to. In the ultimate, there is no self and other, no dualism of samsara and nirvana, no difference between a buddha and a stranger sleeping on the sidewalk.

We have so much fear of loss. We fear losing our money, our reputation, our privacy, our security, our loved ones. We are terribly afraid of illness and death in this culture. We fear things that haven't even happened yet. We buy insurance to try to prepare for the unknown. As long as we are living in the relative world, with all of this dualism, we will fear suffering. If we have the realization that samsara and nirvana are two sides of the same coin, then we will no longer be afraid. In the ultimate, there is nothing to gain and nothing to lose. This is why the Buddhist teachings emphasize practicing without hope or fear; both can be obstacles on the spiritual path.

In the view without thought or expressions,
one is deluded by the activity of hearing and contemplating sutras and tantras.

As we have discussed, the wisdom view is inexpressible; it is free from all conceptual thinking. Jetsun Rinpoche is warning us not to be deluded by the activity of hearing teachings and contemplating sutras and tantras. He is pointing out that it is easy to fall into the trap of allowing the teachings to generate even more conceptual thinking. If the teachings are not helping us to have fewer thoughts, then we are misunderstanding the view. If our study of the sutras and tantras is increasing our attachment to ideas and generating more and more opinions, then we are deluded in our understanding.

The accumulation of knowledge can be a great liability. We run the risk of becoming more attached to thinking, and this can become a much greater obstacle to spiritual experience. Instead of the mind liberating itself, it is actually becoming more and more trapped by ideas. This is how education can actually be detrimental on the spiritual path. An intellectual person may have a much harder time gaining direct insight because they are so buried in ideas. They might have more realization of wisdom if they were living a simpler life, practicing one mantra day after day while working as a shepherd or a farmer.

The risk for intellectuals is that they become more and more opinionated and run the risk of becoming fanatical. They may become convinced that there is only one way of interpreting religion, or only one set of ethical values or moral principles. Instead of having an open mind, intellectuals may become more and more conservative and closed to opposing views. Study and contemplation can delude the mind and become major obstacles to experiencing wisdom.

In the meditation free from extremes,
one is deluded by making physical and mental effort.

Great yogis have taught that meditation is like water that is left undisturbed. You can imagine meditation to be like a lake or ocean without any wind or waves. When the water is without any movement, then all the dirt can sink down to the bottom of the lake, allowing the water to become very pure and very clean.

The more ease we have in our concentration, the more the mind resembles a clear lake. But early in our practice, we may sometimes bring too much force and effort to our meditation sessions. We may approach meditation in the same way we approach sports: putting in all our strength and pushing ourselves to the limit. This can actually disturb the mind and body. You can imagine it being like someone swimming really hard in a lake and splashing water everywhere, creating lots of movement and commotion that stirs up masses of dirt and sand, making the water even cloudier. In this way, exerting too much effort in meditation just makes it harder and harder to meditate; instead of gaining some clarity, we will actually stir up more thoughts and emotions and become even more physically uncomfortable and frustrated.

In the ceaseless natural activity of conduct,
one is deluded by becoming lost in misconduct and wild behavior.

What is natural conduct? Natural conduct arises from ultimate awareness of the true nature of our own mind. Natural activity arises from wisdom. The nature of the mind is pure. The more obstacles we remove, the more our conduct will arise from that natural purity.

If we are not connected to that inherent purity, our conduct will often be so unnatural. We may act in many artificial ways in order to conform to social pressures and expectations. We may even betray our own values in order to move up the career ladder or achieve financial security. We may have been raised with so many familial and societal expectations placed on us that we may not even know how to be authentic. We may feel that we are always acting out a role instead of being true to our nature. We may be so caught in the cycle of emotional action and reaction that we cannot glimpse any true freedom of action.

If we are in touch with the inherent purity of the mind, then that purity will be expressed verbally and physically. We will experience freedom from societal pressures, and we will feel liberated from the cycle of emotional reactivity. Such an expression of purity will be unceasing—just as the nature of the mind is unceasing. In summary, proper conduct is natural conduct, which is the expression of the true nature of the mind.

In the result, the inseparability of samsara and nirvana,
one is deluded by becoming lost in siding with hope and fear.

When we have seen the true nature of the mind, we recognize that samsara and nirvana are inseparable; they are two sides of the same coin. If we have not seen the nature of the mind, then we remain caught in dualism. We remain trapped in these polarities of good and bad, heaven and hell, ugly and beautiful, samsara and nirvana, and so forth. Jetsun Rinpoche is reminding us that once we have realized the buddha nature within ourselves, we will go beyond both hope and fear.

4

Bliss Without Delusion

The view of great Madhyamaka,
being without definitive propositions, is bliss without delusion.

MADHYAMAKA IS CONSIDERED to be the highest Buddhist philosophical view. As we have discussed previously, the philosophical conclusions regarding right view should serve to free our minds from concepts and opinions. When the mind has more freedom and independence, there is an experience of peace and bliss.

Unfortunately, ideas and opinions often become fixed entities; they become intellectual property. Mental and material property actually limit our freedom. We remain bound to that land, to those objects, or to those ideas. We become so attached, which gives rise to fear of losing that property. We pursue copyrights, trademarks, and patents. We purchase homeowner's insurance and security cameras, and put up high fences. We publish papers and defend our conclusions.

It is said that the great Madhyamaka view does not have any proposal, any thesis, any conclusion. That is what Jetsun Rinpoche means by the word "proposition." When we propose something, we become bound to that proposal and we lose some freedom. If we "propose" to another person, we make a promise to marry them. We then become bound to that other person. When we propose a theory, we become bound to that idea and to demonstrating that we are correct. By becoming attached to something we are trying to prove, we lose our mental freedom.

Understanding emptiness means true mental freedom and independence. Through understanding the truth of interdependence, the mind actually realizes freedom. The true meaning of interdependence is realizing that nothing inherently exists. When we cling to ideas, we are deluded because we are clinging to something as inherently existing. The best Madhyamaka philosophers have freed themselves from any premise, any proposal, any mental property. The highest view is non-binding because it is based on emptiness and on the correct understanding of interdependence. Because it is non-binding, this highest view gives rise to an experience of great bliss of total freedom and wisdom without delusion.

The meditation relaxing body and mind,
being without effort, is bliss without delusion.

In these lines, Jetsun Rinpoche is referring to the highest level of meditation that arises from that wisdom view. As we have discussed, in the beginning we need dedication and discipline to commit to a daily meditation practice. Meditation can be so physically, emotionally, and mentally uncomfortable. Without discipline, we would give up within weeks or months; we would not be able to train the mind. That is why discipline, effort, and diligence are very important early in our practice. Even remaining in a correct meditation posture can be extremely challenging at first.

When we first try to meditate, we may get knee pain and back pain; our eyes might tear up constantly; we may feel distracted, itchy, or restless. We may experience the arising of so many thoughts and memories that we have pushed down for decades. When we begin to pay attention, we may find that the thoughts are rushing faster than ever, and we may think we are failing in our practice. That is why it is good to make the effort to persevere and return to the cushion day after day—even when it is so uncomfortable, even when we would rather watch TV and drown out the uncomfortable thoughts and emotions that are arising in our practice.

We may want to quit because we had thought meditation was supposed to make us feel peaceful and relaxed, and now it is having the opposite effect! This is why effort is very important early on. Meditation will not always be comfortable or enjoyable. We may have days when we feel more at ease and think we are really doing well, and we may get attached to that peaceful feeling. The next week, we may be having issues in a relationship and suddenly our meditation is horrible again. Suddenly, all of these negative emotions start surfacing, and our ability to concentrate evaporates. We feel so discouraged, because we have become attached to the positive meditation experiences we've had in the past.

On the other hand, we should not be placing too much pressure on our practice. That is why it is generally better, when we are beginning, to do many short meditation sessions rather than forcing a longer session. It is much better to meditate for a few minutes than it is to sit down and force an hour-long meditation when we are novice meditators. Too much pressure will cause stress, and this will be counterproductive to building a healthy daily practice.

At the highest level of realization, meditation is effortless and relaxing. That experience will only come after many years—or lifetimes—of practice. As long as there is too much effort, there will be no relaxation. It is important to clarify that Rinpoche is not talking about ordinary sleepy relaxation. Meditation here in the West is often taught merely for stress reduction and physical relaxation. Meditation has lost the vital aspect of mental training of awareness and concentration. There is nothing wrong with stress reduction and relaxation, but we should not confuse that state with a high level of meditation. It might feel good to space out, to be relaxed and sleepy, and to let go of our muscle tension at the end of a long day, but that is not the kind of relaxation Rinpoche is referring to here. He is speaking of the very highest level of meditative realization, the highest level of mental awareness and concentration.

The perfection of practice takes time—just like any other skill. For example, someone who is very accustomed to driving may find it very relaxing. When they feel stressed, they may actually want to get in the car and take a long drive to relax. For someone who has just started learning how to drive, though, it may take so much effort and they may feel very nervous; it may feel hard to multitask; they may feel so afraid of getting into an accident that they cannot relax.

It is the same way with training the mind. In the beginning, it may take so much effort to get ourselves onto the meditation cushion each day. Our mind might come up with so many excuses—we can get very rebellious! Even on the meditation cushion, our mind might still avoid meditating by falling asleep, making a to-do list for tomorrow, or replaying a conflict with a colleague over and over in the mind. There are so many ways to avoid meditation—even while seated in good meditation posture for hours! We can go to a two-week silent meditation retreat and still avoid meditating. That is why we also need to have a lot of patience along with the diligence. We have to care for the mind as we would for a young child. Children can be so rebellious; they can have so many tantrums; they can have such a hard time sitting still. The mind can be the same way when we are first developing our meditation practice.

In the beginning, we have to put in the effort; we have to apply ourselves as we would apply ourselves to raising a child. But when meditation reaches the high level that Rinpoche is referring to, we will feel physically light and mentally very supple and at ease. All these energetic blockages in our body will be freed, and energy will move very naturally. There will be a great sense of bliss, ease, and subtle awareness. We will bear witness to whatever is occurring without judgment and without attachment or aversion. We will remain in the bliss of the ultimate wisdom free from all extremes of delusion.

The conduct, the causal ground of desire and anger,
being without accepting and rejecting, is bliss without delusion.

Conduct includes our physical, verbal, and mental actions and activities. As we have discussed, all of this conduct arises from the mind. The more in touch we are with the inherent purity of the mind, the purer our conduct will be, and the less reactive we will be.

That does not mean we will no longer act; we will still engage with life, but we will have freedom of action; we will have gone beyond the root destructive emotions of desire, anger, and ignorance; we will witness things as they really are; we will recognize the empty nature of all things. If someone becomes angry at us, we will not respond reactively. We will not generate any negative emotions even if someone yells at us. We will have mental equanimity and observe what is happening with compassion and clarity. We will not dismiss the suffering of a person who is angry with us, but we will also not increase that suffering or internalize that anger. This equanimity is the result of many years of mental training.

In the beginning we will not have that equanimity. When someone becomes angry with us, we will immediately feel a need to defend ourselves and to reject the other person. We may escalate the situation by responding with anger and increasing the negative emotions and negative karma. That's why we have the five rules, or precepts, in our Buddhist practice. That is why we take the vows not to kill, not to steal, not to use wrong speech, not to commit sexual misconduct, and not to use intoxicants that cloud the mind. These precepts are helpful when we are starting out on the path, when we do not yet have that connection with the inherent purity of our mind, when our conduct can be so reactive and cause so much suffering for others.

Without that equanimity and awareness, we will tend to react emotionally to everything around us. We will cultivate so many likes and dislikes. We may become more and more entrenched in our views and aggressive in our partisanship. We are reactionary because of our ego, and the ego is conditioned by so many different factors in our childhood and culture. Tradition and culture are built around the framework of ego and, likewise, the ego is then conditioned by those influences. Our country, our environment, our language, our belief systems, our family culture, and our socioeconomic status: all play a major role in shaping our sense of self.

The ego is filled with all of these conditions, and because of this, we never experience equanimity. This conditioning trains us to always accept or reject things; that's how societies function. But Jetsun Rinpoche is reminding us that through proper conduct, it is possible to be entirely freed from that reactivity and to experience profound peace and bliss without delusion.

As long as we have ego, we have the causal ground of desire and anger. As long as we have desire and anger, there will be no end to our cycle of action and reaction. The true nature of the mind is without ego; it is without anger and desire. When we uncover that innermost purity of the mind, then we are freed from emotional reactivity. Our mental, verbal, and physical activities will no longer be creating karma. This does not mean that we will no longer respond to situations or engage with life; it means that we will no longer be reacting based on negative emotions, and we will therefore no longer be creating negative karma.

The result, *mahamudra*,[17]
being without hope and fear, is bliss without delusion.

Jetsun Rinpoche is referring here to the three trainings: the training of wisdom—referred to in these verses as "view"; of meditation; and of discipline—referred to here as "conduct." As we have discussed, these three trainings purify the corresponding root defilements of ignorance, anger, and desire. The result of realizing that purity is the experience of *mahamudra*. Mahamudra is the experience of the union of clarity and emptiness. It is the state in which we experience "bliss without delusion," because both hope and fear have been transcended. In Mahayana, this experience of clarity and emptiness is referred to as *madhyamaka*.

---

17. *Mahamudra* (*phyag rgya chen po*), or "great seal," refers to realizing the union of clarity and emptiness in the form of the deity in highest yoga tantra practice.

In the *anuttarayoga* vehicle of Vajrayana according to the Sakya school, however, it is called *mahamudra*.

In Vajrayana practice, even a short sadhana will include these three trainings of right view, right meditation, and right conduct. We will practice the right view by integrating the four emptinesses into the sadhana practice. We will train in right meditation through our generation and completion practices. We will train in right conduct according to whatever sadhana we are practicing; for example, if we are practicing Vajrayogini we will practice left-sided conduct (*samayas*).

Once we realize the union of clarity and emptiness through our sadhana practice, we experience mahamudra. Mahamudra is the realization of the true nature of our own mind. In that union of clarity and emptiness, we are free from all desire and anger, and so there is nothing to fear and nothing to hope for.

If there is no proliferation, that is the view.

"Proliferation" here basically refers to the same thing as the "propositions" referred to a few verses back.[18] As we discussed in relation to that earlier verse: if there are no propositions, then there is freedom. Whenever we propose something, we have attachment to some idea. In a similar way, proliferation refers to all the potential extremes. All philosophical conclusions can fall into the four extremes of existence, nonexistence, both, or neither. If we have attachment to nonexistence we may fall into nihilism, we may think there is no point to anything, and we may abandon right conduct. If we have attachment to existence, we may become eternalistic in our views and we may fail to recognize the empty nature of all phenomena. Even a belief in an ultimate dualism or nondualism can become an obstacle to realizing emptiness.

When we are attached to something, that thing becomes an obstacle to experiencing the ultimate truth. There is no proliferation in the

18. "The view of great Madhyamaka, / being without definitive propositions, is bliss without delusion."

ultimate, because the ultimate view is free from all extremes. The ultimate view is beyond thought, beyond any mental or physical property, beyond the realm of ego. When there is a dissolution of the ego, the mind is freed from all proliferations.

If there is no distraction, that is meditation.

As we have discussed, meditation is a method for cultivating and increasing attention in the mind. Without attention, the mind cannot transcend all of the distractions that obscure its own true nature. Meditation is the cultivation of attention along with memory and awareness. Memory is like a hook, and awareness is like a rope. Memory helps us to not forget the object of meditation, and awareness helps us to tie that memory to the object of meditation. Memory and awareness help us to maintain our attention moment to moment. The more we cultivate memory, awareness, and attention, the more we will experience mindfulness and wisdom. At the highest level of meditation, meditation masters remain in a totally undistracted state; their meditative awareness is constant without any distraction.

If activity is abandoned, that is conduct.

As we have discussed, when we engage in right conduct, we stop creating negative karma. We may still be speaking and acting, but our activities will no longer be motivated by negative emotions. We will be able to *respond* rather than simply *react* emotionally to any situation.

Refraining from activity does not necessarily stop the production of karma because thoughts continue to generate a lot of karma if the mind is not purified. As long as we are still producing karma, that means we still need to train in right conduct. Conduct, in this context, refers to maintaining all of the precepts of Hinayana, Mahayana, and Vajrayana that we have taken.

It is very challenging for us to abandon activities. We are so busy; we cannot just relax and be at peace; our mind and emotions are pushing us to act and react constantly. Abandoning activities does not mean avoiding positive actions rooted in love and compassion. The teachings say that in order to abandon nonvirtues, we actually need to rely on *virtuous* action. Virtuous actions also generate karma—but it is *positive* karma. Although we rely on virtuous actions as the antidote to nonvirtue, there comes a point when we will need to transcend even that dualism; we will need to transcend even virtuous actions. This transcendence is considered perfect conduct of samaya. Jetsun Rinpoche is referring to conduct that goes beyond even our conceptions of good and bad. That is perfect conduct, because it arises from right view, from ultimate wisdom.

Until we realize ultimate wisdom, we need to rely on generating good karma through positive activities in order to stop increasing our negative karma. When we have perfected those positive qualities, we go beyond all concepts of good and bad, positive and negative. These teachings here arise from that highest realization of wisdom.

If mind itself is comprehended, that is the result.

When we experience mahamudra, the union of clarity and emptiness, we comprehend the true nature of the mind. When the mind realizes its own true nature, then it has realized the result. Until we have an experience of the union of clarity and emptiness, we will still be experiencing things through the limits of the conceptual mind.

If doubt is cut, that is view.

Doubt is considered to be one of the primary defilements that force us to be reborn in samsara again and again. The pursuit of knowledge can often result in more and more doubt. The more intellectual we are, the more we probe and dissect everything and the more doubts we may have. It is only through *experiential* wisdom that we are able to gain some certainty of the nature of ultimate reality. When our meditation is based on right view gained through direct experience, we will become very strong in our faith.

If our meditation is not based on right view, then our practice will be very shaky. Right view is essential to liberating our mind from the defilements. Without wisdom, we cannot free our mind from ignorance; we cannot free ourselves from doubt. When we realize wisdom, we are freed from ignorance and doubt.

If there is no clinging and attachment, that is conduct.

Attachment arises from ignorance, and that attachment generates so many negative karmic activities. Many nonvirtuous actions like killing, stealing, lying, and other misconducts are committed due to desire and attachment. For example, animals are killed because we are attached to the taste of their meat. Jetsun Rinpoche is saying that if there is no clinging and no attachment, then right conduct will arise from that equanimity.

If the qualities are complete, that is the result.

Through cultivation of right view, right meditation, and right conduct, we will develop all of the enlightened qualities. By "qualities," Jetsun Rinpoche is referring to the realization of the unity of clarity and emptiness. The result is the realization of buddhahood with enlightened physical qualities of minor and major signs, speech with sixty tones, and wisdom of knowing both the relative and the ultimate truth of all phenomena, including inconceivable enlightened activities to benefit sentient beings.

In general, for a being who has realized the view,
if there is nothing whatsoever to meditate on,
that great meditator is without a practice.
If there is no conduct to perform,
in the yoga free from conduct,
there is no result whatsoever to be pursued.

The supreme view has no view;
philosophical conclusions are not needed here.

The supreme meditation is without meditation;
concentrating mind is not needed here.

The supreme conduct is without conduct;
misconduct is not needed here.

The supreme result has no result;
hope and fear are not needed here.

Generally, for a yogi who has realized the right view, there is no longer any need for practice. Such an awakened being has perfected meditation and is thus always in that state of awareness; there is no longer any separation between meditator, meditation, and objects of meditation. Just as in the perfection of giving—where we reach a point where there is no longer any gift, any giver, nor any receiver—in perfect meditation, we transcend the "three wheels" of subject, object, and action.

In our daily sadhana practices, we are actively cultivating this experience. When we dissolve the deity back into emptiness during the completion stage, we refer to this as "meditation beyond thought." In that empty state, there is no longer a meditator, no longer a deity, no longer a practice, and no longer anything to meditate on; there is nothing to practice when we have gone beyond thought.

We are not at that stage yet; we are still practicing within the relative world. We have not had that experience of ultimate awareness, and so we still need all of these practices to train the mind. Perfect meditation is meditation *without* meditation. This is difficult for us to understand from our relative world. At our level, we still need to accumulate merit—we still need to practice giving, ethics, patience, diligence, and meditation. We need to practice these positive activities as antidotes to all of our negative karma and emotions.

We need to give because we still have a lot of attachment, grasping, and stinginess. We need to practice right conduct because we still have a lot of desire. We need to practice patience and meditation because we still have a lot of anger and aversion. We need to practice diligence because we still experience laziness and indifference. We need to practice meditation because we still have distractions. In the Mahayana path, the first five of these six practices are considered part of the *method*, and when they are integrated with the sixth—wisdom—they are called the six *paramitas* or perfections. The six paramitas involve going beyond the relative and defiled conception of there being a practitioner, a meditation practice, and an object of meditation. Similarly, when supreme view, supreme meditation, supreme conduct, and supreme result are integrated with wisdom, they are well gone beyond (*parasamgate*).

Moreover, in reality[19] there is no object to see;
now, also, the view is not viewed.

In the original nature,[20] there is nothing to meditate on;
now, also, meditation is not meditation.

In the natural state,[21] there is no conduct;
now, also, conduct is not conduct.

Jetsun Rinpoche is reiterating that when someone has seen the clear-light nature of the mind, then they have gone beyond all philosophical conclusions. When one is enlightened, there is no longer a right or wrong view. An enlightened being has gone beyond meditation prac-

---

19. "Reality" means the nature of things free from extremes in the context of the view.
20. "Original nature" (*gnyug ma*) is the basic nature of the mind free from extremes in the context of meditation.
21. The "natural state" (*dbyings*) means the nature of things free from extremes in the context of conduct.

tice, and they are free from the dualism and the constraints of conduct. This only applies to someone who has realized ultimate reality. We are not at that level yet, so there is still some need for philosophical study. We also need to meditate and we need to live our lives according to the natural law of karma.

There are four major philosophical schools in Buddhism, each with very different conclusions about ultimate reality. Whatever tradition we are studying in, we will naturally assume that our view is the only correct conclusion. If we are studying within the Vaibhashika, we will think that their philosophical conclusion is the ultimate truth. But if we then study Sautrantika, we may see that the conclusions of the Vaibhashika philosophy are not ultimate. However, if we study the Chittamatra, or "Mind-Only" philosophy, then the Sautrantika will no longer seem to be the ultimate conclusion. If we progress to the Madhyamaka philosophical views, we will then find faults in the Chittamatra. But if you are fully enlightened, if you are a buddha, you have gone beyond all four of those philosophical schools. To the awakened yogi, ultimate reality is beyond all conclusions, beyond all philosophical views. To the enlightened mind, there is nothing to discuss; there is no right or wrong view. That is what Rinpoche means when he says, "the view is not the view."

Once you are fully awakened, there is no longer any need for meditation practice. Once you have uncovered the original clear-light nature of the mind, the dharmata, you will see the empty nature of all things. The purpose of all of our meditation practice is to uncover that original nature. Once we uncover that purity of mind, we are always in a meditative state, always in a state of ultimate awareness. There is no longer any need for practice.

In that natural state, there is no longer any conduct. In this context, "conduct" refers to physical conduct, verbal conduct, and mental conduct. As we have discussed, once someone is fully awakened they have purified all their karma and have even gone beyond neutral karma.

Once we have gone beyond karma, we no longer need to be concerned with conduct. We are not creating any karma with our mental, physical, or verbal actions. We are not being motivated by karma and we are not generating any new karma. That is why Rinpoche says, "now, also, conduct is not conduct."

If the view has no center or limits,
one might surely think it is space.

Until we have a direct experience of ultimate reality, we rely on similes to give us some insight into that wisdom. Buddhist texts often use the simile of space to describe ultimate reality. Space is the best example of the empty nature. Indeed, the *Heart Sutra* says, "The wisdom gone beyond is like space."

Although we have not traveled to outer space, most of us have seen some images. As our telescopes become more refined, we can get an even greater sense of the vastness of that emptiness within which so many galaxies come and go. But outer space is only an example. When we become awakened, we understand that inner space is just as vast as outer space; our empty nature is as infinite as the universe. But if all of our exploration of outer space does not help us to see the inner space, the clarity and emptiness of our own mind, then it can be misleading. We must use that understanding of outer space to see the true nature of the mind.

Buddhist teachings have many stories that remind us not to be misled. The teachings remind us not to get trapped in the relative world. For example, the teachings say that if the guru is instructing the disciple to look at the moon while pointing his finger, but the disciple remains looking at the teacher's finger or looking at a reflection of the moon on the water, then the disciple will remain trapped in the relative world. They will never see the actual moon if they are only looking at reflections or at the teacher's instruction. This is a reminder to us not to get lost in these similes, to remain aware that they are only examples. It is up to us to gain direct experience of that wisdom. Pointing to outer space is merely a way to cultivate some awareness of inner space.

**If there is no movement or wavering in meditation,
one might surely think it is a mountain.**

In a similar manner, Buddhist teachings sometimes use the simile of a mountain to give us a sense of the steadiness of perfect meditation. As Jetsun Rinpoche says, "If there is no movement or wavering in meditation, one might surely think it is a mountain." If we remain looking at the outer mountain instead of the inner mountain of the stabilized mind, then we are like the disciple staring at the guru's finger or the moon's reflection.

There is a shamatha meditation teaching on the "four unmoving conditions." In meditation, the *object of meditation* is unmoving, the *mind* is unmoving, the *eyes* are unmoving, and the *physical posture* is unmoving. All of these components of meditation are as solid and as still as a mountain. When the body is still, it can help us to slow the mind. That is why we have instructions on seven points of meditation posture, also known as "the seven points of Vairocana." These instructions help us stabilize our energy through our meditation posture, and that helps the mind to also find stability and concentrate on the object of meditation.

In meditation, even our eyes must become still. Through practice, we can learn how to remain focused on the meditation object with our eyes partially open and unblinking. As long as our eyes are still blinking, we are experiencing some distraction. When our eyes are still, it can also help to stabilize our concentration.

Although these instructions on the four unmoving conditions are related to shamatha meditation—which is the most basic meditation upon which all the other practices are developed—these instructions are valuable even in our advanced practice. If we are doing advanced visualizations as part of a sadhana practice, we can use these instructions to deepen our concentration on the visualizations and to anchor our physical body. We can use the simile of the mountain to deepen our understanding of this unmoving and unwavering concentration.

When we are in the presence of a mountain, we can feel the solidity of that earth; we can feel the grounded energy of that bedrock.

This is how steady our mental concentration can become. But we must not think that concentration is the final goal of meditation. We need to cultivate concentration in order to see the true nature of the mind. That is why we also need insight meditation, also known as vipashyana meditation. This includes the Vajrayana completion-stage practices in our sadhana, which help us to see the clear-light nature of the mind. To experience that insight, we first need to establish an unwavering and unmoving mind.

If there is no obscuration of the clarity of experience,
one might surely think it is the sun and moon.

In this context, "sun and moon" refers to insight meditation, to the experience of clarity. First, we need unmoving shamatha meditation. We need that stable mountain of concentration in order to do the generation stage practices in our sadhana. But we must also develop insight meditation in order to do the completion practices.

We can only see the sun and the moon when there are no obscurations. At twilight or at dawn there will not be clarity. Likewise, we can only see the inner sun and moon when there is mental clarity. If our inner experience is like dusk or if our mind is cloudy, we will not have the experience of insight. Clarity and insight should be there in the mind all the time. We use the example of the sun and the moon, but this is a simile for the clarity within the mind. When the mind is clear, like the sun during an autumn day or the moon during an autumn night, we can view all that arises within that space very clearly.

In tantric practice, we also use the sun and moon to illustrate the stages of awakening. We speak of the sun as the "red path" and the moon as the "white path." The sun and moon also represent the male and female elements, the semen and the blood. At the time of death there is a dissolution of the elements. All of our emotions related to the "eighty gross thoughts" are purified and dissolved. There are three occasions during which one can experience the clear-light nature of the mind: during the dying process, during the completion stage practice, and—for some people—during sleep.

As we have discussed, death is one of the best opportunities for experiencing that clear light. The clear-light nature of the mind is only realized when the eighty gross thoughts related to the root defilements of desire, anger, and ignorance are purified. This is how we purify all appearances. There are four stages of this awakening: appearance, increasing, near-attainment, and ultimately awakening to the clear-light nature of the mind.

If there is no accepting and rejecting in one's conduct,
one might surely think it is the ground of the earth.

Conduct is often described through this simile of the earth or the field. When the field is tilled, there are no crops; nothing is growing; there is not much to accept or to reject. Just as one must till the soil before the seeds can be sown, the Buddhist teachings say that before we can develop all the spiritual qualities, we first need to prepare the ground. From the prepared earth, the seed can sprout, become a healthy sapling, grow into a tree, and ultimately it can bear fruit. Conduct is the ground, it is the foundation, the basis of everything.

The earth by itself, however, cannot produce the seeds that we want. Even if the field is tilled, we must still plant the seeds. We should not make the mistake of thinking that conduct is about doing nothing. Conduct is not about remaining neutral or remaining in ignorance. This would be like tilling a field and then becoming lazy and expecting the crop to plant itself! Neutrality and equanimity are two different things.

Neutrality is related to the root destructive emotion of ignorance. From that ignorance arises desire and anger, attachment and aversion, and acceptance and rejection. We conduct our lives in samsara by classifying everything into three groups: desirable, undesirable, and neutral. We grow attached to some people and we hate other people. We accept some objects and experiences, and we reject others. But this attachment and aversion is there in the first place because we have ignorance.

Sometimes we have this misunderstanding that if we remain in ignorance, we will have achieved equanimity. Neutrality can be mistaken for equanimity because it may feel free of the extremes of desire and anger. But neutrality is still based in ignorance, and as long as we have ignorance we also have the other root defilements. Those emotions may be dormant, but when we are challenged we will see how quickly attachment and aversion can be reactivated within us.

On the other hand, equanimity is rooted in wisdom. When we have purified all of the negative emotions, we will experience that unceasing state of equanimity. That is the true ground, the true earth in which all that we plant will flourish.

If we remain in ignorance, we can ignore many things. In such a state, although we may seem relaxed or detached from emotions, it is not the same as equanimity and nonattachment. We have to transcend all attachment and aversion to arrive at nonattachment. But we cannot get there by merely avoiding or ignoring desirable or undesirable things. Because we have not entirely purified our root ignorance, we go through life accepting or rejecting objects and experiences. Acceptance is based on attachment, on the destructive emotion of desire. Rejection is based on aversion, on the root destructive emotion of anger.

As we have discussed, acceptance and rejection are interdependent; desire gives rise to anger. We experience anger when our desires are not fulfilled. When we do not get what we want, when we lose our pleasurable experiences and happiness, we experience pain, and that pain gives rise to anger. When Jetsun Rinpoche says, "If there is no accepting and rejecting in conduct, surely one might think it is the ground of the earth," he is saying that when we experience equanimity we are free from both accepting and rejecting. Therefore, we should be careful not to mistake ignorance and neutrality for equanimity. Equanimity is the earth in which the healthy tree can grow and bear fruit.

In Buddhism, there are three levels of conduct, each of which has its own set of commitments. There are (1) the vows of *pratimoksha*, or self-liberation; (2) the bodhisattva vows, and (3) tantric samaya commitments. The conduct at the level of self-liberation focuses on actions of body and speech, the bodhisattva vows focus more on mental discipline, and the tantric samaya is a perfect discipline based on the equanimity of wisdom.

All of these similes—space, mountain, sun, moon, and ground—are merely examples to help us cultivate those deeper qualities within us. These examples are all relative. We cannot find ultimate reality in the outer world. We must use these examples to cultivate and recognize our inner qualities and, ultimately, the nature of our own mind. Only when we realize this clarity and emptiness within us will we experience ultimate reality. These similes are only relative; they cannot give us the experience of ultimate truth.

If there is no hope or fear for the result,
one might surely think one has turned away from grasping.

When someone is completely free from grasping, they are also free from hope and fear. Fully enlightened buddhas are free from all forms of grasping and, as a result, they have transcended hope and fear. In Sachen Kunga Nyingpo's teachings on *Freedom from the Four Graspings*,[22] he writes,

> If you're attached to this life, you are not a spiritual person;
> if you're attached to samsara, you don't have renunciation;
> if you have self-grasping, you do not have bodhichitta;
> if you have grasping, you do not have right view.

---

22. Tib., *Zhen pa bzhi bral gyi gdams pa*. See *Mind Training: The Great Collection,* trans. Thupten Jinpa, Wisdom Publications (Somerville, MA: 2005), 517–24, for a translation of the root text and a commentary on it by Jetsun Rinpoche Dragpa Gyaltsen.

We can gauge our spiritual progress based on how much attachment we have and how many spiritual qualities we have cultivated.

What kind of hope is Jetsun Rinpoche talking about here? We have so much hope that things will turn out in a particular way. We have so many future dreams, so many goals. We have this idea that we will arrive at happiness as soon as we finally achieve our dream house, our dream job, our dream family.

But as we all know from personal experience, as soon as those dreams become a reality there is always something new to worry about. Maybe we dream of owning a mansion. If we work very hard and are very fortunate, maybe we will finally buy that enormous house. But then we immediately have new goals and new problems: now we may worry about how to pay the mortgage; we may have to hire many people to care for the property; we may notice that our neighbor has a better garden or a bigger house—and suddenly we become dissatisfied with our dream home.

There are always new problems in samsara because everything in samsara is conditioned; everything is impermanent; everything that is born will also die one day. We will one day have to let go of everything we own. From the moment we are born, we are moving closer to our death. From the moment we meet someone, we are moving closer to saying goodbye. Some people may feel that it is very morbid or negative to think that way, but from a Buddhist perspective this understanding of impermanence can allow us to wake up.

If we fully understand that nothing can stay the same, that all phenomena will come and go, then we can begin to shift our focus. We can begin to become aware of the unconditioned space of our true nature. With that awareness, we also begin to lose our fear of death; we begin to understand that our physical body will grow old and die, but the nature of the mind remains unconditioned.

If we study the life stories of the thousand buddhas, we learn that many of them came from royal families. Just like Shakyamuni Buddha, many of these buddhas were born into great wealth and luxury and later renounced everything to become awakened.

Why were these princes so successful in becoming buddhas? If we have everything we desire and we are still not satisfied, we may realize that material comfort and pleasure cannot bring us fulfillment. As a result, it may be easier for us to wholeheartedly renounce that life and to pursue our spiritual practice. If we have everything we could dream of and we are still unhappy, then we will truly understand that the spiritual path is the only way to achieve peace and liberation from suffering.

On the other hand, if we have always struggled just to find enough food to eat or a safe place to take shelter, we may still imagine that achieving wealth and comfort might solve all of our suffering. Renunciation may be more challenging if we have struggled for survival, because deep down we may still carry some craving for comfort, pleasure, and material wealth. In order to be free from grasping, we have to realize at the very deepest level that we cannot attain peace and joy through pursuing happiness and pleasure.

Renunciation is not the same as giving up. Maybe we have tried very hard to become successful or to gain financial security. Maybe our businesses have failed or the economy has collapsed. In such situations, we can become so frustrated and despairing that we also give up all hope or fear. That form of giving up is not perfect freedom. If we become so depressed that we no longer have any hope for the future or any fear of death, we have not achieved any liberation.

Perfect freedom from hope and fear can only be realized through our spiritual growth and through the cultivation of wisdom and compassion. We are not renouncing out of despair; we are renouncing in order to achieve liberation for the sake of all sentient beings. These lines we are discussing are all related to the three trainings of right view, right meditation, and right conduct. The result of these trainings is the realization of our true nature—the awakening to our inherent wisdom.

Meditation may or may not have been integrated into the view,
but when meditation is integrated into the view,
there is no distraction in the ultimate original nature.

The integration of meditation and view is very important. Jetsun Rinpoche is explaining this integration from the perspective of the meditator's path, wherein the right view is realized through meditation. As we have discussed, there have been many highly realized meditators who were not scholars; they may never have studied all of the philosophical schools. Instead, they may have spent many years in practice perfecting their shamatha meditation. Having become established in that concentration meditation, they then cultivated insight meditation, ultimately awakening to their inherent wisdom.

Some yogis are able to gain such direct insight of right view through their meditation practice alone, without much scholarly study. By meditating for many years, they are able to fully integrate that wisdom into their practice. "When meditation is integrated into the view" means that when we have a direct experience of wisdom, "there is no distraction in the ultimate original nature." Once you have recognized the clear-light nature of the mind, there is no longer any possibility of distraction.

As long as we are susceptible to distraction, we have not perfected our meditation. Whether we will have a direct realization of right view, of ultimate reality, depends on the stability of our meditation. As long as the mind is wandering, we will not awaken to that wisdom.

Once we realize the ultimate original nature, the dharmata, the clear-light nature of our mind, we are beyond all distraction; there is no longer any mental chatter; there is no longer any hope or fear; all of the destructive emotions have been purified. That is only possible when meditation is integrated with the wisdom of the right view.

View may or may not have been integrated into meditation,
but when the view is integrated into meditation,
there is no grasping to the taste of *dhyana*.[23]

23. *Dhyana* (*bsam gtan*) is concentration meditation.

Jetsun Rinpoche is now explaining the integration of right view and meditation from the perspective of the scholarly path. From this approach, the scholar first investigates all of the philosophical conclusions through analytical meditation. Through study and analysis, the scholar then tries to integrate that understanding into their meditation experience. If the view is integrated into meditation, then the result is the same as it is from the meditator's path. The scholar will also awaken to the ultimate wisdom, to the clear-light nature of the mind.

Some yogis start with meditation and some yogis start with philosophical study, but the result of perfect integration is the same: the awakening to the wisdom view. If we only study and never practice, we cannot have that direct experience. If we only do shamatha meditation but we do not gain any insight through vipashyana meditation, then we cannot become aware of our innate wisdom. Integration of view and meditation is essential. Without that integration we cannot have a direct experience of the ultimate reality. Our practice and study will not be complete, and it will not help us to go beyond samsara and to experience liberation.

Here in the West, we often translate the word *vipashyana* as "mindfulness meditation." That translation has lost the deeper meaning related to insight, to wisdom view. The Pali word *vipassana* and the Sanskrit word *vipashyana* are translated in Tibetan as *lhak thong*, which means "seeing more." "Seeing" has to do with that insight into wisdom.

If we have perfected our concentration meditation, then the mind becomes clearer. As a result, we begin to have insight into impermanence, we gain clarity about the root causes of our suffering, and we can ultimately become aware of our empty nature.

We become aware not only of the empty nature of the mind but of all five aggregates: form, feeling, ideation, formation, and consciousness. If those aggregates are defiled, they remain causes and conditions of our suffering in samsara. If we recognize that their true nature is emptiness, that they are insubstantial, then we can experience liberation. When we have this realization, then "there is no grasping to the taste of dhyana," and there is no longer any attachment to our shamatha meditation.

If our shamatha meditation is very highly developed, we may even remain in the meditative state of dhyana of the form realms, and the absorption of the formless realms. We may experience some level of peace in that absorption and may mistake that peace for awakening. Because it is enjoyable, we may remain in that state for so long, grasping onto that experience of concentration and absorption.

This is why we also need insight meditation. In order to experience wisdom, we need to see beyond that grasping and beyond that absorption. View and meditation must go together; we cannot separate them. Without the stability of shamatha meditation, we cannot have insight. Although we need a strong foundation of concentration, shamatha meditation alone will never give us that direct experience of wisdom. We also need to cultivate insight. This is why we need to perfect both the generation and the completion stages in our sadhana practice.

Without generation-stage practice, we cannot have a good completion practice. Without completion practice, without that dissolution stage, our generation practice will still be full of grasping. We may have very strong concentration in our visualization of ourselves as the deity, but without any completion practices we risk grasping onto that divine pride. We may use that generation stage to increase our attachment and identification. We may enjoy that experience, thinking, "I am Tara," or "I am Vajrayogini." If we are attached to the form of the deity without doing the dissolution practices, we will never have insight into the nature of emptiness.

View and meditation may or may not have been integrated into conduct,
but when view and meditation are integrated into conduct,
the experiential realization of meditation and post-meditation arises.

Not only do we need to integrate meditation and wisdom view, we also need to integrate these into our conduct. When all three trainings—view, meditation, and conduct—are integrated in our practice, then "the experiential realization of meditation and post-meditation arises."

Normally in our lives, we may sit for our daily meditation practice; but even if we sit for two hours every day, what are we doing in the remaining twenty-two hours? This is why we need to also cultivate right conduct. Conduct is more protective for the practitioner because conduct is continuing all the time.

Once we fully integrate all three trainings—wisdom, meditation, and conduct—then we are practicing twenty-four hours a day. With such integration, there is no separation between the hours of formal meditation practice and all of our other time; we are always in that awakened state; we are in meditation every hour of the day; we are seeing with that wisdom view at all times. We are also conducting our lives with ethical conduct twenty-four hours a day in accordance with whatever precepts and vows we have taken. That is when "the experiential realization of meditation and post-meditation" can arise. Our life and our spiritual cultivation are no longer separate; the practitioner and the practice have become one and the same.

This is the reason why we have all of the various downtime yogas to aid us in continuing that meditation throughout the twenty-four-hour period. In Vajrayogini practice, we have eleven yogas to transform all of our mundane daily activities—including sleeping—into spiritual practice.

Of what benefit is a high view,
if realization does not arise in the mind?
Of what benefit is good meditation,
if it does not become an antidote to the defilements?

We may esteem our philosophical views; we may say, "My view is very high!" But there is no benefit in that view if it does not help us to experience wisdom. We may think we are having a very good experience of meditation because it is making us feel so calm and relaxed. But if meditation is not helping us to purify the root defilements, then it will only increase our desire; we will become attached to that enjoyment, defeating the purpose of meditation.

The purpose of meditation is to purify all of the active negative emotions as well as all of the negative "sleeping emotions." Even when we are not having an immediate experience of anger, as long as anger is not purified it will be a sleeping emotion in us that can be activated at any moment. Jetsun Rinpoche is asking profound questions here that can help us to explore our own practice and gauge the level of our integration of the view and meditation.

Of what benefit is precise conduct,
if wisdom is not connected with compassion?

As we have discussed, there are many vows we take on the Buddhist path. We have the pratimoksha vows—vowing not to harm sentient beings. In the Mahayana and Vajrayana we also take the bodhisattva vows in order to achieve enlightenment for the sake of all sentient beings. Even if we have taken bodhisattva vows, if our conduct is not based on bodhichitta, if we are not acting out of loving-kindness and compassion, then our conduct is still limited. For conduct to be complete, we should not only refrain from causing harm, but we also need to act out of deep compassion in order to help sentient beings as much as possible. It is only when we become highly realized through tantra, that we can go beyond all dualism. We can go beyond all ideas of right or wrong conduct to see every being as a buddha, to hear all their speech as mantra, and to realize everyone's concepts as wisdom, according to the "continuous" samaya conduct.[24]

Of what benefit is primordial buddhahood,[25]
if one's faults are undiminished even on the surface?

---

24. This refers to ceaseless deity yoga practice, even in one's downtime.
25. "Primordial buddhahood" (*ye sangs rgyas*) is the unconditioned buddha nature pervading all sentient beings.

Although we all have buddha nature inside us, we should not be misled and take pride in thinking that we are already a buddha. Before we can realize our primordial buddhahood, we must purify all of these faults, negative emotions, and karma.

In tantric practice, there are all of these visualizations that we use in order to see ourselves in the image of the deity, as a buddha. This is a method of taking the result—buddhahood—into the path. But we still need to walk that path! Although tantra has very skillful means of reminding us of our basic buddha nature, we will not develop any deeper realization if we do not integrate that into the path. If our practice is not decreasing our defilements or purifying our negative karma, then it is not benefiting us; it is not helping us gain any insight into our primordial nature.

When the meaning of non-arising is realized,
one has arrived at the limit of the view.

Here, Jetsun Rinpoche is helping us to gauge the depth of our understanding, the validity of our view. We have to look within ourselves and question whether the nature of our mind is arising and whether it is ceasing. When we have realized that the nature of the mind, the clear light, is non-arising and non-ceasing, then we have realized the limit of the wisdom view.

When both meditation and post-meditation do not exist,
one has arrived at the limit of meditation.

As we have just discussed, we know that we are remaining in the awakened state if there is no longer any distinction between our life and our spiritual practice, if we are integrating the practices twenty-four hours a day, if there is no difference between meditation and post-meditation. Then, we are living a mindful life, always aware of the clarity and emptiness of our own nature. If that is occurring, it is a sign that our meditation practice is perfected and has arrived at the limit of meditation.

When destruction and protection are neutralized,[26]
one has arrived at the limit of conduct.

When we are in a state of equanimity arising from direct experience of wisdom, we are free from ignorance, free from desire and anger, and free from attachment and aversion. When we are free from these negative emotions, we are free from the need to destroy or protect. We do not have enemies to destroy; we do not have loved ones to protect. We have perfected our conduct and have arrived at the limit of conduct.

When one has obtained both the dharmakaya and the rupakaya,[27]
one has arrived at the limit of the result.

When we attain buddhahood, our wisdom and compassion can manifest in three bodies or *kayas*. Through the loving-kindness and compassion of bodhichitta and through the perfect accumulation of merit, we can obtain the rupakaya, which includes the two form bodies of an enlightened being. As we discussed, these two aspects are the nirmanakaya and the sambhogakaya. The nirmanakaya—the "emanation body"—appears in order to benefit ordinary sentient beings in samsara. The sambhogakaya—the "enjoyment body"—appears in order to benefit highly realized bodhisattvas in the pure lands.

Once we have accumulated wisdom and we realize the clear-light nature of the mind and dharmata, the nature of all phenomena, we attain the dharmakaya—the "truth body." That is how we know that we have arrived "at the limit of the result": we experience the ultimate reality of a buddha's enlightened mind in all its manifestations.

---

26. "Destruction" refers to destroying one's enemies. "Protection" refers to protecting one's followers.
27. Rupakaya is the result of the merit accumulation, physically appearing in Buddha realms and in samsara.

5

Examining the Mind

One should examine one's own mind for the view;
See if permanence and annihilation exist or don't exist.

WHEN WE ENGAGE IN the trainings of wisdom, meditation, and discipline, we can begin to experience significant changes. The whole purpose of Buddhist study and practice is the transformation of the mind. Buddhist study is not about collecting knowledge and information. As we have discussed, if we study in order to collect information, how much are we actually learning? Memory and intelligence are not the same thing. We may be able to memorize so much information, but if it is not helping us transform then it is not very useful spiritually.

Spiritual education has very different goals than academic education. In the academic world, we may memorize a huge amount of information, write so many papers, and generate many opinions. We may be considered very successful according to those values. But from a Buddhist perspective, if that knowledge is not helping us to cultivate our mind, then we are not really learning or understanding.

Modern education has become so utilitarian; we treat it almost like a tool or a weapon. We use education to sharpen our defenses, to polish our concepts and opinions, and then to defend our views. As a result, education may actually be strengthening the ego and increasing the negative emotions. We may become renowned scholars, we may achieve worldly success and financial benefit, we may have many doctorates, but is this cultivating more positive qualities in our mind? We may actually see an increase in aggression and arrogance. We may see the mind becoming more closed to differences in opinion and becoming less flexible and open to learning. From a spiritual perspective, we may have a PhD, but we are not considered wise if there has been no inner transformation.

In the Buddhist training of wisdom, we study, we contemplate, and then we integrate that study into our practice and into our daily lives. Instead of the mind focusing on the outer world, the mind focuses inward in order to understand its own true nature. Modern academic education, on the other hand, is focused outward. It is focused on learning about the world, the universe, other people, and the history of ideas.

The understanding of right view requires that we learn about ourselves so that we can transform and go beyond ourselves completely. When Jetsun Rinpoche exhorts us to "see if permanence and annihilation exist or don't exist," he is asking us to look into our mind to see if we have fallen into the extremes of eternalism or nihilism. Only when we use the mind to examine its own true nature will we begin to understand ultimate reality. Is there any permanent existence of the mind? Is there any nonexistence? This kind of inquiry is what leads to the greatest transformation. The right view can only be cultivated by looking inside our own mental world and asking whether the mind is existing, or nonexisting. Through this inner study we cultivate the training of wisdom, the understanding of clarity and emptiness.

One should examine one's own mind for meditation;
See if distraction exists or doesn't exist.

Although we often use external meditation objects to develop our concentration, meditation is never a practice of looking at the outer world. Meditation is about becoming familiar with our own inner world. By observing ourselves and the habitual patterns of our own minds, we become familiar with how much distraction there is within us. If there is still a lot of distraction in the mind, it means our meditation is not very effective yet, and is an indication that we need to continue practicing. If we look inside the mind and there is *no* distraction, that means our meditation is becoming stronger. As the mind develops more focus and concentration, we will begin to have more glimpses of a true meditation experience. On the other hand, if our mind can still easily be overtaken by thoughts and emotions, then that is a sign that we need to do more meditation.

One should examine one's own mind for conduct;
See if vulgarity exists or doesn't exist.

Ordinarily, we tend to understand conduct in terms of outer activities, such as physical or verbal conduct. Jetsun Rinpoche is reiterating that conduct begins within the mind; if the mind still has negative, vulgar emotions, that means we still need to strengthen and practice mental discipline. If we discover that the mind is increasingly filled with positive emotions and good thoughts, then that means our discipline is working. Whatever we say and do arises from all of those subconscious thoughts and emotions. All of our conduct arises from the motivation and volition in the mind. As we have discussed, the purer our mind is, the purer our conduct will naturally be.

One should examine one's own mind for the result;
See if the ability to endure hardship exists or doesn't exist.

What kind of result can be expected in a practitioner who has trained in meditation, view, and conduct? The result will be someone who is not judgmental or reactive. When faced with undesirable situations, the practitioner will maintain equilibrium and patience. The result of these trainings is a mind that is able to bear witness without engaging emotionally, without accepting or rejecting.

On the other hand, if our practice of meditation, view, and conduct is not successful, then whenever we are faced with hardship we may have so many emotions: we may become angry, we may be filled with regret, we may be very fearful or very hopeful, we may be attached to a certain outcome, we may not have the patience to endure hardship, we may feel such strong resistance to whatever is unfolding.

Good practitioners have very profound patience. When the soon-to-be Buddha was seated under the Bodhi tree attaining enlightenment, the demon Mara appeared in many forms and tried to disturb, distract, and deceive the Buddha in every possible way. Mara tried to elicit desire by sending his three beautiful daughters to throw flowers and to seduce the Buddha. Mara tried activating his anger by being aggressive and threatening him with weapons. Mara tried to evoke doubt and fear in the Buddha by questioning his views and sending wild beasts and natural disasters. But the Buddha remained unshaken by all of these attempts due to the strength and wisdom in his mind. He remained in meditation under the Bodhi tree, bearing witness to what was unfolding around him without being disturbed.

We are not at that level of wisdom yet. If someone is attacking us, we react and defend ourselves. If someone is seducing us, we may be unable to resist the attraction. Like moths who cannot stop flying right into a flame, we are often unable to resist desirable objects. Our minds are still not very disciplined, so we fall prey to all kinds of sensual pleasures. We have not seen the ultimate reality, the nature of emptiness, so we are always grasping and clinging.

There are so many kinds of addictions in ordinary life. Some addictions, such as abusing drugs or alcohol, can be life-threatening. But often we don't realize the impact of all of the other things we are addicted to. Maybe we are addicted to social media, or television, or shopping, or food. This is all a result of not seeing the ultimate nature of reality yet.

We are so easily deluded by our strong emotions. When we are infatuated with someone, we become selectively blind to the risks or to their faults. That deluded mind is the opposite of the goal of training in wisdom. Wisdom helps the mind to see the empty nature of ultimate reality, but negative emotions delude the mind completely. When we have a deluded mind, we are not disciplined and we do not have mindfulness. We are controlled by emotion and become dependent on objects, relationships, substances, or activities. We may even commit crimes in order to achieve more of what we desire.

If our mind is trained in wisdom, meditation, and conduct, we will have an enduring peace and balance in the mind. The "ability to endure hardship," refers to that unshakable peace. The result of the three trainings is the realization of our own buddha nature, and that clarity and emptiness allows us to be at peace regardless of what hardships are occurring.

View is the guide of the mind;
meditation is the path of the mind;
conduct is the friend of the mind;
the result is the host of the mind.

At our level, it is very difficult to experience peace. We are constantly distracted; we are always reacting; our minds are still very restless and undisciplined. And why are we restless? We are restless because our consciousness is always focused *outward*, pursuing things outside ourselves. We are pursuing things in the outer world and yet, the more we consume, the more insatiable we become. As we have discussed, trying to satisfy desire is like drinking salty water; the more we drink, the more thirst we have. We cannot satisfy the mind through pursuing desirable things outside the mind. Our habitual pattern is to consume something based on desire and then to inevitably become frustrated and restless and move on to desiring something else. In this way, we become trapped in a very vicious cycle. The minute a marriage becomes difficult, we begin looking for a better partner. The minute our dream home begins to have issues, we immediately start looking for a bigger and better house.

As long as the mind is pursuing happiness through grasping at outer objects, there is no way the mind will ever be satisfied. Only when we focus the mind *inside* and get to know our own true nature will we begin to feel a deep sense of fulfillment and peace. In a sense, we are returning to our true home, to our true resting place.

The mind is so accustomed to wandering around outside itself pursuing objects and ideas. It is so busy looking outward it does not get to know itself. It is always restlessly searching for happiness and satisfaction. Through practice, we can bring the mind back to its ultimate home. If the mind is blinded by delusion, it cannot find its own true home. It is only through developing the wisdom view that we can guide the mind. That is why Jetsun Rinpoche is saying, "view is the guide of the mind"; with the training of wisdom, the mind will find its way home to its true nature.

If we are wandering around outside and our vision is obscured, it will be very hard to get home. The wisdom that we are training in is the mind's own eye. To get back home, we need the right view, but we also need the path of meditation. But even if we have good vision and the proper path, the journey is long and we may get very discouraged and weary. That is where conduct is such a good friend to us along the way. Conduct supports this journey home; it gives us the discipline to persevere even when the journey is challenging. Physical discipline, verbal discipline, and mental discipline are all very trusted friends on the path. Proper conduct supports the mind through all of the obstacles along the way.

What is the result of that long journey? The result is that we are welcomed home to our original nature. The original nature of the mind is the true host of the mind. When the mind realizes its own true nature of clarity and emptiness, it has finally come home to the ultimate reality, where the mind will be entirely at peace.

We all have the potential to bring the mind home because this true nature is already within us. Bringing the mind back to its original state is the goal of all of our practice. It is not about discovering something new; it is about uncovering our true nature that is already within us. That is the only way that we will truly find peace and rest. As long as we are wandering in the outer world looking for happiness, we will never be satisfied. In just four lines, Rinpoche is giving us a concise and profound teaching. Through contemplating and understanding these lines we can understand the very heart of our practice.

Meditation has the ability to transcend all of the habitual patterns in the mind. It has such incredible healing power. With it, we can reverse so many negative patterns of thinking and acting; we can become aware when we are walking down the wrong path, and apply the antidotes. But it is only through practicing day after day that we can begin to experience this transformation. We can imagine that meditation is like going into a very dense forest each day and slowly clearing a path home. Practice and perseverance are the only way to accomplish that path.

Conduct helps us determine who are the true friends of the mind. Conduct helps us see which thoughts and actions are helping us along that path and which activities are actually harming us. We need to understand this properly. We often mistake enemies for friends along the way. Certain activities may give us momentary pleasure so we consider them friends. But in reality, those activities may be making us more deluded or lazy; they may be the cause of more desire or anger. We can mistake temporary satisfaction as a sign of good conduct, but that is a very limited understanding. We often do not see that we are increasing negative emotions through these pleasurable activities.

If an enemy is running at us with guns and knives, we will know immediately that they mean to harm us. But if someone approaches us with gifts and compliments, we may be fooled into thinking they are a friend, even if their intentions are negative or manipulative. They may appear very pleasant but in reality, they are hurting us. These kinds of false friends are the worst enemies because they deceive and harm us and we do not even know to be alert to the dangers.

The mental world is no different. Many of the things that bring us temporary happiness are actually enemies disguised as friends; we may not recognize that they are actually the root cause of increased desire or anger. It is very important to observe which thoughts and activities are enemies and which activities are friends. Conduct is the friend of the mind that helps us determine this. Conduct helps to discipline those negative emotions and helps us determine which thoughts and activities are helping us along the path.

Through traveling that path in our daily practice, we will come home to our true nature. The result is not something up ahead somewhere—it is not about achieving something new. The "result" is coming home to our true dwelling place in the ultimate nature of the mind, in that union of clarity and emptiness.

I heard a story that will help to illustrate this point. Once, there was a young man who was carrying a lamp outside and searching intently for something he had lost. An old mystic asked the young man what he was looking for. "I am looking for a needle I have lost," replied the young man. So the mystic asked him where he had lost the needle, and the man replied that he had lost the needle inside his house. At this, the mystic said, "Well, if you have lost the needle inside your house, then why are you looking for the needle outside in the yard?" This story helps to remind us that the result—buddhahood—cannot be searched for and found outside. Instead, if we look inside our mind, then we will see that the result—the clear-light nature—is the host, and the mind is the guest.

The sky of the view is considered to be high;
the ocean of meditation is considered to be deep;
the field of conduct is considered to be tilled;
the crop of the result is considered to be ripened.

If we are flying very high in the sky, we will be able to see everything. Like that, our view should be as expansive as the sky. The wisdom view provides such a vast perspective. With this view, we will see the truth of everything. In contrast, if we are walking through a dense jungle our view will be very limited.

The five experiences of shamatha meditation are often described through water imagery. Early in our shamatha practice, we may experience a rushing torrent of thoughts when we try to concentrate. This first experience is described as being similar to a waterfall. The second experience, where we may begin to notice a slowing of those thoughts, is said to be like a river. The third experience, where the thoughts are more settled but occasionally still disturbed by the springs, is likened to a spring-fed pond. The fourth experience is like the ocean with waves; our concentration at this level is deepening and we are beginning to experience that spaciousness and vastness of the ocean but there are still waves, we are still experiencing some thoughts. The fifth experience of shamatha meditation is like the "ocean without waves." When we reach this final experience of an ocean without waves, our concentration is completely stable, the mind is totally calm, and there are no thoughts or distractions. At this highest level of shamatha practice, our meditation is very strong; even in the depths of that "ocean," there is no longer any movement, and we can experience a deep concentration within the mind.

Our conduct should be like tilled fertile ground, from which any crop can grow. For us, that crop is all of the spiritual qualities that we are cultivating within us. If the ground is well prepared, then whatever we plant in those fields will sprout, grow into a healthy plant, ripen, and eventually we will experience a good harvest as the result. Through all of these outer examples, Jetsun Rinpoche is giving guidance about how to train in view, meditation, and conduct.

Although I do not possess the best understanding,

In this line, Jetsun Rinpoche is expressing his humility. We can see that, although he has profound spiritual realization, he does not have any arrogance about his understanding. If someone has a lot of ego and pride they will be more apt to say, "Oh, I know everything!" But for someone who is wise, they will understand that the more they know, the more they will realize there is more to learn. When they have a very deep understanding like Rinpoche, they may even be able to say that they do not know. Someone with limited understanding may be more likely to be arrogant and to claim they have all of the answers.

We can see this danger in academia; scholars may do research on just one subject and yet they may make conclusions regarding all of Buddhist philosophy. But to accurately reach conclusions regarding Buddhism, one must first study over one hundred volumes of teachings by the Buddha in the Kangyur, and then, based on that, study the treatises and commentaries in the Tengyur—which comprise over two hundred volumes. On top of this study, one must also cultivate a deep meditation practice. At that point, perhaps the scholar may reach a more complete conclusion!

If our study is too narrow and we specialize in just one text or philosophical school, our understanding will not be very well-informed. We may experience pride or arrogance because we know this one text so well. But Jetsun Rinpoche is a yogi; even though he has profound spiritual realization he is always expressing his humility.

yet by studying with learned gurus and
by accumulating the knowledge of hearing and contemplation,
my understanding of realization arose.

Jetsun Rinpoche is showing us the importance of studying all of the scriptures and shastras, and of hearing, contemplating, and practicing the oral instructions. He is emphasizing that it is only through learned gurus, through study and contemplation, and through incorporating all of that into our practice that we will obtain realization.

Understand that a human body is difficult to obtain,
like a sea turtle [surfacing through] a yoke.

These lines are referring to the preciousness of obtaining a human rebirth. According to a Buddhist teaching, the chances of being reborn as a human are as rare as the chances that a blind turtle swimming in a vast ocean surfacing only once every hundred years will surface perfectly with his neck inside a yoke that is floating randomly on that ocean.

Not only is human rebirth rare and precious, it is even more rare to have a human rebirth with all of the endowments for spiritual practice. There are so many things that are allowing us to do spiritual practice, for which we should feel very grateful. Most importantly, we are endowed with a mind that is not clouded by illness and is able to learn, study, and practice. If we are suffering from dementia or other injuries or illnesses of the brain, we may be unable to understand or concentrate. The brain needs to be able to function in order to cultivate the mind. Although the nature of the mind is already pure, in order to access that purity we need a healthy brain. The greatest gift we have is a brain and mind that are alert and aware enough to practice and learn and to uncover the true nature of the mind.

We should also feel grateful if we are endowed with a situation that gives us time to pursue spiritual practice. If we are focused solely on survival, we might find it very difficult to concentrate and practice. We should feel grateful if we are endowed with positive living conditions. If we are suffering from war or famine, we will be very distracted by hunger and danger, making it harder to practice.

Mind and body are interdependent in this life—they complement each other. We all have our own mental characteristics, emotions, psychological tendencies, and physiological characteristics. We also have all of the sense organs, and we should be grateful if we have healthy sense organs. Healthy eyes, ears, nose, and so forth are a great gift. We can understand these as results of past karma and we can practice gratitude for all of these positive conditions that support our practice.

Here, it is important not to misunderstand karma. We should not feel shame if we have physical or mental disabilities. We should not understand this as some form of punishment. We can use these challenges as fuel to cultivate compassion for the suffering of all beings and to do whatever is possible in our spiritual practice in this life. Maybe it will take longer if we have some of these obstacles, but we should not let this be discouraging; we should do whatever we can. We can practice gratitude for whatever we have and cultivate positive emotions even if conditions are challenging.

If we have many obstacles to our practice, we can still cultivate gratitude for the preciousness of this human rebirth. Even just being born in a human form is a result of many good things we have done in past lifetimes, so we can cultivate gratitude for this life and for what we have done in the past that generated this rebirth. This human life is very rare and very precious.

There is a saying that "health is more important than wealth." This is very true when it comes to our practice. We may be millionaires, but if our mind is clouded by illness, all of that wealth will not help our practice. Having a stable mind and a healthy body are a great fortune. They are far more valuable than any other assets. If we have some physical challenges, it may consume a lot of our energy and it may be more difficult to practice. We often take our health for granted and only think about it when something goes wrong. It is good to remember to be grateful while we are healthy and not to take it for granted, especially because we know how impermanent this body is. Eventually we will all grow sick and old. We will all die. It is good to cultivate awareness of impermanence and to use this precious lifetime for spiritual practice.

Everything is always changing: our body is always changing; conditions around us are always changing. Many people think, "I will practice meditation and do retreats when I retire and have more time." We should not assume that we will live to retirement age. We should not wait for some future time when it will be more convenient to begin our practice. We should remember that any day could be our last day in this human lifetime.

Life can change in an instant. If we follow the news, we will be reminded every day about impermanence. Situations are always changing. Everything can be normal and then suddenly there is a massive storm or a traffic accident or a terrorist attack or a global pandemic.

Things are changing globally, and things are changing at a very personal level all the time.

Understand that it is difficult to find a guru,
like the jewel of Takshaka's crown.

Jetsun Rinpoche is reminding us that encountering an authentic teacher and cultivating a spiritual practice is even more rare and precious than obtaining a human life. In fact, it is the most extraordinary opportunity in this lifetime. Takshaka is one of the eight Naga kings who wears a precious jewel in his crown. Finding an authentic guru who is connected to an unbroken lineage of gurus is as rare as this jewel in Takshaka's crown.

Nagas are powerful beings who dwell in the underworld. They are celebrated and revered in cultures across Asia. In Buddhism it is said that the Nagas have a strong impact on weather. Because of this, in Tibet and India, whenever there is an issue with the weather, practitioners try to make offerings and show friendliness to these beings in the underworld. They try to be friendly with snakes and fish and frogs and other beings associated with the Nagas. It is believed that weather is actually influenced by the underworld and by all of these elements.

Our lives depend on what is arising from the earth and from the domain of these Naga creatures. It is said that the underworld is the owner of our wealth. We can see how all of our oil comes from underground. All of our precious jewels, our gold and diamonds, and all of our minerals are coming from the underworld. When we disturb the Nagas, we are also disrupting the ecosystem.

We celebrate Naga days in order to honor these kings of the underworld and to make offerings to them. We do this by going to the roots of the trees and offering milk to the snakes; we go to the water and offer food to the frogs. Through these offerings we show our goodwill and friendliness to these beings. If we disrupt these beings, they will also disturb us. There is so much disruption in our ecosystem these days; we are creating so much toxicity in the ground; we are disturbing the underworld with so much mining and drilling and development and dumping of waste. From a Buddhist perspective, these activities are very upsetting to the Naga beings, who will then bring trouble for us.

These changes of the body with four seasons—
understand them as the secret sign of death.
Understand that everything is left behind when passing away,
like a person being exiled to an enemy country.

Although we have a precious human life with eight freedoms and ten endowments and are connected with the Dharma through the guru, just like the changing of the four seasons, our life is still rushing toward death. Whatever we have materially accumulated, including our body, we will have to leave behind at the time of death. We will be forced by karma to be exiled to the fearful bardo, and will experience painful rebirth in different realms in samsara.

Understand that everything is born from karma,
like the colors of a peacock's feathers.
Understand that there is no birth in samsara
if emptiness by nature is realized.

The relative world is like the colors of a peacock's feathers; both the inhabitants and their location in the world are created by the karma of beings. This is the reason why the great Indian master Vasubandhu says in the *Abhidharmakosha*, "different world systems are born from karma." But if one realizes the ultimate nature of emptiness, then one is free from the wheel of life, including birth and death in samsara.

Understand the nature of appearances as emptiness,
like a reflection in a mirror.
Understand the nature of emptiness as appearances,
like a display seen in a dream.

These are the two different ways to explain relative and ultimate reality respectively. Whatever appears to us is due to interdependence. The profound lines of the *Heart Sutra* also express this interdependence by saying, "Form (matter) is emptiness. Emptiness is form. Form is not other than emptiness, nor is emptiness other than form." We are the creators of our entire experience of the universe. We need to understand the nature of appearances. "Appearances" refers to all of the apparent objects in the universe. We are the creators of those appearances in the same way that we are the creators of our own dreams.

As we have been discussing, we are the creators of the entire relative world. Our experience is not universal. Until we understand ultimate reality—the empty nature of all things—we will be living in a very relative world. It is relative in the sense that our experience is not the universal experience. For example, we may think of water as something for drinking and bathing. We may also be afraid of water when there are floods or ocean storms. But for fish, their experience of water is entirely different from ours. For fish, water is their home and they will die if we take them from the ocean. If our experience of water were ultimate reality, then all beings would have the same experience of that appearance.

Due to our individual and collective karma as human beings, we create our human experience of the relative world just as we create our dreams. There is an interdependence here between subject and object. If we busy ourselves learning only about the outer world of objects rather than getting to know the nature of our own minds, we won't experience any spiritual transformation. From our limited understanding, we cannot see that apparent objects are empty. Objects feel very real to us. There is no way for us to see the empty nature of appearances if we have not recognized it within our own mind first.

At the moment, outer objects have so much power over us; we do not realize that we are the creators of those appearances. We have not realized any freedom because we don't understand the empty nature of all phenomena. We can only recognize that emptiness when we have seen that purity in our own mind. When we discover the clear nature of the mind, everything that appears will become pure vision.[28]

When we have the realization of clarity and emptiness in our own mind, objects will no longer have any power over us. We will be able to view all appearances as illusory, like images in a dream or reflections in a mirror. By nature, they are empty; but if we do not have the inner realization of emptiness, then the outer appearances will seem to us like independently existing objects.

Understand the nature as completely pure,
like the golden luster of whey.
Understand conceptuality as adventitious,
like clouds, dirt, or rust.

Once we have the realization of the nature of our own mind, then the nature of the subject and the object will be the same. Jetsun Rinpoche gives us the example of whey. When we make cheese, we boil the milk and everything congeals together; what remains is this clear golden liquid whey. In a similar way, the reality of both the outer object and the inner subject is pure. Human nature is as pure as the golden luster of whey. By nature, we have so much goodness inside us. The nature of the mind is so pure. Our minds are obscured by all our concepts and emotions, like clouds or dirt or rust obscure what lies beneath them. The nature of the mind is as pure as space, but clouds come and go, temporarily obscuring that clear sky.

What Rinpoche is reminding us is that anger is temporary, delusion is temporary, all of the negative as well as the positive emotions we have are temporary. We are pure by nature. This is actually very liberating. Whenever we feel overwhelmed by negative emotions, it helps to remember that these feelings are impermanent. If we have the patience

28. There are three types of vision: the impure vision of sentient beings, a yogi's experiential vision, and the pure vision of the buddhas.

to relax, to not grasp onto or reject those feelings, they will come and go just like clouds.

If we are feeling rage, the best thing to do is to have patience and to allow the anger to pass—and it will pass, because the conditioned world is always changing. Negative emotions will always pass like clouds, because they are not in the true nature of the mind.

Understand conceptuality as samsara;
understand nonconceptuality as nirvana.

As long as we are caught in the conceptual world, there will be so much anguish and suffering. We will be creating more and more karma through our thoughts and actions. When we stop thinking, we also stop suffering; suffering is present because of thinking. If we want to free ourselves from suffering, we have to stop thinking. That's why the teaching is saying nonconceptuality is nirvana.

Whenever we can stop thinking, even for a few moments, we will experience peace. We will have little glimpses of nirvana. In our highest experience of meditation, there is no thought; there are no emotions; there is an experience of profound peace. Thoughts and feelings create all of our suffering. Mental suffering is the most serious. Mental pain can be even more severe than physical pain. Mental pain and suffering is rooted in negative thoughts. Maintaining that space without any thoughts during meditation is actually a source of healing for the mind. As a result, it is also a source of healing for the body. When the mind is at peace, the body is also at peace.

Understand samsara as suffering;
understand liberation as bliss.

Understand that both happiness and suffering do not exist;
understand primordial emptiness as free from origin.[29]

29. "Free from origin" means "unconditioned."

Liberating the mind from thought is blissful. Being caught in cycles of thinking generates all of our suffering and keeps us trapped in samsara. Thoughts arise because of our self-clinging; all thoughts have some relationship to our ego. Due to that ego involvement, thoughts can perpetuate so much mental pain. Jetsun Rinpoche is reminding us that in ultimate reality, happiness and suffering do not exist. Primordial emptiness, that freedom from conditioned existence, is ultimate reality. It is the ultimate bliss of liberation.

6

Bliss Again

Generally, if comprehension arises in the mind, bliss;
if the view is realized, also bliss.

The ripened illusory body[30] is bliss;
if there is no disease, again, bliss.

Relying on the seclusion of retreat is bliss;
if activities are abandoned, also bliss.

Livelihood agreeing with Dharma is bliss;
if wrong livelihood is abandoned, again, bliss.

IF WE HAVE A realization of ultimate reality—the natural emptiness of all things—then we will have the wisdom to transcend all reactivity in our lives. At that point, whatever unfolds in our lives, good or bad, we can simply bear witness to it; we can remain at peace. The

30. "The ripened illusory body" refers to our body as a result of the ripening of karma.

word "bliss" here is referring to that peaceful experience of realizing the wisdom of empty nature that has gone beyond both pain and pleasure, beyond both happiness and unhappiness.

As we all know, life often feels like a roller coaster. Our emotions are always changing: sometimes we have very high emotions and we feel excited and happy; sometimes when things go wrong, or even when they merely change, we can feel emotionally low and depressed. This is how we are living, always on this emotional ride. Once we have a realization of wisdom, we will be stable in spite of that roller coaster. When we have exciting emotions, we won't become too happy. When we have low points, we won't become too sad. We will transcend both of these extremes and maintain peace and equanimity in our lives.

High and low are interdependent. When we experience high emotions, it is inevitable that we will feel low again at some point. That is because everything is always changing. Happiness is a form of suffering, because whatever brings us happiness in the relative world will always change: our marriage will change, our home will change, our work will change, our body will change, our children will change. Nothing can stay the same.

Our lives are conditioned this way; there will always be sickness, old age, and death. We will always be faced with gains and losses. What *can* remain stable is our response to those changes. Whether we are able to experience life without accepting or rejecting things, without attachment or aversion, depends on our level of spiritual realization.

Ordinarily, if we have no pain or disease, we may take our health for granted. We may not even remember to be grateful for or mindful of the body. But if there is sickness, then usually we become very focused on the body, and we often feel resentful of circumstances. These negative emotions will increase our physical and mental suffering. Jetsun Rinpoche is teaching us that whether there is sickness or health, both can be approached in the same way. We are transcending this dualism.

Rinpoche is also encouraging us to renounce mundane activities and to remain in seclusion. For those who have higher realization though, it doesn't matter whether they are surrounded by people or in a solitary retreat; they can experience the same peace in all situations. Whether we are busy or idle, both are the same if we have the wisdom to know the empty nature of activities. We will experience the same equanimity and peace regardless of circumstances.

Livelihood is important in our relative world; our work is how we provide food and shelter for ourselves. If we don't have work we may suffer; we may experience homelessness, for example. For someone without spiritual realization, begging for food and sleeping on the street may seem like terrible suffering.

On the other hand, for someone with a high level of realization, they may experience bliss even when they are wandering through dirty streets begging for food. As we've discussed, there is a long tradition of wandering yogis who have experienced very high realization of wisdom while living without any home, work, or belongings. The Buddha was born a prince and had so much luxury, surrounded by pleasurable experiences, yet he abandoned everything to become a wandering yogi, surviving on whatever food was offered to him.

Even now, in countries like Thailand, it is normal for monks and nuns to go out on the street every day to ask for food offerings from laypeople. At some point, when our realization of wisdom is very strong, we can experience bliss in any situation, neither accepting nor rejecting, because we see the empty nature of phenomena. We will no longer *need* a job, a home, or any worldly belongings. Whatever circumstances arise, we will be able to relate to them with the same equanimity.

As long as we are still caught in the dualism of accepting and rejecting, of attachment and aversion, we will experience great resistance to disagreeable objects and circumstances. Rejecting what we are experiencing creates so much inner suffering. Although the Buddha was begging on the street, he did not experience that as suffering; he had a level of mental freedom within that situation and there was no longer any judgment of good or bad experiences. The Buddha was free from the five wrong livelihoods.

**The desire-objects of the youthful body and mind are bliss;
if one is connected with the method, also bliss.**

If a practitioner has integrated the skillful methods of bodhichitta and the tantric practices, then even desirable objects can cultivate the great bliss of wisdom within them. For a highly realized practitioner, even if they consume desirable objects—even if they eat delicious foods or experience other sensory pleasures—those experiences will not generate more desire and more attachment to those objects. At our level, because we do not see the ultimate reality of the object, whenever something gives us pleasure and happiness, we become more attached to it. We cling to positive experiences and become more dependent.

Jetsun Rinpoche is saying that if we know the empty nature of objects, then we have freedom even if we engage with such objects. From the view of ultimate wisdom, even if we are consuming something wonderful, it will leave no karmic traces; it will not generate more craving. It is like walking somewhere without leaving any footprints. With such an understanding, we will not engage with the object based on negative emotions, nor will we be reinforcing habitual patterns.

Someone who has the realization of wisdom can experience things freely without being driven by karma and emotions. From the outside, it may appear that they are just indulging in a delicious meal like everyone else. But their experience of that meal and the results of eating it will be very different. It will leave no karmic imprint and will not act as a condition for further craving. At the next meal, if they are given food that is very undesirable, the yogi will not experience aversion or disappointment; there will be no expectation, and they will consume that disgusting meal with the same bliss.

But for us, because we do not see the reality of the object, once we taste something delicious we immediately become attached to that experience. We may crave that meal again for many years. The pleasurable experience leaves karmic imprints, increasing our desire. If we return to the same restaurant and it does not taste as good as it did the first time, we will be frustrated and disappointed. But for highly realized yogis, desirable and undesirable experiences are the same. Whatever they consume does not leave any trace in their mind; it does not increase their desire or attachment, and it does not give rise to future craving or disappointment.

Friends with agreeable view and conduct are bliss.
Practicing in solitude is bliss.

Friendship has so much influence on us. Ordinarily, when we spend time with people who share our views and opinions, we experience pleasure and happiness. Our friendships generally arise based on mutual interests and shared belief systems. In this way, many relationships begin with very agreeable circumstances. But many friendships and marriages are destroyed when people begin to have significant differences of view or opinion.

For yogis who are living with a realization of ultimate wisdom, whether a friend is agreeable or disagreeable does not make a difference. Because the friendship arises from ultimate reality, it is not conditional. From a place of ultimate wisdom, a friend does not become an enemy. Such highly realized yogis are also not dependent on others; whether they practice in solitude for many years or in a busy place, they will experience the same bliss.

Food and wealth without grasping and attachment are bliss.
Having no definite residence is bliss.
Friendship free of obligation is bliss.
If one obtains freedom, bliss!

Generally, we equate security with having an abundance of food, owning a home, and reliable relationships. We think that the more wealth we have, the more food we have, the more security cameras we have on our homes, the more it will insure our safety and our status. We do not realize that all of this grasping is actually making us feel more and more insecure. There is no way to buy enough insurance to feel completely at peace. The nicer our home is, the more afraid we may become of losing it to wildfires or storms. The more valuable our possessions are, the more worried we may become about someone stealing everything. Most of our relationships increase our dependency on each other rather than our independence and freedom. Freedom without obligation is great bliss, but being dependent on each other actually increases our insecurity.

Due to our attachments, when we lose some wealth or security we may experience acute suffering. But for those who don't have any attachment or grasping, loss or gain will not impact their well-being; they will still have mental security. Realizing the empty nature of objects liberates them from all clinging and fear. They realize the impermanence of all conditioned things. As a result, even if they have a wonderful home and it burns to the ground, their bliss will be undisturbed. They understand that we come into this life alone and without any possessions. Likewise, we will not be able to take anything with us when we die. We cannot take any of our loved ones, our wealth, or our possessions with us; only our mind will continue after death.

The nature of all conditioned things is impermanent. Even if we have been very fortunate and prosperous in our lives, none of that can travel with us. We spend so much of our lives accumulating wealth and material security, but none of that can prevent old age, sickness, and death. It is better to cultivate the mind in this lifetime, for the mind is all that will continue.

In ancient times, in some civilizations it was customary for a king to be buried with many of his possessions. We can see in these ancient burial sites that kings were entombed with their horses, their gold, even their servants. They may have believed they would be more secure bringing all of those attachments with them. But the reality is that none of their possessions or servants could assist those kings after death.

7

Both Have Occurred at the Same Time

I am not someone who possesses merit,
but both my obtaining a complete human birth,
and the spread of the Buddhadharma—
both of those occurred at the same time.

HERE AGAIN, JETSUN RINPOCHE is expressing humility and reducing his arrogance by saying he does not possess merit. He is not taking any personal pride in these auspicious conditions. But, as we know, a precious human birth is only possible if we have accumulated significant merit in past lifetimes. "The spread of the Buddhadharma" here means that the Buddha's teachings are available in the world to be met with.

Rinpoche gathered enough merit to be born as a human being. Not only that, but he was one of the founding masters of the Sakya school. He was not only a great scholar, but he was a great yogi. He was born at a time when the Dharma was spreading everywhere in his area of Tibet.

We can see that his precious human life possessed all of these signs of accumulated merit from past lifetimes.

There is a prediction in the sutras regarding how long Buddha Shakyamuni's teachings will last in this world. Even if we are fortunate enough to be born during the existence of the Dharma in the world, we will not connect with that Dharma if we don't have the sufficient karma and merit.

This great song by Jetsun Rinpoche is also called a *doha*. Doha is a Sanskrit word that means "couplet." Sometimes couplets can have double meanings and they can also feel similar to navigating a maze. Sometimes the dohas of the mahasiddha Gorakshanatha are even called *Gorakh dhanda*, which is translated as "Gorakh's maze."

Rinpoche is directly pointing out how two events have happened at the same time. Indirectly, he is clarifying how all of these events have occurred simultaneously due to the accumulation of merit. Rinpoche is also reiterating how difficult it is to achieve a human rebirth. The meeting and occurring of two conducive events at the same time makes the human birth even more precious and valuable. Only someone who has accomplished both the accumulations of merit and of wisdom can have such auspicious meetings and simultaneous occurrences.

In the following lines, Rinpoche shares his own experiences on the spiritual path. His personal experience can also serve as a reference for us on our own journey. Several factors were essential on his path and will help to guide us. These factors include achieving human birth; producing renunciation; searching for teachers and gurus; learning the meanings of scriptures; finding the guru and receiving empowerments; receiving transmissions and oral instructions; the arising of certainty in the Dharma; the arising of devotion to the guru and receiving his blessings; the arising of the wisdom within; accomplishing both the generation and completion stages; accomplishing the paths of accumulation, application, and seeing; and integrating realization and practice continuously during post-meditation.

Both turning away from clinging to worldly dharma,
and the arising of enthusiasm for spiritual Dharma—
both of those occurred at the same time.

Generally, the Buddhist spiritual path formally begins by taking refuge. The main purpose of taking refuge is to produce renunciation for samsara and worldly "dharma." Only when we have produced renunciation, will our enthusiasm to practice Dharma increase.

Jetsun Rinpoche makes an important distinction here between the "eight worldly dharmas" and the holy Dharma. Although we may appear to be practicing Dharma when we practice the eight worldly dharmas, our purpose is still not spiritual; we have not renounced worldly life. But it is well known that Rinpoche was a great yogi and had genuinely renounced all of the worldly dharmas. "The arising of enthusiasm for spiritual Dharma," refers to the arising of diligence in practicing the Buddha's teachings.

Both having left one's country abandoned,
and meeting the guru in exile—
both of those occurred at the same time.

Jetsun Rinpoche is referring to a long tradition in India and Tibet of wandering yogis who found their gurus while traveling away from their hometown or country. Yogis are not nationalists; they often abandon their home or country just as Buddha Shakyamuni did while he was still prince Siddhartha, renouncing his own kingdom and proceeding to meet with different teachers.

Wandering yogis abandon all security. For the sake of pursuing spiritual practice and benefiting all sentient beings, they abandon their worldly life, renouncing everything and going into exile to search for their guru. The stories of the eighty-four mahasiddhas of ancient India describe how these great masters lived as wandering yogis. Although they owned nothing, they attained a deep inner security and peace due to their spiritual practice and realization.

Both hearing the scriptures,
and understanding their words and meanings—
both of those occurred at the same time.

Jetsun Rinpoche is referring to understanding the words and the meanings of the Buddha's sutras as well as of the shastras of the great *panditas*, which comprise scholarly commentaries on the sutras. For example, we can understand the meaning of the *Heart Sutra* much better by studying the *Abhisamayalamkara*. The purpose of studying the Buddhist sutras and shastras is not to memorize and simply repeat their words. The purpose of studying these Buddhist scriptures and treatises is to understand and experience their deeper meaning. In Rinpoche's case, that study and that profound understanding occurred at the same time.

Both finding a Vajrayana guru,
and obtaining the four *abhishekas*[31] completely—
both of those occurred at the same time.

Not only did Jetsun Rinpoche find his guru, he also received all of the four *abhishekas*—the profound Vajrayana empowerments. In order to realize mahamudra through the practice of the generation and completion stages in our sadhana, we need to receive all four empowerments. These four empowerments are comprised of the vase, secret, wisdom, and *turiya*—also called *chaturiya*—empowerments.

The Sanskrit word *abhisheka* literally means "sprinkling and pouring." "Sprinkling" refers to the power of abhisheka to cleanse us of all our negativities. "Pouring" refers to the way that these empowerments pour the potentialities of wisdom into us. Abhisheka includes four

31. *Abhisheka* (Tib. *dbang* ["*wang*"]) is the method for achieving enlightenment in this lifetime by creating a special dependent origination between the cause (aggregates, elements, and *ayatanas*) and the result (the kayas and wisdoms); it also introduces the student to Vajrayana.

sprinklings to purify the negativities. These sprinklings purify the physical, verbal, mental, and all remaining negativities.

With the four pourings, we receive the potentialities for all four buddha manifestations or *kayas* within us. These kayas are the nirmanakaya, or emanation body; sambhogakaya, or enjoyment body; dharmakaya, or truth body; and *svabhavakaya*, or essence body. Rinpoche is saying that finding the guru and obtaining empowerments both happen at the same time. This can only result from the accumulation of much merit in previous lifetimes.

Both the bestowal of the oral transmission and instructions,
and the arising of profound certain knowledge—
both of those occurred at the same time.

The highest teachings within the Sakya school emphasize four kinds of validations that can give rise to a profound certainty of the Dharma knowledge within us. The first validation is based on the student's direct spiritual experience in their practice. The second validation is based on the strength of the student's experience, which then validates the authenticity of the guru. The third validation is based on the shastras and oral instructions taught by the guru. The fourth validation is based on those shastras being validated by the Buddha's words in the scriptures (sutras). When Jetsun Rinpoche says, "profound certain knowledge," he is referring to all four of those validations occurring.

Not only did Rinpoche receive the empowerments, he also received the oral transmissions and instructions. Those oral transmissions and instructions contain the pith experiential teachings from the gurus that can help our practice. Based on such oral transmissions and instructions, Rinpoche attained certainty in the Dharma.

Both arousing devotion for the master,
and the entry of blessings into the mindstream—
both of those occurred at the same time.

According to Buddhist teachings, there are three levels of mental satisfaction related to devotion. The first level of mental satisfaction related to devotion is based on the student's personal realization and experience. This experience is gained through the practices received from the guru who bestows the oral transmissions and instructions. When the student gains some spiritual realization through these practices, the student's devotion is strengthened. The second level of mental satisfaction of devotion is gained when the student's experience and the guru's oral transmissions are validated by the shastras. The third level of mental satisfaction of devotion is gained when the student's experience, the guru's oral transmission, and the shastras are all validated by the Buddha's direct teachings in the sutras. Jetsun Rinpoche is referring to the entering of blessings into the mindstream due to these three satisfactions of devotion.

Both cutting doubts about the outer objects,
and the arising of spontaneous wisdom—
both of those occurred at the same time.

Here, Jetsun Rinpoche is referring to how we can eradicate our misunderstandings and doubts regarding outer objects and, simultaneously, experience the arising of spontaneous wisdom. Without any deeper investigation, all of the objects we perceive through our sense organs may appear real. Due to our emotions and karma, we become attached to objects when they are agreeable to our ego and when they make us feel good. But if we examine things more closely, we realize that all of these objects do not exist independently.

Instead, we experience outer objects *interdependently* due to our six sense consciousnesses—the five physical sense consciousnesses plus the mental consciousness—and corresponding sense organs. We cannot find sense organs, sense objects, or sense consciousnesses inherently existing independently. By having this realization of relative interdependent origination, and by understanding that ultimately the nature of our experience is emptiness, we are able to cut through doubts and overcome misunderstandings related to outer objects. At the same time, we can only cut our doubts regarding outer objects if we have realized the nature of the mind, where spontaneous wisdom arises.

Both having clarity in the creation stage deity,
and experiencing the realization of the completion stage—
both of those occurred at the same time.

The highest tantric sadhanas include both creation and completion stage practices. Before we engage in these two main practices, we do the preliminary practices in order to accumulate merit based on common and uncommon foundations. Next, we practice the accumulation of wisdom based on purifying the subject—the practitioner—and the objects—all other things—into emptiness.

For our main practice, we generate ourselves in the form of the deity. Once the generation of the deity—related to the vase empowerment—is stabilized through concentration, we then do the completion practices, which are related to the remaining three empowerments: the secret empowerment, the wisdom empowerment, and the turiya empowerment.

Realized yogis such as Jetsun Rinpoche can practice and experience both the generation and the completion stages simultaneously. Indeed, his biography mentions that he was never separated from the samadhi of the two stages of generation and completion. It is said that even during the course of one complete night and day, Rinpoche practiced seventy different deity mandalas.

Both having the heat of bliss[32] blazing in the body,
and the arising of appearance and emptiness in the mind—
both of those occurred at the same time.

---

32. The "heat of bliss" (*bde drod*) refers to the bliss that results from engaging in the completion-stage practice of inner-heat yoga, or *tummo* (*gtum mo*).

Jetsun Rinpoche is saying that because he has accomplished the path of accumulation, he has progressed to the second path—the path of application. As we have discussed, the path of application has four levels: heat, peak, patience, and supreme dharma. Due to the *tummo* practice of the completion stage, Rinpoche has experienced "heat," the first level on the path of application. This is where he experienced bliss related to the four ascending and four descending joys. As a result, he achieved what is called the isolation of body.

Next, due to accomplishing the *pranayama* breath practices, Rinpoche experienced "peak," the second level on the path of application. At this level he achieved the isolation of speech. When Rinpoche describes the "arising of appearance and emptiness in the mind," he is referring to patience, the third level on the path of application. At this level, he has achieved the isolation of mind. When Rinpoche experienced the impure *illusory body*, he realized the supreme dharma, the fourth level of the path of application.

Both understanding delusion as relative,
and understanding emptiness as ultimate—
both of those occurred at the same time.

According to the highest tantric practices like Chakrasamvara, completion-stage practice involves five experiential stages. The first stage is the experience of the isolation of body; the second stage is the experience of the isolation of speech; the third stage is the experience of the isolation of mind; the fourth stage is the experience of the clear-light nature of the mind; and the fifth stage is the experience of union.

In the experience of union, one realizes the union of relative and ultimate truths. This advanced level of experience can help a yogi to always remain as a witness to everything that is unfolding without reacting, regardless of whether the object is good or bad, positive or negative. We can infer from these lines that Rinpoche has had the experience of union where he can see the union of relative and ultimate truths.

Both losing awareness of the object,
and being connected with the hook of recollection—
both of those occurred at the same time.

In these lines, Jetsun Rinpoche describes how advanced yogis can experience the faults of meditation practice and their antidotes simultaneously. For beginners especially, many faults arise in one's meditation practice. In shamatha meditation, for example, there are five faults that can arise: laziness, forgetting instructions, dullness and agitation, under-application of instructions, and over-application of instructions. To counter these five faults, a set of eight antidotes are often given. The first four are antidotes to laziness and include interest, diligence, faith, and pliancy. The fifth antidote is remembering, which is the antidote to forgetting instructions. The sixth antidote is awareness, which is the antidote to dullness and agitation. The seventh antidote is volition, which is the antidote to the under-application of instructions. The eighth antidote is equanimity, which is the antidote to the over-application of instructions.

At Rinpoche's level of experience, he is always in the meditative state and is able to apply the antidotes to the faults simultaneously, applying the "hook of recollection" at the exact moment that he "los[es] awareness of the object."

Both being robbed by misfortune,
and the arrival of friends, the antidotes—
both of those occurred at the same time.

In this verse, Jetsun Rinpoche is expressing how yogis can incorporate all misfortunes into their spiritual practice. In the mind-training text *The Wheel of the Sharp Weapon*,[33] bodhisattvas are likened to peacocks, who can eat poisonous plants and yet become even more colorful and beautiful. Other beings die when they eat toxic things and cannot

33. *Blo sbyong mtshon cha 'khor lo*, by Yogi Dharmarakshita.

transform those poisons, but bodhisattvas thrive in their practice when faced with misfortunes in their lives. Yogis can use misfortune as an opportunity to strengthen their spiritual practices, but ordinary beings often fail when confronted with challenges and misfortunes.

Whatever misfortunes we may experience in our lives, we can bring them into our spiritual practice as allies. For example, if we have an enemy, the presence of that person can help us to practice patience. Whatever hardships and challenges occur in our lives, the possibility exists to transform these poisons into medicines. Everything in our lives, good or bad, can be integrated into our spiritual path and used to deepen our practice and help us cultivate more positive qualities.

Both losing desire in objects,
and being connected with skillful means—
both of those occurred at the same time.

Here, Jetsun Rinpoche is referring to utilizing skillful methods in Buddhist practices. In Hinayana Buddhism, all practices are based on renunciation—giving up harmful or unskillful behaviors. For example, if you are confronted with your enemy, the practice is to renounce interacting with that person. In the bodhisattva practices of Mahayana Buddhism, on the other hand, practitioners focus more on using the skillful means of bodhichitta with wisdom and compassion to transform an encounter with an enemy into an opportunity to practice patience.

In Vajrayana, the practitioner, through sadhana practice, transforms a meeting with an enemy into an opportunity to see the buddha nature in that enemy. Sakya Pandita said that skillful means are like a bow and arrow; one can shoot the obstacles perfectly when one has both the bow-like method of compassion and the arrow-like wisdom working together.

Through skillful means and tantric anuttarayoga practices, we can incorporate all of our desire, all of our craving for sensual objects, as well as our anger and our feelings toward our enemies, and then our ignorance and our feelings toward neutral objects into our spiritual practice.

In anuttara practice, all of the objects and emotions related to desire, anger, and ignorance can be simultaneously seen as interdependent yet empty by nature. All of these "negative" emotions can be used to increase our wisdom and further our spiritual practice. Skillful means enable us to turn these poisons into powerful medicine. The more poisonous the emotions, the more potential they have to be transformed into potent medicines.

Both experiencing happiness and suffering,
and understanding them as illusions—
both of those occurred at the same time.

As we have discussed, there are five basic feelings according to Buddhist psychology: happiness, unhappiness, pain, pleasure, and neutral feelings. We can reduce these feelings into three categories according to how we perceive them: agreeable, disagreeable, and neutral.

All five feelings are included in the second aggregate—the aggregate of feeling. Feelings are central to how samsara works; running around chasing after pleasure and happiness and trying to avoid pain and unhappiness keeps us stuck in samsara's endless cycles. But the ironic thing about feelings is that they are like two sides of the same coin. Happiness and unhappiness cannot be separated; pain and pleasure cannot be separated; they always go together—one always brings the other.

Furthermore, all feelings whether positive or negative are rooted in the afflictive emotions: pleasure and happiness are experienced due to desire; pain and unhappiness are experienced due to anger; and neutral feelings are experienced due to ignorance. The key point here is that these negative emotions and the feelings that arise from them, are all impermanent; by nature, all feelings are insubstantial and empty. This is why Jetsun Rinpoche says that whatever feelings are experienced, they are all illusions in the sense that they are not independently existing. When causes and conditions come together, we can experience illusions and dreams. And like illusions and dreams, feelings are not independently existing.

Both seeing the suffering of sentient beings,
and the arising of profound compassion—
both of those occurred at the same time.

Compassion is the practice of helping others to become free from suffering and the causes of suffering. According to Buddhist teachings, there are three kinds of compassion. The first kind of compassion focuses on the suffering of sentient beings. The second kind of compassion is more actively focused on providing material support for suffering beings—for example, providing medicine for a sick person. The third kind of compassion is directed toward uprooting the *causes* of suffering.

This third compassion is also called "objectless compassion." This is the most profound compassion because it is based in the wisdom of emptiness, which can uproot ignorance—the ultimate cause of all suffering. Advanced yogis, like Jetsun Rinpoche, can manifest all three kinds of compassion simultaneously in order to help all sentient beings become free from suffering and the causes of suffering.

Both producing an argument with an opponent,
and the dawning of proof inside oneself—
both of those occurred at the same time.

Religious debate has a long tradition in India. Among scholars within the same religion, debate is used in order to help students understand and integrate what they are learning, and can help to clear up misunderstandings and doubts. Sometimes scholars from different religions debate one another in order to try to convert their opponents.

In Sangphu Monastery in Central Tibet, a form of debate was developed by master Chapa Chökyi Sengge (1109–1169) to help students advance their understanding. This debate style became very popular within Tibetan monastic colleges. Studying debate and logic also helped students to become very confident in refuting erroneous doctrines using reason and proof.

The process of debate can help to increase and validate spiritual understanding within us. But Buddhist debate is not designed to increase our opinions and conceptual thinking or to make us more attached to our views—quite the opposite. The purpose of debate is to help us question our views and validate our inner realizations.

Both revealing the spring of merit,
and turning away from attachment to food and wealth—
both of those occurred at the same time.

Jetsun Rinpoche is describing here how his merit is increasing, like a spring of water bubbling up from the source and, as a result, he is experiencing an abundance of food and wealth. But rather than increasing his attachment, stinginess, and greed, this abundance is arising at the same time that Rinpoche is turning away from all of those negative emotions. And as he is turning away from attachment to material objects, his abundance simultaneously increases. Rinpoche may instead be using his food and wealth to practice eating-yoga and to make *ganapuja* offerings in order to transform them into further accumulations of merit and wisdom.

Both abandoning misconduct,
and doing whatever conduct is pleasing—
both of those occurred at the same time.

If we study the three types of vows—pratimoksha, bodhisattva, and samaya vows—it may seem at first that there are many contradictions among them regarding right conduct. But it is important to remember that the higher vows always supersede the lower vows. Jetsun Rinpoche has taken upasaka vows and bodhisattva vows, and he has also taken tantric samaya vows because he is a highly realized tantric practitioner. Because he has taken the highest vows that supersede all the other vows, there will be no contradiction, even if his conduct appears to be misconduct according to the pratimoksha vows. "Whatever conduct is pleasing" means whatever is pleasing *to our spiritual practice*, referring to practicing according to those highest vows.

Please, may hearing and wisdom also meet;
please, may scripture and reason also meet;

Jetsun Rinpoche is reiterating, based on his spiritual realization, that while learning through hearing and contemplation is important, it is more important to cultivate deeper wisdom. If our study remains purely intellectual, we will not experience any of the transformation and liberating insight that comes from cultivating deeper wisdom. Therefore, it is very important for us to integrate our studies with the realization of wisdom.

The Buddha's words in the sutras and tantras are regarded as the ultimate scriptural authority. His words are cited in order to prove whether something is right or wrong. However, Rinpoche is advising that while we can quote from the scriptures, meeting them with logical reasoning—using both inferential logic and direct logic—is also important. Otherwise, if we rely only on scriptural authority without using reason, we may cultivate mere blind faith.

On the other hand, using only logical reasoning without relying on spiritual authority may merely increase our conceptual thinking. As we have discussed, the Buddha himself encouraged us to investigate his teachings through logical reasoning in order to prove their genuineness, similar to how goldsmiths, in order to prove the purity of their gold, traditionally used methods like burning, cutting, and rubbing the gold to test its purity.

please, may the lineage and the guru also meet;
please, may practice and oral instruction also meet;

Here, Jetsun Rinpoche is reminding us of the value of being connected to an unbroken lineage. A lineage originating from the enlightened Buddha that can be traced all the way down to one's root guru is necessary in order to receive the transmission of blessings. Lineage also helps to certify the authenticity of the guru and to increase our confidence that the teachings and practices that he or she teaches descend authentically from the enlightened source. It's very important to have a guru who has a pure lineage because without a lineage we will not receive the blessings.

Oral instructions are given in order to help guide us in our practice. But if we receive many oral instructions without committing to any practice, it will not be very beneficial. Thus, practice and oral instructions need to come together, just as the lineage and guru must also meet for the authentic teachings to be transmitted. Any sadhana or other spiritual practice we are doing should be based on the upadeshas—the oral instructions.

please, may diligence and faith also meet;

The Buddhist spiritual path has three stages of faith: clear faith, wishing faith, and unshakable faith. We experience the stage of clear faith when, having seen the positive qualities of the outer refuge objects, our minds become clearer and purer, without any active defilements. Then, wishing to integrate those spiritual qualities within us, we experience wishing faith. Ultimately, if we continue in our practice, we will experience profound inner transformation and experience the ultimate refuge objects within the nature of the mind: the clarity is Sangha, emptiness is Dharma, and the union of clarity and emptiness is Buddha—then one has unshakable faith.

Although we may have wishing faith, without diligence in our practice we cannot achieve the qualities of unshakable faith and achieve buddhahood. "Diligence," here, means having enthusiasm to practice virtue. Diligence helps us to accomplish virtue, helps us progress along the five spiritual paths, and is the strongest antidote to laziness.

The Buddhist scriptures describe three kinds of diligence. Armor-like diligence refers to the power of making a heartfelt resolution to practice in order to achieve enlightenment. This diligence is like armor due to the way that this core resolution acts to protect us from laziness. The second diligence—that of application—concerns the need to constantly apply ourselves to spiritual practice. Thirdly, there is the diligence of discontent, which is concerned with overcoming discouragement when faced with obstacles and not being content with small virtues and small achievements on the spiritual path. When the practitioner achieves all three faiths and all three diligences, they will make an unshakable commitment to their practice to achieve buddhahood.

please, may fame and qualities also meet.

There are some teachers who have lots of spiritual qualities but are not well known and do not have any students. For example, there are many hidden yogis who are focused on their own practice but are not directly benefiting other students. On the other hand, there are some teachers who, although they are very famous, are not actually very learned and lack many qualities; although they are serving the Dharma, their benefit to their students will be limited. Jetsun Rinpoche is emphasizing here that fame and qualities complement each other; they must go together in order to benefit others.

No comprehension will arise
from hearing without wisdom.
No certain knowledge will arise
from reason not connected with scripture.

As we have discussed, there is no use in going to listen to many Dharma teachings unless they are helping us to experience transformation and develop wisdom. Instead, if the more we learn, the more arrogant and proud we become, then all that learning has not helped us to have any realization.

Logical reasoning can be useful in overcoming doubt. But if we find that we still have doubts after exhausting logical reasoning, then we must rely on the Buddha's words to help us to achieve certainty in the Dharma. Jetsun Rinpoche is advising us that in order to obtain certainty in our understanding of the Dharma, we need to rely on *both* logical reasoning *and* scripture, with each acting as a support for the other.

No blessings will come
from the guru without a lineage.
There will be no achievement
with faith without diligence.

As we just discussed, we need to rely on a guru who has a pure lineage originating from the Buddha if we wish to achieve enlightenment. We should see our guru manifesting in the form of a buddha in our practice. In this way, we can receive the Buddha's blessings transferred directly down through the entire lineage of the gurus to our own root guru.

The Sanskrit word *adhisthana*[34] is usually translated as "blessing" or "consecration" in the context of Vajrayana, but literally translated it means "abiding" or "present." This reminds us that, in the context of lineage, if we have very strong faith and devotion in our guru as the Buddha, we will be able to feel their *presence* in us. In our practice, we visualize the guru just above the crown of our head, abiding as the *kulapati*—the father of our spiritual family. A guru without a lineage originating from the Buddha cannot transmit blessings coming from Buddha Vajradhara—the primordial buddha.

On the Buddhist path, there are five "powers" that enable us to progress: faith, diligence, memory, meditation, and wisdom. Cultivating and *deploying* these powers is extremely important to our practice. As we have discussed, although we start the spiritual path with faith in the refuge objects, we will not make any progress on the path without diligence. Diligence is also essential to cultivating the remaining powers of memory, meditation, and wisdom.

---

34. Tib. *byin rlabs.*

There is no benefit for oneself
from oral instruction without practice.

The Indian master Atisha, who was the founder of the Kadampa tradition in Tibet, which is famous for its propogation of mind-training teachings, once made a remark about how Tibetans often received many initiations and empowerments but did not commit themselves to one particular practice. As a consequence of this lack of committed focus, Atisha declared that these practitioners were not likely to experience any realization. On the other hand, meditators in India tended to focus their sadhana practice on a single *istadevata* (*yidam*) deity, with the result that many became mahasiddhas. Jetsun Rinpoche is reminding us that it is far more beneficial for us to commit to one yidam practice after receiving empowerment and oral instructions rather than moving from one practice to another.

There is no benefit for others
from good qualities without fame.

For those practitioners who are primarily practicing on the level of the pratimoksha vows of individual liberation, the purpose of practice is to attain self-liberation in order to achieve nirvana. Those, however, who are on the Mahayana and Vajrayana paths, take bodhisattva vows in order to achieve complete enlightenment for the benefit of others.

There are three kinds of bodhisattva vows: the king-like, shepherd-like, and sailor-like. The king-like vow means that first you achieve buddhahood and then, with that king-like power, you benefit sentient beings. The shepherd-like vow means that you remain a bodhisattva instead of achieving buddhahood, tending to sentient beings like a good shepherd tends to their sheep. The sailor-like vow means that you travel together with other sentient beings, helping them cross the waters of samsara and trying to achieve buddhahood simultaneously. All of these vows are focused on benefiting others.

Jetsun Rinpoche is saying that although we may have cultivated many spiritual qualities, if we are not well known, we cannot directly benefit others according to our bodhisattva vows. This is the reason why many hidden yogis don't have many disciples while the traveling teachers become famous and collect many students.

8

Which Is First?

Without an egg, where does the chicken come from?
Without a chicken, where does the egg come from?
Which is first: chicken or egg?

JETSUN RINPOCHE IS USING the well-known example of the chicken and the egg to explore cause and result in the relative world. Buddhists believe in interdependent origination in the relative truth, which asserts that there is no first cause that is itself uncaused. The example of the chicken and the egg demonstrates the futility of trying to prove which came first.

In the non-arising nature,
if there is no creation by conditions,
which is first: cause or result?

In the above lines Jetsun Rinpoche is contrasting the ultimate truth of emptiness of non-arising nature with the relative truth. Cause and result are born from one another. If the chicken is born from the egg, and the egg is created by the chicken, we cannot say that either one came entirely before the other because each depends on the other for its existence. From a Buddhist perspective, however, we are not interested in who came first; we are interested in realizing the non-arising of the chicken and the egg. Rinpoche is saying here that chicken and egg are interdependent and appear as real to us in the relative world. But in ultimate reality, we can see the non-arising—the empty nature—of both the chicken and the egg. In that non-arising nature, there is no question of which came first because there is no beginning to non-arising—there is no first cause.

We should also understand that our conditioned experience of apparent objects does not reflect some universal truth. We call this creature a "chicken," and we define it by all of these characteristics using human categories and language. But a chicken does not know it is called a "chicken"; it does not define itself by those characteristics. The chicken's perspective of its identity and utility is radically different from the human perception. Therefore, we cannot say that our experience of a chicken is universal. Even among humans, some people keep chickens as pets, some people treat chickens merely as a source of meat, and some people keep chickens only for eggs. Some people may be afraid of chickens. In this way, we can see that how we refer to and perceive objects is based on our particular conditioned reality. When we take all of the conditions and causes away, we cannot find a chicken or an egg. Such an absence of causes and conditions is only possible when we realize ultimate reality and have an experience of the purity of our own mind.

In the original purity of mind itself,
if both conceptuality and wisdom do not exist,
which is first: the Buddha or sentient beings?

Jetsun Rinpoche is emphasizing that the original nature of dharmata is nondual, free from both relative truths and ultimate truths, concepts and wisdom, and Buddha and sentient beings. Our conditioned mind gives rise to all apparent objects, but the nature of the *mind itself* is beyond all concepts. When we dwell in the ultimate reality, there is no such thing as a chicken or an egg. Abiding in this meditative perfection, we go beyond both cause and result. In this state, there are no longer any concepts or projections that create the phenomenal world.

Likewise, because there is no cause and result in that awakened state, there is no difference between the Buddha and sentient beings. The Buddha does not precede our capacity for buddhahood; buddhahood is already within the nature of the mind itself. There is no difference between the Buddha and sentient beings in the unconditioned original purity of the mind.

Since dharmas do not exist from the beginning,
if the result, buddhahood, never occurs,
which is first: dharmas or the Buddha?

Relatively, we can conceive of dharmas—anything that possesses characteristics—and Buddha as different things. But ultimately, the nature of both is emptiness and, therefore, we cannot say which came first.

Since, ultimately, nothing whatsoever exists,
if both delusion and non-delusion do not exist,
which is first: relative or ultimate?

Relatively, we can assert a difference between delusion and non-delusion, and between relative and ultimate. But in the ultimate nature, all are empty and we cannot, therefore, assert that any member of these pairs is prior to the other.

Since in the ultimate there is no Buddha,
by whom was the Tripitaka taught?
If no Dharma was taught by the teacher,
how are there volumes of scriptures?

In the ultimate, the Buddha realized the nature of dharmata—which is the ultimate reality and the empty nature of all dharmas and can't project any inherent existence. Relatively, due to auspicious causes and conditions, the Buddha manifested in his form body—the nirmanakaya—and gave the teachings collected in the Tripitaka to the sentient beings of the world.

If it is said, "Cessation is nonexistent;
all will die and be born;
the conditioned is ultimately nonexistent,"
how can it be that a result is produced from action?

Relatively, whatever is born and conditioned will die. But ultimately, karma—including cause and result—is empty by nature.

If the nature does not arise from the beginning,
how will there be cessation?

Here, Jetsun Rinpoche is referring to the *ultimate* nature, in which there is neither beginning nor cessation. Cessation can only occur for something that has arisen. Death can only happen if something has been born. But if the nature of the mind is without beginning, there will be no cessation of that original purity. Only the nature of the mind is unconditioned. Rinpoche is saying that all conditioned things are relative and imperfect because we are still stuck in the realm of the chicken and the egg; we are still caught in the dualism of the conceptual world.

Aside from the dharmadhatu,
nothing whatsoever actually exists.
In that immutable dharmata,
how can there be birth and death?

By asking these questions, Jetsun Rinpoche is confirming that enlightened beings are free from birth and death. In comparison, in our experience here in samsara, we remain constantly cycling through birth and death.

If all dharmas are false,
why do we think them reliable?
If all dharmas are true,
how is it that everything is deceptive?

Jetsun Rinpoche is confirming that relative truth is not ultimate truth. And even within relative truth, there is both perfect and imperfect relative truth. For example, if someone has jaundice, it is said that they may see snow as being yellow in color. That is considered imperfect relative truth. However, the majority of people can see that snow is white, and that is considered perfect relative truth. Both the imperfect relative truth and the perfect relative truth are unreliable and deceptive because both are not the ultimate truth.

If samsara is suffering itself,
performing nonvirtue is extremely deluded.

Relatively, life in samsara is suffering due to deluded karma. But ultimately, samsara is empty. There is a passage in the *Hevajra Tantra* that says, "Because of delusion, samsara has form; without delusion, having purified samsara, samsara becomes nirvana."

If it is said there is no liberation to higher realms,
performing virtue to cause that is deluded.

Ultimately, nirvana is a state of cessation, which is unconditioned wisdom. The *Abhidharmakosha* mentions three unconditioned dharmas of space and two wisdoms of nirvana that cannot be caused by virtue. But, relatively, performing virtue can purify negativities so that we realize that unconditioned wisdom. Performing only virtue and merit helps one to achieve a higher rebirth in the higher realms, but to achieve nirvana and complete enlightenment, the merit should be integrated with wisdom."

If the result of karma itself is true,
the nature, emptiness, is deluded.

Karma is always relative and cannot be established as independently existing in the ultimate. Otherwise, proving its nature as emptiness in the ultimate is delusion.

The moon in the water is not the moon in the sky,
but without depending on that [moon], that [reflection] does not appear.
Similarly, the nature of all things
is taught as the two truths.

There are no dharmas other than
those included in the two truths;
but because the nature is neither true nor false,
grasping to the two truths is deluded.

Jetsun Rinpoche is saying that even ultimate truth is not something to become attached to. Ultimate truth was taught by the Buddha so that we could transcend the relative truth of conditioned existence. As we have discussed earlier, the Buddha gave us all of these methods that can serve as a staircase that enables us to progress on the spiritual path. But the staircase is not the goal; it is only the method. Eventually we need to go beyond the staircase itself to reach the final goal.

In order to transcend the ultimate, we need to see the original perfection within us. Relative truth and ultimate truth are ways of training the mind; we should not get attached to the ultimate truth. If we imagine ultimate truth as the top step of that staircase, then we should be careful not to get attached to that top step. If we are attached to it, then we will never go beyond the staircase.

9

Never at Any Time

Desire-objects, the salt water of craving,
will never satiate [craving] at any time;
like a leper looking in a mirror,
if one turns away from attachment, one is sated.

THIS NEXT SECTION OF Jetsun Rinpoche's doha contains seventeen four-line verses relating to the base in samsara, the different methods and practices as paths, and the result that is enlightenment.

In the first of these verses, Rinpoche addresses the central problem of craving. The first pair of lines refer to a general condition of samsara, and the second pair of lines describe the method of liberating oneself from those conditions. Humans live in the desire realm and we have become habituated to chasing after desirable objects. Everything we do is motivated by desire. As we have discussed, trying to satisfy desire is like drinking salty water: the more we consume, the more we want. Our Buddhist practices are skillful antidotes to this insatiable craving. In some schools of Buddhism it is taught that the way to achieve freedom from the thirst of desire is to renounce and turn away from all desirable objects by looking into the undesirable aspects of those desirable objects. But in Mahayana practice, negative emotions are transformed into positive emotions through the practices of tonglen and bodhichitta. And in Vajrayana practice, we learn to *incorporate* craving and desire into our spiritual practice to go beyond both negative and positive emotions and see wisdom.

The ripples of the river of *duhkha*[35]
will never be removed at any time;
like the smoke of a methodically extinguished fire,
if one turns from nonvirtue [one's duhkha] is removed.

We all aspire to find happiness—it is a primary motivator in our lives. We want to avoid suffering and find fulfillment. Whether we are poor or rich, educated or uneducated, wherever we come from, we all share this wish for happiness.

Happiness is very elusive, though. We often believe that as soon as we accomplish a goal, or achieve our dream job, or find a wonderful partner, we will finally be happy. We don't seem to realize the nature of impermanence and the fact that everything is always changing. Even a wonderful marriage will face so many tests and challenges. Even our dream job cannot stay the same forever. We often feel that our goal is just ahead of us, and that as soon as we finish our degree, or buy our home, or have children, or move to a new town, we will finally be satisfied.

Because everything changes, the more we pursue these external sources of pleasure and happiness, the more we will also suffer more pain and restlessness. If we look closely at our lives, we can begin to see that our methods for achieving happiness are flawed. If our methods were correct, then they would bring perfect happiness and pleasure. We would experience the bliss of the awakened state that does not rely on outer circumstances.

If we look back on our lives, however, we can begin to see that all of the sources of pleasure and happiness that we found were also the causes

35. *Duhkha* is Sanskrit for "suffering."

of further suffering. Because our happiness was reliant on outer circumstances, it was very tenuous. Our children may have brought us so much happiness when they were young, but now they have become rebellious teenagers. Or maybe the relationship has remained strong but they have moved far away, causing us to suffer so much from that separation.

Maybe we dreamed that when we finally finished our PhD, we would feel satisfied. But we may instead struggle to find a fulfilling job and suffer from financial stress from student debt. Maybe we finally purchase our dream car, and for a year we are so satisfied. But then one day we back into a fence post by mistake, and now all we can see are the ugly scratches.

When we examine our lives in this way, we can begin to question our methods. Are we pursuing happiness in the wrong way? Is there a fundamental misunderstanding in how we are living our lives? Are we struggling because we cannot accept the truth of suffering and because we do not understand the causes of suffering? Even while we are experiencing temporary pleasure and happiness, we are sowing the seeds for future pain and unhappiness. Even when we engage in very positive and altruistic activities, if we are attached to an outcome, it will still cause us suffering.

Most of our pleasure and happiness is based on nonvirtue. What is more powerful, pain or pleasure, happiness or unhappiness? We tend to notice pain and unhappiness much more than we notice happiness. When we are happy, we generally become oblivious to those seeds of unhappiness. The expression "ignorance is bliss" is true in the short term. But the more spiritually awakened we become, the more we can begin to see both sides of the coin. We begin to see the causes of unhappiness even while we are experiencing happiness. Now, you may think that this will increase your suffering, that you will not be able to enjoy yourself anymore. But this increased awareness actually gives us more equilibrium; we will not be shocked when things change; we will not feel that it is unfair when challenges arise; we will be much more balanced as our awareness deepens.

If we remain deluded, we will not see all the causes and conditions that give rise to pain and unhappiness. Such ignorance is very similar to addiction. When we are intoxicated, we may temporarily feel satisfied and happy. But the minute the drug or alcohol leaves our system, we will feel even more unhappy and our craving will increase. The more unhappy we feel in that drug withdrawal, the more desperate we become for the drug.

We are addicted to happiness and pleasure in our daily lives. We may not notice it because it is not as acute as a drug addiction. But if we look closely, we will see that we are driven by desire and craving. When our desire is fulfilled, we experience temporary satisfaction and happiness. It is worth reiterating again and again: no amount of salty water will quench our thirst! The more we consume, the thirstier we will become. We are addicted to happiness and pleasure.

Through spiritual practice, we can begin to glimpse our freedom from that addiction. At first, it will only be very small moments of freedom; but the more we practice, the more our mind will begin to let go of the grasping of desire. When we are no longer intoxicated by these temporary pleasures, when we are no longer caught in this vicious cycle of chasing happiness, we can begin to know our own mind. We will begin to have some freedom from negative emotions and we will produce less negative karma, slowing down the cycle of craving.

Jetsun Rinpoche is reminding us that we need to free ourselves from the causes of suffering if we want to experience liberation. Happiness and pleasure are actually causes of suffering. Until we can deeply integrate this truth, we will not have any freedom. If we want to experience joy—the unshakable bliss that Rinpoche is referring to—then we have to free ourselves from the root causes of suffering. We have to free ourselves from nonvirtue. We have to stop generating more negative karma as a result of that nonvirtue. After abandoning nonvirtue, we also have to accumulate merit through virtuous activities.

When we free ourselves from negative karma, then we may begin to experience that true joy. Joy is not the result of fulfilling our cravings; it is not temporary; it is not dependent on outer circumstances. Joy is liberation from the cycle of desire. It is the result of abandoning nonvirtue and engaging in virtuous activities. Beyond joy, there is a bliss that is beyond all activities, beyond all dualism, beyond the conceptual mind.

From the river of birth, aging, sickness, and death,
one will never be freed at any time;
like constructing a bridge over a river,
if one realizes non-arising, one is liberated.

According to the Buddha, birth is one of the four major sufferings we experience. Although we don't remember being born, it is a very painful experience for the mother and for the infant. Aging is also very painful. The slow weakening of our body causes mental and physical suffering, our sense organs gradually diminish, our eyesight weakens, we lose our hearing, our teeth begin to decay and fall out, we lose our stamina, we begin to have daily aches and pains, it becomes harder to walk, and so forth.

Old age, sickness, and death are painful because they get in the way of us fulfilling our desire. Even birth goes against our desire; maybe we do not want to be reborn in samsara to suffer again and again; maybe we don't want to leave the safety and comfort of the womb. Because we are born, we are subjected to the other sufferings of sickness, old age, and death.

How can we be freed from these conditions? Jetsun Rinpoche says here that if we can realize non-arising, then we are liberated. What does this mean? Let's take the sense faculties as an example. We have an eye organ because we have not realized the empty nature of the eye. We have not realized the non-arising of all of our sense organs. The *Heart Sutra* lists all of the sense organs as non-arising: "no eye, no ear, no nose, no tongue, no body . . ." and so forth. If we understand the profound meaning of this sutra, we will be freed from all of that suffering. If we realize the non-arising of all things, we will be liberated from those causes and conditions for suffering.

We are born because we have not realized non-arising; we have not realized our true nature so we are forced to take rebirth. The only way to free ourselves from forced rebirth is to realize the non-arising, empty nature of all things. By realizing clarity and emptiness, we will be freed from birth, aging, sickness, and death.

We all know that we will die, but we probably don't know how or when we will die. Most of us resist the idea of death and hope to live a long life. But the longer we live, the more we will experience that slow degeneration of our bodies. How can we become more peaceful and accepting of that degeneration? We cannot halt that process, but through spiritual practice we can gain much more freedom within it. If we are not attached to the body, we will not suffer as much as it ages and changes. If we are not attached to this life, we will not fear death. If we accept that illness is a part of life, we will not become angry when we, too, become sick. We will not feel like it is unfair that we are suffering; we will not take it personally. We will experience peace because we understand that sickness and aging are inevitable. In this way, our relationship to suffering can slowly be transformed through our spiritual practice.

I have lived in many cultures. I was born in Tibet, grew up in India, and now I have lived in America for decades. In Tibet and India, spirituality is very ingrained in the culture. I have seen how that faith allows people in extremely hard circumstances to be more accepting and at peace. If someone is overwhelmed by hardship, it can take such a toll on their mental health. But spirituality can provide a very strong foundation that allows people to be very mentally healthy in spite of terrible hardship. Without that spiritual foundation, people may be much more prone to mental suffering.

Some of the most terrible mental suffering actually occurs in wealthy countries. The ways that we interpret suffering, process trauma, and understand and treat mental illnesses varies significantly between cultures. Faith increases our capacity to accept change, enabling us to not become angry when we experience loss and suffering. Acceptance allows us to maintain some equilibrium throughout all of the challenges we face.

I have observed that many Tibetans accept very difficult circumstances from the perspective of karma. They do not become enraged when something goes wrong and they do not resist what is happening, and this brings them some relief. They do not expend all of their energy feeling upset, or angry, or blaming someone else. That is very good for them mentally; it allows them to preserve their strength to face that hardship. We see how this approach has allowed Tibetans to survive unimaginable suffering after the Chinese invaded. Tibetans lost their country, their livelihoods, their family members; there was brutal torture; even their sacred sites were demolished. But amid this terrible loss and suffering, they generally did not become consumed by anger; they did not allow their faith to be destroyed.

If you have faith in karma, you understand that challenges are the ripening of your own negative karma. You do not feel that God or someone else is trying to punish you. You accept the situation, even if you do not understand what caused it. You understand that you have lived countless lifetimes and that the karma that is ripening now could be the result of causes many lifetimes ago. Without such an understanding of karma, we have a tendency to blame someone or something else. This often increases our negative emotions and mental disturbance.

It is very common for people to blame the faults of their parents for their own unhappiness. Understanding karma is not about condoning the horrible actions that others have committed against us. There are many terrible parents, and so much child abuse and neglect. By understanding karma, we are not saying that we, or anyone else, deserves to be abused. Understanding karma has more to do with liberating ourselves from the abuser; if we remain angry at the abuser, we remain tied to them for our whole lives. If we understand karma, we can transform our trauma and suffering. We can use the compassion born out of that suffering to care for other suffering beings.

We can see how it is often the people who have suffered the most who have the greatest impact on humanity. Their compassion becomes very fearless and very limitless. If we remain caught in our anger and blame, it will be poisonous to us. Acceptance does not mean we need to spend time with an abuser; it does not mean we need to engage with someone who has harmed us. Acceptance is about liberating ourselves from that poison.

We create so many problems for one another. As long as we are living in society, we will always have conflicts with other people. If we are unhappy at work, we will want to blame our boss or our co-workers. If we are unhappy at home, we will want to blame our partner or our children. People cause each other so much emotional suffering. There is so much competition, so much comparison, so much judgment. We are very childish that way.

We may think that we can solve this suffering by living in retreat and withdrawing completely from society. But even if we are far away from people, we can still be tormented by the past. We can still carry those struggles and conflicts even into our retreat.

Having faith and an understanding of karma can serve to protect the mind. Although it will not protect us from bad things happening, understanding karma can keep our minds from becoming filled with negative emotions. As long as we are blaming others for our unhappiness there will be no inner peace. We will never be free from that suffering because we cannot change other people; we cannot correct their behavior; we cannot get the apology we deserve; we cannot get someone else to see our point of view.

There is a risk of misunderstanding karma. If we focus only on how past karma is affecting our present lives, we may still feel helpless. A correct understanding of karma, however, can give us a tremendous sense of agency. If we begin to focus on generating positive karma through virtuous activities, we will begin to feel more freedom. The only way to free ourselves entirely though is to stop creating karma altogether; and we stop generating karma only when we realize the wisdom of non-arising.

As long as we are generating karma, we will be forced to take rebirth; and from that, we will have the sufferings of aging, sickness, and death. But if we have the realization of non-arising emptiness, then we will achieve ultimate freedom.

The great ocean of samsara
will never dry up at any time;

like the arising of the seven suns of existence,
if one turns away from craving desire-objects, [one's own samsara] is dried up.

As long as we have craving, we will remain trapped in samsara. As long as we desire happiness and pleasure, we will continue grasping and clinging to outer objects for satisfaction. If we study the Buddhist teachings on the twelve interdependent links, we can see that as long as we have grasping and craving for desirable objects, we will be propelled through this vicious cycle and will remain trapped in samsara. There is no drying up that vast ocean of samsara around us. There is no limit to desirable objects. But through spiritual practice, we can free ourselves from the causes of suffering inside us. By freeing ourselves from craving, our own inner ocean of suffering is dried up and we achieve liberation in our own mind. There is no need to dry up the ocean around us if we are liberated internally. The world can be overflowing with desirable objects, but if we are freed from craving, then those objects will no longer be a cause of suffering.

The difficult conditioned activities of work
will never be completed at any time;
like changing canals for irrigation,
by leaving [the work] as it is, it is finished.

There is an old Tibetan saying: "Activities are never finished until death; but after death, what benefit will they have?" That can be true of so much of what we prioritize in life. We are always racing to get ahead; we are always working so hard and trying to succeed; we are consumed by countless activities. But how meaningful is most of that activity? What can we actually bring with us? The finish line of all of our striving will still be death for all of us. Only what we have cultivated spiritually can go with us after death.

Of course, many activities are necessary for our basic survival. We all need to eat; most of us feel dependent on shelter; in order to maintain a home, we need to work and pay the bills. But even when those basic needs are met, many of us are not satisfied, so we chase after more activities. We want to be promoted; we want recognition; we want a pay raise. Whatever it is, we often find ways to increase our activities. We are always restless. American culture idolizes progress. We esteem moving up the corporate ladder. Whatever job you have, you should be looking for a better job. Whatever home you have, you should be dreaming of a bigger home. This is how we spend so much of this life.

It is common to see higher levels of happiness in cultures that don't have this same obsession with wealth and individualism. Some of the happiest people on earth live very simple lives. Many people who do hard manual labor all day will come home more satisfied and content than a CEO making millions who flies home on a private jet. Wealth and success do not increase happiness. The more activities we do, the more stress we often feel. In order to relieve that stress we feel the need to distract ourselves with movies and vacations. We forget how to truly relax and sit still. We are not at peace with ourselves.

Jetsun Rinpoche is referring to all of these seemingly endless conditioned activities; he is saying that anything that is not furthering our spiritual cultivation should be abandoned. How much of what we do in a typical twenty-four-hour period will actually matter after our death? For most of us, spiritual practice comprises a very small portion of our time.

If we want to have more peace, we should simplify our lives. The fewer activities we commit to, the more time we will have for contemplation and spiritual practice. If you are someone who genuinely enjoys being busy, then you can choose virtuous activities. Shantideva wrote that if your life is used for virtuous things, then it will be good to live a very long life. But if you are doing many negative things, then it actually would be better for you to have a short life so you do not increase that negative karma.

We sometimes engage in very negative activities because we think this will increase our chances of survival. Many people equate wealth with security. The more wealth they have, the more they may think they are protected against death. They want to have more health insurance, more home insurance, more security measures. But in order to obtain that wealth, they may engage in very negative business activities. We can see how large corporations are often very corrupt. Some people will steal, or even kill, in order to increase their sense of security. Big corporations will promote terribly addictive drugs in order to increase their profits. With that profit, the executives may feel they will have more security. But according to Shantideva, living a longer life in this negative way will actually be very destructive for that person. It would be better for such a negative life to be short so they do not commit so much harm.

But if someone is engaged in very positive and altruistic activities, then it is good for them to live a very long life; they will benefit so many beings and create so much positive karma. If their activities are based in wisdom, these activities will be transformative for those around them. That wisdom will continue on in their mindstream, even after death.

It is important to ask ourselves whether our activities are a form of spiritual laziness or whether they are helping us to cultivate wisdom. So much of what we do in ordinary life is actually a form of distraction. We may look very productive but, from a spiritual perspective, we are being very lazy. We often avoid what is most important in this life: the cultivation of compassion and wisdom for the sake of all sentient beings.

The dense darkness of ignorance
will never be removed at any time;
like a lamp in a dark room,
if the sun of wisdom arises, [ignorance] is removed.

The sun of the wisdom of selflessness
will never arise at any time;
like the dawning of the rising sun,
if the supreme dharmas arise in the mindstream, [wisdom] dawns.

Meditation is the process of learning about our own mind. We are not chasing knowledge about the universe. As we have been discussing, from a Buddhist understanding it is far more important to learn about ourselves and how our mind operates. The more we know our own mind, the better chance we will have of truly knowing others and the world around us.

As we have noted, our education system is usually focused on learning about everything *outside* ourselves, on pursuing external knowledge and memorizing information. Educated people know so much about our physical world. We have created airplanes, computers, and the internet. We have discovered so many lifesaving medicines and surgeries. We have traveled to the moon! We are landing rovers on Mars. We are capturing images of black holes. These are incredible accomplishments, but they do not help us to understand our own minds; they do not help us find liberation.

Out of all of our discoveries, all of our technological progress, how much of it is bringing us more peace and happiness? Is technology, in fact, even giving us more free time? Computers are supposed to save us time, but we now waste so much time on our phones and consuming random information on the internet. Is all of this rapid access to information making us happier or healthier? Instead of bringing us closer together, social media seems to be increasing the divisions in our country. The internet has become a tool for increasing fanaticism. There is so much anger being generated by these arguments online.

These discoveries are not necessarily making us happier. We are spending so much less time in nature; we are sleeping poorly; we are eating fast food; we are losing our ability to connect. Teenagers are texting instead of spending time building social skills with their peers. All of these discoveries and inventions are directed toward pursuing external knowledge. We have a false belief that understanding and controlling the external world will bring us more peace and happiness.

Where I grew up in Tibet, we did not have any of these modern facilities. Life was very simple there. Compared to Tibet, we here in the West have more daily pleasures and comforts; our life is more convenient in many ways. But I have to ask myself, are any of these things making me more peaceful? It is very convenient to have electricity and to be able to travel quickly by car or plane, but has reaching a destination more quickly brought us more peace?

Here in the West it seems we are focused on making everything faster, easier, and more convenient. We are always trying to get faster internet, faster transit, faster delivery. We value speed so much in this culture. But if we look closely at our lives, has this technology and this instant gratification brought us more peace and relaxation? Many of us are using our free time to surf the internet instead of to meditate! We pay a price for all of this comfort, pleasure, and convenience; it can be very unsettling to the mind. We have such high rates of stress; we have more depression and anxiety and insomnia; we have more feelings of social isolation. Although life may be more comfortable in the developed world today, life was much less stressful in traditional Tibetan culture.

Being dependent on outer technology makes us more prone to stress. We depend on a car, and then when the car breaks down or we get into an accident, we have stress. We depend on email, and then when the internet isn't working we feel so frustrated. We depend on electricity, and then when storms come we cannot cope without heat and light. We don't know how to survive without these luxuries anymore. We have lost the ability to be self-sufficient. We have also lost the ability to nurture community because we can just hire strangers to build our homes, fix our cars, and tend our gardens.

When we become more dependent on technology and less dependent on community, we often feel less secure. We worry about becoming sick or growing old alone. We worry what will happen if we can't survive financially. We worry that our families will be too busy to care for us if we need help. When our lives are preoccupied with obtaining *outer* security, we lose touch with ourselves and our own *inner* development. Modern life seems to be moving further and further away from the cultivation of wisdom. We are losing the ability to connect; we are losing community; we are losing the ability to be quiet and create space for contemplation and spiritual practice. All of this "progress" is not necessarily good for humanity.

It is becoming so much easier for people to live in isolation. So many people spend hours alone at night watching TV; they order food delivery; they work from home on their computers all day; they text instead of seeing friends. This isolation can be very corrosive to our wellbeing. No matter how fancy our homes are, how fast our cars are, how much money we have, we still long for connection and social support. Technology cannot fulfill that need for community.

We have misunderstood the meaning of self-sufficiency. In the old days, it meant that we were self-sufficient as a community; we could survive together; we could help one another through difficult times; we could share our skills with one another; we could care for the sick and the aging in our own homes.

Although we feel that we are self-sufficient in our modern lives, we are actually becoming very isolated—and feeling more and more vulnerable as a result. Loneliness can be very bad for our health. We are the loneliest generation, and this loneliness and isolation makes us more prone to physical and mental illness. We could fall into a very deep depression and no one would know that we are suffering, because we are so independent and isolated. Teenagers may be on social media and texting on their phones all day, but their rates of loneliness, depression, and suicide are very high.

Meditation allows us to turn the focus inside while also deepening our compassion for others. Maybe for the first time, we begin to slow down and notice how our mind is working. Instead of distracting ourselves from difficult emotions, we begin to learn how to sit with them. This is very hard to do; there are so many easy ways to avoid our meditation practice. When we feel uncomfortable emotions arising in our practice, we may feel desperate to get on the computer and distract ourselves. But if we are patient and meditate for short periods, we will begin to feel more at ease with our own thoughts and feelings.

There is a vast inner world that we can explore and witness through meditation. We do not need all of the outer technology to explore this inner universe. We have these ancient meditation techniques and yogas—these inner technologies—that help us reveal our inherent wisdom. The more meditation we do, the more freedom we gain from dependence on the outer world. We may still use all of the modern comforts, but they will not have as much power over us anymore. If our car breaks down, we can maintain our mental peace. If the internet fails, we are not frustrated. If the electricity goes out, we can be very content to sit in the dark. The more we explore this inner world, the more freedom we will have from our dependence on outer technologies.

The more we get to know our own mind, the more accurately we will see the world around us. Jetsun Rinpoche is reminding us that knowing our own mind and seeing our inherent wisdom is completely possible. The more awakened we become through meditation, the more clearly we will see the world around us.

Our practice is measured by five sequential "paths:" the path of accumulation, the path of application, the path of seeing, the path of meditation, and the path of no more learning. We start our spiritual practice with the path of accumulation in order to accumulate merit and purify negative karma. When we accomplish that, we then enter the path of application to purify the destructive emotions. The path of application has four levels: heat, peak, patience, and supreme dharma. When Rinpoche speaks of supreme dharmas here, he is referring to that fourth level of the path of application. The path of seeing refers to seeing the wisdom of emptiness and is realized after the supreme dharma.

The painful defilement of concepts
will never be extracted at any time;
like an experienced doctor extracting an arrowhead,
if one possesses the powerful antidotes, [defiled concepts] are extracted.

These lines are describing the importance of applying the correct antidotes. If you are an experienced surgeon—if you work in an emergency room where you treat many victims of shootings, for example—you will be able to extract bullets or arrows very skillfully. Likewise, if we apply the antidotes to our practice, then our practice will become more successful.

When Jetsun Rinpoche says, "the painful defilement of concepts will never be extracted at any time," he is referring to both the "sleeping" defilements and the "active" defilements. Our active defilements manifest in all of our eighty gross thoughts, which arise due to the three destructive emotions of desire, anger, and ignorance. How can we extract those concepts? How can we purify that inner chattering?

To purify those concepts, we have to apply the antidotes. We apply shamatha meditation to purify all of the overactive thoughts and emotions. Like extracting a deeply embedded arrow, we apply insight meditation— vipashyana—to dig out those deeper sleeping emotions. The antidotes of shamatha and insight meditation, which are included in our sadhana practice, can purify all of the eighty concepts and their causes, the root defilements.

The knot of avaricious selfishness
will never be untied at any time;
like untying a knot of silk,
if one understands that possessions are illusory, it is untied.

As we have discussed, desire is one of the strongest emotions we experience. Stinginess often accompanies desire. Once we obtain a desirable object, we want to guard it and keep it for ourselves. It is said that those whose minds are completely possessed by stinginess will be reborn as hungry ghosts. The realm of the hungry ghosts is one of the six realms we can be reborn into. Hungry ghosts have very big stomachs and very tiny throats; they have an insatiable hunger and thirst but can never be satisfied. They have a poverty-stricken mind, and their hunger and thirst can never be fulfilled. This kind of scarcity mindset arises out of insecurity, which is rooted in self-clinging.

Jetsun Rinpoche is saying that only when we realize that possessions and properties are illusory, will we be able to let go of our stinginess and greed. At our level, it is very hard to understand that all of these things we are attached to are actually illusory. Until we understand that ownership and possessions are empty by nature, we will continue to grasp. If we are a millionaire, we will want to become a *billionaire* instead. We will never be content; we will always be afraid that we may lose our fortune.

Meditating on impermanence and death can help us understand this illusory nature. As we have discussed, nothing we possess can go with us after death. No amount of fortune can keep us from old age and suffering. It is good to remember impermanence when we are stressed or experiencing financial loss or insecurity. By accepting the truth of impermanence and change, we can loosen our attachment to property and possessions.

From the prison of samsara's three realms
one will never be freed at any time;
like a prisoner being released from a cell,
if one is liberated from the iron chains of the grasper and grasped,
one is freed.

Human beings cherish freedom. Especially here in the West, we esteem individualism and independence. We have this false belief that capitalism gives us more freedom. We think that the more things we possess, the more independent we will be. Relative to some societies we *do* have a lot of freedom: we have freedom of expression; we have freedom of religion; we have freedom to own whatever we want. But Jetsun Rinpoche is reminding us here that as long as we are driven by negative emotions, the mind really has no freedom at all.

We may live in a palace; we may have every luxury imaginable; but if our mind is in pain, then we are still a prisoner of our emotions. If the mind is not freed from negative emotions, we will never experience true independence. The methods we use to gain independence within a capitalist society often make us more imprisoned. Our hunger for success and wealth and recognition actually fuels our negative emotions. The further up the corporate ladder we climb, the less mental and emotional freedom we are likely to find. The higher we climb, the more fear there is of falling down.

If we compare ourselves to animals, it is worth questioning whether we have more mental freedom than they do. Humans put animals through unimaginable suffering: so many animals have been domesticated and forced to serve the needs of humans; we have taken so much freedom away from animals. Yet, animals often have more mental peace than humans. Animals are more capable of living in the present moment. Animals are often more resilient in the face of trauma.

The more we do in the name of independence and security, the more trapped in the spiderweb we often become. Even if we get to the point where we want to leave everything, we are too trapped in the web to escape. That is how samsara is; we are prisoners in this cycle of suffering. Until we let go of grasper and grasped, until we are free from this dualism of subject and object, we will remain imprisoned.

The city of nirvana
will never be reached at any time;
like a guest entering onto a path,
if one is connected with the beginning of the path of liberation,
one will arrive.

The ultimate freedom of nirvana is possible within each of our minds. We all have the potential for true liberation and true joy. Such freedom can only be achieved through cultivating inner wisdom. Jetsun Rinpoche is saying that as long as we enter the beginning of the path of liberation, we will eventually arrive. On this path, it is imperative to be connected with the four refuge objects: the Guru, the Buddha, the Dharma, and the Sangha. Such liberation can seem like an extraordinary and impossible dream to us in our current lives, but Rinpoche is reminding us that all we need to do is enter the path. Through spiritual practice, we can all experience that inherent freedom.

The guru, the spiritual friend
will never be met at any time;

like Dharmodgata and Sadaprarudita,
if a past accumulated karmic connection exists, [the guru] will be met.

To achieve liberation, we need a good guide; that's why the spiritual teacher is so important. It is the guru who can guide us to the beginning of that path. The Buddha always cautioned his followers not to get attached to him. He warned that his teachings should not be held dogmatically and should not become another "ism." The Buddha said he was merely showing us the path; it is up to us to walk that path.

There are many stories about how teachers and students have met each other. Jetsun Rinpoche is pointing to the famous story that demonstrates the ideal relationship between a teacher (Dharmodgata) and his student (Sadaprarudita). According to the Buddha's teachings, nothing happens by chance or by luck; everything has to have a cause or condition in the past. Therefore, finding a teacher in this lifetime and receiving the teachings is always due to karmic connections established in the past.

The stream of nectar of oral instruction
will never be drunk at any time;
like finding a drink because of being thirsty,
if a suitable student abandons [mundane] activities, [that student] drinks.

Teachers and students need particular qualifications for their meeting to be beneficial; it is a mutual relationship. The teacher's main responsibility is to give the teachings, to give the oral instructions based on the authentic lineage and based on the teacher's experience. It is the students' responsibility to commit themselves to spiritual practice with dedication and devotion. With such diligence, spiritual practice can become the center of their lives. When one is very diligent with practice, mundane activities are naturally abandoned.

If the connection is strong between teacher and student, there can be tremendous transformation. In the story of Marpa and his student Milarepa, we see how even a killer can be transformed, become a great yogi, and attain enlightenment. The power of the student-teacher karmic connection can be very strong and transformative. The test of the relationship is the strength of the faith that arises. When we have met a true, authentic teacher, a strong faith will arise in us, and we will receive great blessings through our practice.

Nondual mahamudra
will never be realized at any time;
like a camel meeting with her calf,
if the mind is recognized, [mahamudra] is realized.

As we have discussed, mahamudra is the realization of the ultimate nature of the mind, the union of clarity and emptiness. In Sanskrit, *maha* means "great," and *mudra* in this context means "seal" or "stamp." Thus, mahamudra means "great seal"; once we have realized that union of wisdom and emptiness, we can "seal" that onto all phenomena, our realization of clarity and emptiness being integrated into everything we experience.

Faith has the power to transform anything. Even if we have faith in an impure object, such faith still has much power to change us. There is a well-known Tibetan story of a mother who sent her son to India to obtain a relic of the Buddha. The son did not succeed, and he brought her a dog's tooth instead, telling her it was a tooth from the Buddha. The mother had so much faith in this impure object that she was completely transformed—even the object became sacred.

For those who have very strong faith, seeing mahamudra, the nature of the mind, is entirely possible. There are two paths to this realization: one based on devotion and one based on intelligence. Whatever path you are on, you have to make the most of your strengths and be aware of the risks. The end result is the realization of nondual mahamudra.

If we don't have faith, if we are skeptical and filled with doubts, achieving realization may be a much more challenging process. It is very common for someone with high intelligence to be so filled with intellectual questions and doubts that the path gets more and more obscured. The great enlightened masters have used many methods to cut through conceptual thinking and help students realize the nature of their own minds. Realizing the nature of the mind is the purpose of all our practice; it is the purpose of the teacher–student relationship.

The leaves of the words of conventions
will never be exhausted at any time;
like [closing up] business activities due to exhausting one's merchandise,
if conceptuality is exhausted, [words] are exhausted.

Speech is essentially a way to convey thoughts to one another; it is not a method for conveying *experiential* wisdom. As we have often discussed, language is a product of conceptuality. As long as we are caught up in ideas and opinions, we will not be conveying experiential wisdom. Because all our words are based in thinking, we cannot rely on words to express the ultimate truth—words are too filled with misconceptions. That's why the *Heart Sutra* says that the perfection of wisdom is speechless, thoughtless, and inexpressible. As long as we are thinking and expressing, we are not actually conveying the ultimate truth. Ultimate truth is beyond thoughts and words. Ultimate truth is inexpressible.

You may be wondering, "What, then, is the use of having a teacher? What is the use of all these teachings?" The teachings are useful as a reference; they can guide us to the beginning of the path and can give us some trail markers along the way. But they cannot convey to us the actual experience itself. A teacher cannot give us the understanding of wisdom, but the teacher can guide us and provide methods that will help us on our journey to discovering our own true nature.

The teachings and practice of mahamudra are found in the Sakya, Gelug, and Kagyu schools of Tibetan Buddhism. Since we are studying in the Sakya lineage here, I will clarify the understanding of mahamudra according to Sakya teachings. Mahamudra refers to the realization of the nature of the mind—but the way to realizing that nature of mind differs between the schools.

According to the Sakya school, mahamudra can only be realized through tantric practice. Within tantric practice we have four different levels: *kriya*, *charya*, *yoga*, and anuttarayoga. According to Sakya teachings, mahamudra can only be realized through the highest anuttarayoga sadhana practices, such as Hevajra, Chakrasamvara, or Vajrayogini. The anuttarayoga practices are those that include the generation of oneself as the deity, as well as the completion practices in which this divine identity is dissolved back into emptiness. Through these practices, it is said that one will realize the nondual wisdom of mahamudra. The Sakya tradition states that there is no realization of mahamudra except through these highest Vajrayana practices. The Kagyu and Gelug schools have mahamudra in both sutra *and* tantra.

Jetsun Rinpoche is speaking of the realization of mahamudra attained through the guru's instruction and the practice of highest Vajrayana anuttarayoga. That realization of mahamudra is ultimate because it is the union of clarity and emptiness. In that ultimate realization of mahamudra, there is no mind. Mahamudra has gone beyond all words and concepts; conceptuality is exhausted; words are exhausted.

The rawhide of one's mindstream
will never be tamed at any time;
similar to medicine for one with disease,
if one practices according to Dharma, [the mindstream] becomes tamed.

As long as we have ego, we will have self-clinging. Thoughts will arise as a result of those negative defilements. As we have discussed, the root defilements, the "three poisons," are desire, anger, and ignorance. Ignorance is based on our misconceptions about the self. From that ignorance arises desire and anger, attachment and aversion. Because these root defilements are the source of all of our concepts and suffering in samsara, we have to apply something to treat those poisons.

All Dharma practice is essentially concerned with treating these root defilements of desire, anger, and ignorance. The Buddha gave us many antidotes to these three poisons. As we have discussed, the Buddha provided three trainings: the training of discipline, to treat our desire; the training of wisdom, to treat our ignorance; and the training of meditation, to calm our anger. These three trainings can cure the poisons and free the mind from the diseases of the defilements.

Possession of the three kayas and the five wisdoms
will never be obtained at any time;
like a kingdom from gathered merit,
if the two accumulations are completed, those [kayas and wisdoms] are obtained.

The "three kayas" refer to the three bodies of the Buddha: the dharmakaya, the sambhogakaya, and the nirmanakaya. The five wisdoms arise from the transformation of the five aggregates—form, feeling, ideation, formation, and consciousness—into the wisdom of the dharmadatu, the wisdom of equality, mirror-like wisdom, the wisdom of discernment, and the wisdom of all-accomplishment, respectively. Essentially, these lines in Jetsun Rinpoche's song are referring to personal transformation. When our mind is transformed and we see our true wisdom and empty nature, we have achieved buddhahood. Such realization is only possible when one has achieved the accumulation of merit and wisdom.

In our ordinary lives, we are generating so much karma. All of our mental activity is generating mental karma. Through that mental activity, we may speak and create all of the verbal karma. We also do so many bodily actions, creating so much physical karma. In order to purify all of the negative karma of body, speech, and mind, we have to replace them with positive actions. The accumulation of merit comprises all of the positive karmas we generate at the level of body, speech, and mind that replace the ordinary negative karmas. The accumulation of merit is performed to exhaust the negative karma.

The accumulation of wisdom involves exhausting and purifying the defilements. The accumulation of merit and wisdom together can purify all of our negative karma and root defilements. The result is that we are able to awaken to our inherent buddha nature. The accumulation of merit and wisdom is not something mysterious; it is a very practical process through which we are able to profoundly transform ourselves.

10

Always Practice Dharma

Do monks who have done hearing and contemplation
comprehend the intent of sutras and tantras?
It is dangerous not to cut doubts;
please do not spend [your time] in pursuit of conventional designations.

THESE LINES ARE RELEVANT not only to monastics but to all practitioners. "Hearing" refers to studying, which was traditionally passed down through oral transmission. Once we have heard the teachings, we need to contemplate what we have heard so that we can understand the intent of the sutras and tantras. But study and contemplation are not enough; we have to practice and integrate the profound meaning of these teachings *experientially*. If we are only learning intellectually and not experientially, we will still have doubts and will still be at risk of falling on the side of conventional thinking. If knowledge is only integrated at the intellectual level and has not become the means for realizing the wisdom of emptiness, then we will not benefit from it nor will we be transformed.

Do all teachers who write and teach,
have the benefit of definite knowledge?
Inquire into the sacred oral instruction;
there is a danger that scholars will die in an ordinary way.

As we have discussed, knowledge is only useful on the spiritual path so far as it helps us to realize our true nature. If we simply acquire knowledge without cultivating wisdom, it will be of no help to us—especially at the time of death. We will die an ordinary death without any spiritual experience to help us.

Among Tibetans it is said that one's death will reveal whether one has been a good spiritual practitioner. People who have been transformed through their practice will approach dying in a different way. They may experience more peace and clarity, they may be less overwhelmed by their pain, and they will not experience the existential anxiety that people often experience as they approach death.

Some highly experienced practitioners may even realize buddhahood at the time of death. There are many accounts—both ancient and modern—of yogis remaining in a meditative state for days or even weeks following their clinical death. In this and other ways, great yogis will show signs of their awakened nature at the time of death, including manifesting a rainbow body.

Death can be very frightening to someone without a spiritual practice or faith. We can observe how hard it is for people to talk about death and dying. For great practitioners, the time of death is viewed as one of the most precious opportunities for achieving enlightenment. Practitioners will be very comfortable with impermanence and will have meditated on death for many years. As a result, the process will feel familiar, and they will not experience anxiety.

If we have avoided contemplating death throughout our lifetime, then we may feel very shocked and frightened when we are dying, and that fear and anxiety can increase our physical pain. This mental and emotional suffering can increase our negative emotions. According to Buddhist understandings, the emotions we have at the time of death will influence the nature of our rebirth. This is how we remain trapped in samsara, forced to be reborn again and again due to these negative emotions.

If we do not have any spiritual practice, our mind may become very disturbed at the time of death. We may have strong anger that we have never processed, we may have strong attachment and clinging to our loved ones and to our possessions, and we may have especially strong attachment to our sense of self, to our ego. Death may feel very frightening for the ego. If there is no belief in an afterlife or in rebirth, the ego-self may feel especially disturbed to be faced with this sense of termination.

Someone who has a strong spiritual practice can face their death with stability and peace and with fewer disturbing emotions. Of course, the experience of death will vary due to one's circumstances, what kind of illness one is facing, and so forth. Being a strong practitioner does not necessarily mean you will not experience a very painful death, but spiritual practice can alter how your mind responds to that pain, resulting in less anger and resistance to the pain for those with a strong practice.

Jetsun Rinpoche is cautioning us that scholars who have never transformed their minds may risk facing death in an ordinary way, with all the anxiety and uncertainty that this brings. This is because their scholarship may have only served to increase their egos rather than transform their minds. The bigger one's ego, the more it can obstruct one's realization of ultimate truth. Scholars may only have faith in their knowledge; if their knowledge helps them to comprehend ultimate reality, then that is useful. But it is very common for knowledge to fuel the ego, increase doubt, and become an obstacle to making a connection with and having faith in a sadhana practice and enlightened deities.

There are many Buddhist stories that explicitly warn about the doubt and torment that scholars can become trapped in. One story tells of a great intellectual who was renowned as a scholar. One day he fell ill, and it was soon obvious that he was dying. Thereupon, he became so scared, realizing that all of his knowledge could not protect his mind or bring him any peace. Although he had never developed any real faith, as he was dying and experiencing so much emotional pain, he suddenly felt a deep welling up of faith and began to practice and recite mantra.

If we have cultivated some measure of faith throughout our lifetime, we will not have this same existential struggle as we are dying. Through years of practice, we will feel some connection to our teachers, to our sadhana deities, and to the Buddha.

Having a daily spiritual practice is vitally important. Even if we feel that we are mediocre practitioners, just having a daily practice can cultivate a positive connection to the sadhana deity. Then, if we are faced with challenges and we are fearful, that deity will feel close to us and we will have a sense of stability and comfort from that connection. Faith in the deity can protect the mind from all of the negative emotions. The deity represents our own buddha nature, the wisdom and emptiness of our own mind. Jetsun Rinpoche is advising us to seek oral instructions from teachers who are highly realized—like those great yogis of the past.

All [you] great meditators who practice,
please do not enjoy engaging in idle talk;
please do not yearn greatly for food and clothing;
please do not become attached to the taste of dhyana.

Jetsun Rinpoche is reminding us here of the risks we face as practitioners. Although we may want to go into retreat, although we may want to achieve more concentration in our daily practice, we will inevitably encounter the obstacles of craving and attachment. We are so used to engaging with the world, that even when we go into retreat we may continue that mental grasping. Even if we are all alone, we may continue to engage in idle chatter in our own minds. We may be eating simple food on retreat, yet we still may crave our favorite meals. Instead of focusing on meditation, there is a possibility that the mind will continue engaging with the outer world regardless of whether we are practicing in solitude.

As we have discussed, the mind is very rebellious; it has had countless lifetimes to develop habitual patterns and to act based on negative emotions. Practice is about learning to discipline the mind. We can all observe the struggle between discipline and distraction when we try to meditate. The rebellious, distracted mind will often win this struggle early on in our meditation training. When the rebellious mind wins, we lose our discipline and concentration.

When our mind rebels, the best thing we can do is maintain our daily practice. We will all go through many "seasons" in our practice. We may have days or months when our practice feels very strong, and then weeks, or even years, go by when our mind is very rebellious; we may be sitting on the cushion, but our mind may be wandering everywhere. We may be filled with worries or fears; we may be haunted by difficult memories that are suddenly coming up. When we experience such difficulties, the best thing we can do is continue to practice day after day, even when the mind is very uncomfortable and trying to escape. In disciplining ourselves in this way, it is also very important to be very loving and patient with ourselves, like a good parent with their child. If we diligently return to our practice day after day, over time our mind will become tamed, and we will find more steadiness in our concentration and in our practice.

In ordinary life, we are always chasing after sensory pleasures. We chase after delicious foods, beautiful music, wonderful fragrances, and inspiring images; we want to engage with beautiful things and avoid ugly or unpleasant objects. But if we look closely, we will see how indulging in sensory pleasures actually *increases* our cravings. Satisfaction of desire is generally very short-lived because enjoyment of sensory objects does not create a stable or lasting sense of happiness. Instead, we are only increasing our appetite for these pleasures in such a way that it may become more and more difficult to be at ease. In this constant cycle of craving and enjoyment, our minds become increasingly addicted to sensory indulgence, and it becomes difficult to find enjoyment in just sitting still; we feel easily bored and restless; simply being alone with our own mind makes us very uncomfortable.

If you have developed a habit of going out to a bar every Friday night with friends, eating rich foods, and laughing and drinking, you may feel very deprived if you have to stay home. This is because your mind has become conditioned to need these activities. If you are addicted to smoking and suddenly you don't have any nicotine, you will be very uncomfortable. This is the fundamental dilemma with indulging in sensory pleasures. As we have discussed, these pleasures can bring momentary happiness but they are always the causes of future pain and unhappiness. We can see this so clearly in our addiction to technology. Having so much available to us online has not made us any happier or more content. Everywhere we go, there are advertisements that are designed to increase our cravings. The result is that we are ever more restless, and it becomes harder and harder for us to be alone with our minds or to enjoy simple activities.

When we meditate, we withdraw from all of this external craving, engaging instead in an introverted pursuit, trying to find peace in our own mind. And it is important to remember that even this peaceful state within meditation can become addictive. When we get attached to this feeling of peace, we can become upset when we have a "bad day" in meditation. There is a danger that if we get attached to this peaceful feeling, we will never go beyond this sensory experience to experience the true bliss of awakening.

In these lines, Jetsun Rinpoche is warning us not to become attached to those peaceful meditative states, which he refers to poetically as the "taste of dhyana." If we become addicted to these peaceful experiences, it will actually become an obstruction to our practice and to our realization of ultimate truth. If we are attached to these feelings of peace, we will not be able to see emptiness.

All [you] Dharma practitioners who turn away from nonvirtue,
please comprehend the view of sutra and tantra a little;

occasionally follow the guru as an attendant;
always look into your own mind.

It is a common pitfall in monastic training to place too much emphasis on the training of discipline and on rituals without sufficiently cultivating the trainings of wisdom and meditation. On the other hand, people in the West usually focus *too* much on meditation and do not put enough emphasis on discipline. As we have discussed, without good guides along the way, without the Dharma teachings, and without a connection with an authentic teacher and lineage, it will be very hard for us to progress along the spiritual path.

When we talk about Buddhism here in the West, we often equate it merely with meditation, ignoring the trainings of discipline and wisdom. But for a Dharma practice to be complete, it should include all three trainings: discipline, meditation, and wisdom.

Of these three trainings, the training of wisdom is the most important. When Jetsun Rinpoche refers to the "view of sutra and tantra," he is referring to that wisdom. To realize this wisdom, we also need to train in meditation and discipline. These three trainings are complementary and inseparable in Buddhist practice. If our meditation and our discipline are not helping us to realize the view of wisdom, then our practice is not complete; meditation and discipline should act as means for realizing wisdom. If meditation and discipline are not helping us realize wisdom, then we may experience peace, but we will never be liberated from samsara.

In the highest Vajrayana practice, guru yoga is very important. Even following the guru as an attendant can be part of guru yoga practice. It is possible to realize our inherent buddha nature through guru yoga. The external manifestations of the Guru, the Buddha, the Dharma, and the Sangha are really just reminders of these inner qualities. Guru yoga allows us to see our inner buddha nature. Devotion to the guru can be a very powerful method for realizing that wisdom; the more devotion we feel to the relative guru, the more it will help us to recognize the wisdom within us, our own inner teacher and guide.

If there is laziness toward the side of virtue,
[keep] the impermanence of death in mind.

If we do not understand how the natural law of karma operates, we will not put much faith in the Buddha's teachings on cause and effect and, as a result of that lack of faith, we may become very careless. When we do not understand karma, we become completely distracted by entertaining our senses and pursuing pleasure.

Sensory pleasure has so much power in our lives. People are often completely ruled by the pursuit of pleasure and happiness. At our level, happiness and pleasure are inseparable from emotions; they activate and increase our emotions. Jetsun Rinpoche is urging us to remember the natural law of karma, which governs how things come to be due to cause and effect. He is encouraging us to remember that everything is always changing: the outer world is changing, our own bodies are changing, and every day we are moving closer to our own death. Remaining mindful of impermanence and death can interrupt our complacency. A mindful awareness of death can cut through our impulsive pursuit of sensory pleasures. An awareness and appreciation of impermanence can help us remain focused on our spiritual practice.

Mindfulness of impermanence and death are fundamental to Buddhist practice. Our negative emotions can lead us to become quite lazy and complacent. We may appear busy and productive according to societal standards, but this is often a symptom of spiritual laziness. We may be intellectually curious, always searching for new information, positive experiences, and good results.

We may even become complacent in our spiritual practice. We may study Buddhist texts; we may be devoted to a spiritual teacher for many years; we may practice meditation diligently for some time, and so forth. But if we reach a point where we do not feel our practice is transforming us, or where it becomes very difficult physically or emotionally, we may get bored, frustrated, and discouraged, and may even abandon our practice altogether.

Complacency is a pattern that we can see throughout our lives. We chase after excitement and novel experiences that distract us from ourselves and from our suffering. Perhaps we are chasing after mystical experience in our spiritual practice; having had a few glimpses of mental freedom, we may continue to chase that experience for years without achieving it. We can see similar patterns in so many areas of our lives.

For many people, the things they do repeatedly start to lose their interest, leading to a sense of dullness and complacency. For example, we may be very devoted to a partner early in a relationship. We may regularly bring them gifts and feel so much interest and excitement. But after many years of marriage, we may become increasingly bored and frustrated. We may lose all of that enthusiasm and attention we initially had. We can see this pattern in many areas of our lives. If we were given our favorite meal every day for years, we would eventually become very bored with it and would crave something else.

We may be steadily engaged in Dharma study. But instead of becoming a better yogi, many practitioners become more complacent as the years pass, going through the motions of practice while actually daydreaming and spacing out. We may have reached a point where we have become very sleepy and dull in our meditation, and we may feel that our practice is no longer bringing us pleasure. Many students will eventually drop their practice because it does not seem interesting or beneficial anymore. They may feel that their time would be better spent focusing on some new hobby or interest.

Feeling bored, we let go of our practice. Or maybe we stop studying because we have some disagreement with our teacher or a conflict with someone in our sangha—there are many reasons why people decide to leave their practice. This is why it is so important to make a lasting commitment, to have faith, and to be disciplined. We will go through many seasons in our practice: There will be dry seasons; there will be stormy seasons; there will be abundant seasons. Through all of this, our faith and discipline can carry us through the many challenges and obstacles that arise. Having faith and diligence will keep us on track, even during the very challenging times in our life.

Cultivating such faith and diligence is not always easy. We are accustomed to things happening so fast in our culture; we have been conditioned to expect instant gratification. We are so impatient when we do not get the result we want immediately, and we become bored and lonely when we are not getting any satisfaction out of our practice. The more we try to meditate, the more we may experience that frustration. Because we don't want to feel our negative emotions—because we don't want to sit still with those difficult feelings—we will want to abandon our practice and turn on the television or go out with friends.

It can be very painful to get to know our own mind. There are so many layers of suffering we have to peel away in order to reveal that inherent wisdom. People spend so much energy running away from unpleasant feelings, from difficult memories, and from the qualities we don't like in ourselves. Slowing down and observing what is arising in our mind can make us very self-conscious and uncomfortable; we may discover many things we don't like in ourselves; we may feel almost allergic to ourselves as we come to recognize how driven we have been by our ego; we may feel shame and loneliness.

All of these factors can cause us to abandon our practice. We may try to find something else to replace the practice, something that will bring us more peace or pleasure and will allow us to escape the reality of our own suffering instead of facing it. But if we can remain mindful of the inevitability of impermanence and death, it will help us to face reality and it will push us to use our time more wisely while we are living.

In this pithy verse, Jetsun Rinpoche is giving an important teaching about practice and motivation: if we are able to face the reality of impermanence and develop a strong faith in karma, we will remain committed to our practice; when we deny the reality of impermanence, we will stray from our practice and squander our virtue. This is a basic choice each of us has to make in our own lives; either we try to face reality and become more awake, or we ignore reality and sleepwalk through our lives.

This process of waking up and facing reality is not pleasurable. It does not initially bring more happiness and peace. It can be a very painful and uncomfortable process. We have been running from reality for so long that it is very hard to sit down and face the truth. It is very hard when we realize that so much of what we thought was important is really just a distraction; that much of our "productivity" and "success" was really just a form of spiritual laziness.

We are conditioned to want to run away from our problems. But how far can we really run though? Until we solve the basic underlying issue, until we treat the root poisons, our problems will continue to follow us. We may get a new job, a new partner, or move to a new city, but new problems will arise. Although there is no escaping how difficult this life can be, we have the option to stop running from this difficulty. We have the option of getting to know the root causes of our suffering. We have the choice to free ourselves from our negative reactions. We cannot stop all of the many difficult things from happening to us, but we *can* change how we respond. As we become less reactive and less concerned with always running away from emotional discomfort, we will find that we have so much more energy to practice.

Yogis accept the truth of suffering. By facing reality, they become more mindful and awakened—which is the basis of transformation. It is very common for practitioners to try to avoid reality instead and to remain very distracted or sleepy in their meditation. It is easier to avoid strong feelings and sensations when one is sleepy, but it also prevents growth or transformation from happening. By not facing reality, we remain childish and reactive. Ignorance and sleepiness may appear peaceful from the outside but, internally, there is no transformation happening—it is merely another way of escaping reality. Accepting the reality of impermanence and death is a way to cut through ignorance and to become more devoted in our practice.

If desire and anger arise toward objects,
[keep] the dharmata of dharmas in mind.

The three poisons are interdependent. As long as we have ignorance, we will also have desire and anger. We become attached to objects because we do not know the true reality of those objects; we become angry when our desires are not fulfilled. These three—ignorance, desire, and anger—are the root negative emotions that prevent our mind from seeing reality.

In order to transcend these negative emotions, we need to see the true nature, the dharmata. *Dharmata* means "the nature of dharma," with the word *dharma* in this context meaning all phenomenal objects. It is only when we see the true nature of the phenomenal world that we can be free from attachment and anger.

In our current lives, we are attached to external objects because we have not seen the empty nature of all phenomena. We have not seen this empty nature because we have not recognized the true nature of our own mind; we have not awakened to the union of clarity and emptiness. Once we awaken, we recognize that all of these negative emotions are just temporary clouds, coming and going in the mind. But the nature of the mind is clear like space.

When we see the dharmata, the true nature of the mind, then we see that anger and desire and ignorance are just passing through; they are not in the nature of the mind. Jetsun Rinpoche is telling us that realizing this true nature of mind is the antidote to the negative emotions. He is helping us to understand how to become awakened and how to free ourselves from the grip of these negative emotions.

Life is filled with emotions. We tend to think that having many emotions is a sign of life and vitality. But all of those emotions are actually *obscuring* reality. When we get attached to a beautiful object, our desire completely obscures the empty nature of that object. Seeing the dharmata, the true empty nature of the mind—and of the phenomenal world—is the best antidote to negative emotions.

Modern civilization seems to be getting further and further away from seeing that true nature. We are becoming increasingly technologically advanced and complex. But the more complex our surroundings become, the harder it may be to recognize emptiness. If we think about it, has any of the technology in our lives helped us to see the nature of reality more clearly? Has increased technological complexity helped us to experience more peace and satisfaction? In fact, all of this development has not brought us closer to understanding reality; our technological advancements have not increased our wisdom. Many new technologies have come at the expense of humanity and of the earth. Although we have learned to cure diseases and have made incredible discoveries and inventions, all of that development has had consequences. Our earth is being destroyed, and we have lost our sense of interdependence with other living beings.

We—like all other beings and objects—are a product of karma. The more we understand the natural law of cause and result, the more peace we will experience. Modern development has not brought us more peace and more joy; instead there is more fear and more insecurity. By becoming aware of the nature of the mind, we can free ourselves from this vicious cycle of negative emotions and negative karma. Meditation is the only way to experience the true nature of the mind.

If connected with a circle of people and things,
[keep] the deceptions of Mara in mind.

We are part of so many social circles. We are born into a family and as we grow up we develop a wider circle of friends and colleagues. We may also form community with other spiritual practitioners. It is important to contemplate these relationships and to evaluate what kinds of relationships help us to grow and which relationships may be deceiving us. Not all relationships that appear pleasant or enjoyable are necessarily beneficial to us. We have a wide variety of social relationships based on emotional needs, survival needs, and cultural influences. "Mara" refers to whatever is creating obstacles to our spiritual practice. It is important to look closely at all of our social interactions and evaluate when they are helping us to awaken and when they are increasing our negative emotions.

Our spiritual practice helps us to bring wisdom into all of our social interactions. It helps us maintain clarity and equanimity when we are encountering very difficult conflicts. It helps us find some measure of emotional freedom. It helps us focus our energy on spiritual growth and on the cultivation of wisdom and compassion instead of wasting our lives chasing pleasure and happiness.

The Buddhist teachings mention four kinds of Maras: the Mara of aggregates; the Mara of defilements; *Devaputra* Mara, the Mara of the sons of the gods in the desire realm; and the Mara of death. These four are called Mara because they create harm and obstacles to achieving enlightenment on our spiritual path. Jetsun Rinpoche is warning us that our relationships with our "circle of people and things" can become obstacles to our practice, like the deceptions of the Maras.

If, despite whatever you may do, there is no happiness,
[keep] the faults of samsara in mind.

As we have discussed many times, misconception about what will bring us happiness leads to continued pain and suffering. The pursuit of happiness has no end; the minute we achieve a goal, we start dreaming about the next goal; the minute we finish a wonderful experience, we start thinking about how to repeat that experience.

Jetsun Rinpoche is reminding us to keep the faults of samsara in mind when we experience this perpetual unhappiness and dissatisfaction. Moment to moment, life is always changing: our body is not the same today as it was yesterday; we are aging every moment; things are being born and things are decaying. We often resist this change, which is a major cause of suffering. Life in samsara is filled with the suffering of change. Happiness and unhappiness always go together; pain and pleasure always go together. There is no person who is happy all the time, because happiness is a state that is always changing. Rinpoche is not speaking of the state of spiritual bliss and ultimate joy here. Rather, he is speaking of the kinds of happiness and pleasure that are relative and conditional.

We really should not expect so much happiness from this life. Once we see the reality of things, we can better learn how to let go of the expectation that we can reach a state of lasting happiness. That expectation is actually causing us so much more suffering. The nature of life itself is change—wherever there is happiness, pain is going to follow; wherever there is pain, happiness will also be possible. Happiness and suffering are inseparable in samsara. If we can really integrate this understanding, we will not be so obsessed with pursuing happiness; we will understand that pursuing happiness also means increasing our suffering.

When we have a better understanding of the inseparability of happiness and suffering, we will actually feel more peace. We will stop striving toward some imaginary future where things will be better. We will develop more acceptance of the present moment. We will understand that in this moment there is happiness and there is unhappiness. We will recognize that even if we make huge changes in our lives, there will always be new causes of happiness and unhappiness. This is why Rinpoche is urging us to keep the faults of samsara in mind—because it will help us to accept life as it is and to stop resisting change or chasing something in the future.

With Dharma, this life and the next life are blissful,
the *bardo* existence is blissful,
rebirth is blissful;
[these are] very blissful because of birthlessness.
Oneself is blissful, others are blissful, both are blissful;
therefore, please always practice Dharma.

The essence of Dharma is training the mind with discipline, meditation, and wisdom in order to purify desire, anger, and ignorance. With these trainings, our present life, our rebirth, and the *bardo*—the intermediate state between death and rebirth—will be transformed. When we realize enlightenment, which is free from birth and death, not only do we experience bliss, but we also become uniquely able to benefit others and help them to achieve the great bliss of wisdom and compassion. For these reasons, Jetsun Rinpoche is emphasizing that we should make the commitment to practice Dharma all the time.

At the time of obtaining complete human birth,
why is it that one does not practice spiritual Dharma?

Jetsun Rinpoche is asking why we are not using our precious human birth to practice spiritual Dharma. What do we think is the purpose of life? Are we merely focused on basic survival? Are we living just to eat? Or can we fulfill our basic needs in order to do something greater? Buddhist teachings emphasize that the ultimate purpose of life is to achieve complete enlightenment for the benefit of all sentient beings. Of course, to support that, we need to overcome obstacles and experience many conducive conditions in our life. But without any spiritual practice, what is the difference between this precious human life and the life of an animal?

Having been with a sacred guru again and again,
why is it that one has not pleased him?

Here, Jetsun Rinpoche is questioning why some students are not benefiting despite having met with the sacred guru many times. There are numerous stories from India of the tests that Buddhist masters put their disciples through. The great master Tilopa put his disciple Naropa through many trials and tribulations in order to purify Naropa's karma. These trials helped Naropa become a great practitioner and mahasiddha. There are also many famous examples of the importance of the guru–disciple bond from Tibet, including the stories of Marpa and his disciple Milarepa, or Jetsun Rinpoche and Sakya Pandita. Texts like the *Fifty Verses of Guru Devotion* help students learn how to please their guru. In Vajrayana, the guru is envisioned as being a fully enlightened buddha—even taking the form of Kulapati, who is honored even by the enlightened buddhas on their own crowns.

On the other hand, as exemplified in the famous story of Angulimala, if the guru orders the disciple to commit nonvirtues, such as killing and other negative actions due to jealousy and anger, then it is better to stay away from such teachers and gurus. In such cases, Sakya Pandita taught that it is best to remain neutral rather than reacting negatively to those teachers.

Having requested the profound oral instruction again and again, why is it that one has not done any practice?

Jetsun Rinpoche is questioning why some devotees who receive many empowerments and instructions still do not do any practice. This is very common in Buddhist countries, where devotees gather in huge crowds to receive empowerments from a high lama or go to watch groups of monks or yogis performing rituals and ceremonies. Many of those participants don't follow up with a commitment to any particular practice. Instead, they view these empowerments and oral instructions simply as blessings from which they may be able to earn a little merit. Their Dharma practice generally ends there; they are not diligent enough to practice a daily sadhana or to go on retreats.

Having aroused definite knowledge in the Dharma again and again, why is it that one goes back again?

Jetsun Rinpoche is wondering why some scholars who have already gained confidence and certainty in their Dharma knowledge still turn back again and again to their studies. Scholars like to collect more and more information. Indeed, there is no end to learning until we have achieved wisdom. There are stories that describe scholars spending their whole lives learning, yet failing to do any spiritual practice. This is like reading books about cooking for years but never actually cooking a meal or tasting the food. One of my own *khenpos*[36] even expressed regret that he had spent his whole life busily giving teachings, and thus never had time to do any retreats.

---

36. *Khenpo* (*mkhan po*) is a title given to learned masters and teachers in all of the Tibetan Buddhist traditions of Nyingma, Sakya, Kagyu, and Gelug schools.

11

Have No Regrets

Generally, leave your homeland and remain in exile;
even though one is separated from one's country, there is no regret.

MANY STUDENTS LEAVE THEIR family, town, and country in pursuit of spiritual teachers and spiritual practice. As we have discussed, there is a great tradition of wandering yogis in India. Many Tibetan lamas have also traveled to India to study Dharma with the great masters of India. Within Tibet itself, practitioners regularly traveled—and still travel—from their hometowns to other regions of Tibet in order to learn from different gurus. Many monks from Eastern Tibet traveled to the large monasteries in Central Tibet to learn and practice, some even abandoning their hometowns forever.

Jetsun Rinpoche is reminding us that dedicated practitioners who abandon their hometown or country in pursuit of spiritual practice don't have any regrets about living in exile. These practitioners realize that spiritual cultivation in the pursuit of enlightenment is more important than remaining attached to their birthplace. They understand that we were born alone and, ultimately, we will be forced to leave everything behind when we die.

In the next verses, Rinpoche emphasizes the non-regretful dharmas, which are similar to the eight irreversible dharmas mentioned in the sutras. These irreversible dharmas are related to bodhisattvas who have reached the irreversible stage, where they are certain to achieve complete buddhahood without reversing back to the lower levels. Similarly, non-regretful dharmas help practitioners to become great yogis.

Direct the mind always to positive dharmas;
even if one is born in hell, there is no regret.

Jetsun Rinpoche is encouraging us to always practice in order to cultivate all the positive spiritual qualities within us. You may be wondering how, if we have cultivated all the spiritual qualities, it would be possible to be born in hell. The answer is that those who have entered into the way of the bodhisattva may freely choose to be reborn in the hell realms in order to benefit the beings who are suffering there. There are many stories of bodhisattvas who, through profound compassion, chose to be reincarnated in hell realms and places of tremendous suffering because that was the place where they could be of the most help to sentient beings. Instead of feeling regret, bodhisattvas such as these rejoice in helping others.

Rely on the guru as the principal deity;
even if one's resources are exhausted, there is no regret.

There are many examples in the stories of the great mahasiddhas—such as those of Tilopa and Naropa—of disciples relying on the guru as their principal deity, which means that the guru and the yidam deity are inseparable. If we are practicing Vajrayogini as our principal sadhana deity, then we will see Vajrayogini in the form of the guru and we will see our guru in the form of Vajrayogini.

Many yogis have had to sacrifice everything in order to pursue their practice. They have had to give up their homes, their wealth, and their comfort. They have had to renounce everything. Jetsun Rinpoche is saying here that even if we become a homeless beggar, like the Buddha and the mahasiddhas, we will not experience any regret.

Some of the best practitioners have been beggars. Milarepa barely had any resources to begin with; and yet he gave whatever he had to his teacher Marpa. As we have discussed, Milarepa was doing his practice in a cave; he had no elaborate shrine on which to make offerings, and he had no other food except for nettles. But despite these difficulties, he had no regrets because it was through these practices that he became enlightened. He knew the difference between worldly dharma and the holy Dharma. He had no regret, even when all of his resources were exhausted.

Do any devotional service for the guru;
even if [the guru] shows no interest, there is no regret.

Early in our spiritual practice, we may place a lot of importance on the outer refuge objects, and until we recognize the *inner* Guru, Buddha, Dharma, and Sangha, our faith will remain shaky. For example, if we have some disagreement with our guru, we may become dispirited and abandon our practice. In this way, our initial falling in love with the outer refuge objects may lead us to get stuck in a more superficial devotion that only exists at the emotional level.

According to Buddhist teachings, devotional service to a spiritual teacher will generate more merit than serving in worldly causes. The difference lies in how much emotional involvement there is in our service. Fighting for a cause often brings up a lot of anger and generates a sense of animosity toward others. We have a very strong desire for a better outcome for those we serve, and so we often feel anger at broken systems, at oppressive structures, at the government, or at other organizations. Even positive causes can generate many negative emotions in us.

On the other hand, when we perform devotional service to pure objects, we are not expecting any outcome. As our service transforms us, we have less and less need for recognition. We begin to understand that serving the relative guru is a way of honoring and cultivating the guru inside us. In this way, serving the guru serves to transform our attachment to our own ego. When our devotional practice is strong, then even if we have a conflict with the relative guru or with someone in the sangha, our faith will remain stable because we have recognized that these pure objects are within us. Devotional service can be very stabilizing—not only for individual practitioners but for a society as a whole. We can see this in countries with thousands of years of devotional practice: for instance, the practice of Bhakti yoga among the yogis in India.

There are many Buddhist stories that illustrate how transformative devotional service can be. As we discussed in an earlier chapter, Jetsun Rinpoche once became very sick, and his nephew Sakya Pandita became very devoted to his uncle and nursed him back to health. After that, Sakya Pandita wrote that his mind became much clearer; he no longer viewed Jetsun Rinpoche as an uncle but recognized him as his guru, and as a result, Sakya Pandita's inner realization increased.

Whenever we do something based on positive emotions, it has greater power. That is why devotional service is emphasized. Devotional service cultivates the positive quality of wholeheartedness. In this wholeheartedness, there is no holding back, no hope or fear. By giving selflessly, we develop a greater sense of inner freedom. We can perfect our generosity to the point where there is no longer any gift, any giver, or any receiver.

Early in our spiritual practice we may offer service to the guru or to the sangha, but it may still feel conditional. It may still be arising from our attachment. We may volunteer our time with a subtle expectation of recognition by the teacher or the wider sangha. We may become frustrated and overextend ourselves, leading us to feel resentful. It is important for us to offer our devotion from a place of health and stability. It is very common for new students to volunteer too much and then become exhausted. It is important to offer devotion from a place of mental balance and health; it will be much more sustainable and transformative that way.

Devotional service is not a commodity, something that one can scale up and increase its production. That is a very capitalistic view of devotion. Doing prostrations is devotional service; it does not produce anything material. Circumambulating a stupa is devotional service, but it does not produce anything for the temple. Often, the simplest devotional practices are the most transformative. Devotional service is very connected to diligence; through repetition, we are creating positive patterns and habits.

Faith and love can bring the heart and mind together. If we perform service only from an intellectual motivation, it will not be as beneficial. If we do something that we know is positive but our heart feels resentful or resistant, it will not be transformative or sustainable. When the heart and mind act together, it generates so much power in our practice. Even a simple act of prostration repeated again and again in a heartfelt and mindful way can be transformative. When the heart and mind are fully engaged, we will not feel bored or resistant. Instead, we will feel all of the positive qualities that arise from that activity. We may even lose track of time because we are so fully participating in our practice.

Devotional service is not about pleasing someone else. If we serve the guru with the hope that we will receive special attention from the teacher, then we may feel very resentful if the teacher does not seem to notice us. But it would actually be very destructive if the guru were increasing our ego by paying special attention to us. If the guru and student see devotional service as a personal act, it can create a very dangerous dynamic. If the service itself is not helping to free the student from attachment to self and attachment to the relative guru, then the service is not actually being done with wisdom.

Devotional service that arises out of wisdom, that is based on mature love and faith, can become unconditional. When service is unconditional, we transcend the three wheels of gift, giver, and receiver—we are not doing a Tara sadhana to make Tara happy; we don't make offerings to the Buddha to make the Buddha happy! In performing devotional service with mature love and faith, there is no receiver; we transcend the ordinary conditions, we transcend the need for results, and we begin to give from a place of clarity and emptiness.

When we begin to make offerings from this place of higher wisdom, our practice becomes unconditional and, thus, very strong. Our faith is no longer shaky; our devotion to the refuge objects cannot be contaminated by outer conflicts or negative emotions. If our teacher becomes angry, it does not shake our faith in the inner guru. If our sangha falls apart due to some scandal, it does not shake our faith in the inner sangha.

So long as devotion arises out of attachment, there is still ego involvement. The ego is very susceptible to disillusionment, frustration, and relational conflicts. The ego is always looking for recognition; it is always looking to reinforce itself. When the ego meets disagreeable conditions, it will be tempted to drop the entire practice. This dynamic can become especially precarious right as a student approaches a very pivotal change. It is often the case that we cling most tightly to the ego just before we have a breakthrough in our practice. There is often a burst of egoic activity when the ego feels threatened. If we do not meet this ego response with wisdom, then we will tend to do whatever is necessary to protect our ego, even if it means leaving our teacher and our practice.

If our devotional service has been offered with a pure mind, then our transformation does not rely on any particular outcome. With a pure mind, we are able to give without any hope or fear, without any ego. By performing this pure giving, we are transformed, regardless of whether anyone notices or not. Even if our guru is angry, we will not feel any regret, because we have offered with pure devotion and wisdom.

Request the upadeshas in accord with scripture;
even if one cannot practice, there is no regret.

It is common for Western students to want to receive as many teachings as possible. They may be impatient and jump from one Buddhist center to another or read many books without obtaining any oral instruction. But it is vitally important to receive initiation from an unbroken lineage of teachers. Without a direct transmission from an authentic guru, our practice cannot be activated by the blessings of the lineage.

Our practice must be received from a guru and traced back through an unbroken lineage all the way to the Buddha. This is how the teachings that we receive are validated by the Buddha's words as preserved in the sutras and tantras–it is how we can certify that the practice is valid. Otherwise, anyone can just make up a practice. If we do not have that authority and that connection to the lineage, our practice will not bring much realization.

Abandon activities, as the principal virtuous conduct;
even if *siddhis*[37] are not obtained, there is no regret.

After we receive empowerment from a qualified guru, we then have to do the sadhana practice of whichever deity we have been authorized to practice. That sadhana deity is now the center of our life. We recite mantra, we do our daily practice, and even in our downtime we practice yogas of sleeping and eating, and so forth. The more we focus on this practice, the less time we will have to engage in neutral and nonvirtuous activities.

Many yogis renounce all worldly activities and spend their lives in caves just doing meditation. But even as a layperson, we can choose to prioritize our practice, which will help us to renounce mundane activities and to refrain from mindless entertainment. The more practice we do, the more results we will see in our life. But Jetsun Rinpoche is saying here that even if we do not see any results, if we have given our best effort to spiritual practice we do not need to have any regret.

Protect your promises as your principal concern;
even if one is ridiculed by friends, there is no regret.

Jetsun Rinpoche is talking here about resolutions, commitments, loyalty, and faithfulness. Whenever we make promises and commitments

---

37. *Siddhi* (*dngos grub*) refers to both common siddhis (worldly wealth and so forth), and the uncommon siddhi of full enlightenment.

in our life, there will be some sacrifices. Maybe our friends will not understand our choices and our priorities; maybe we will feel very pressured by family or society to engage in worldly activities; maybe we will be seen as strange if we want to spend a lot of time alone in practice. But keeping our promise and commitment to our practice is a great strength. We have to keep that promise when practice is going well—and especially when it is going poorly.

The Buddhist teachings say that childish and ordinary promises are like something written in the sand: wind, waves, and storms will easily blow those promises away. But the great bodhisattva vow, the promise to achieve enlightenment for the sake of all sentient beings, is a promise carved in stone. It can survive so many storms; it can survive disaster; it can survive many years when practice is frustrating, when it does not feel as if we are making any progress.

In general, it seems that we have more difficulty keeping promises and commitments in modern society. We have a more difficult time staying faithful in relationships; we have more trouble staying with jobs and navigating conflicts; we see how hard it is for people to maintain loyalty. There is a weakness to our promises; we have lost some of that capacity of older generations to stick with things even when times are hard. On the one hand, we have more freedom and more choices—but this is not necessarily making us any happier or more fulfilled.

As we lose a sense of community, we lose our trust in others. It used to be that a community held its members accountable because its members needed one another to survive. With the breakdown of community and the increased isolation in society, it is more and more difficult for people to have trust. We worry that people are out to take advantage of us for their own gain. We have a culture with so many contracts, so many lawyers, so much insurance. We have to get everything in writing because we do not have the same code of honor regarding keeping our word with someone. Even the sacred union of marriage is not to be trusted, as reflected in the high divorce rates. Even when someone is very much in love, they sometimes create a prenuptial agreement protecting their wealth in advance in case of divorce.

When we are on the spiritual path, we are making a deep commitment. We have to care for that commitment; we have to tend that spiritual practice as we would tend a very important relationship; we cannot grow complacent. Spiritual practice is a lifelong commitment; we hope that it extends beyond this lifetime and that we continue to progress in our awakening from life to life. In this way, we must commit our hearts and minds to this spiritual path.

When we make many sacrifices in order to pursue our spiritual practice, other people may feel some scorn. Because we are not making much money or succeeding by societal standards, it may seem like we are failing. People may judge us for living very humble lives. People may not understand why we prefer to be home doing meditation practice instead of joining friends out at a party. People may even feel hurt by our decisions, thinking that we are abandoning them. People may even look down on those who commit to a spiritual life, thinking that people of faith lack intelligence.

Even the great yogi Milarepa was not understood by those around him; even his own sister could not understand his choices. When she went to visit him in his retreat cave, most of his body had turned green because he was subsisting on nettles, and he had only the smallest bit of cloth to cover his body. When his sister saw how he was living—that he was basically ragged and starving—she felt sadness and pity for him and said, "My brother, what kind of spiritual practice are you doing? Why are you not like that *geshe* who is a great scholar and travels on horseback with many attendants who hold brocaded umbrellas above his head? Why do you not prefer to practice Dharma like him? Your practice is not helping improve your life; it is not helping your family." Milarepa then sang many mystical songs to explain his realization and to make the distinction between holy Dharma and worldly dharma practice.

Spend your life in the Dharma̩, gathering accumulations;
even if one dies, there is no regret.

Jetsun Rinpoche is encouraging us to spend our life practicing Dharma, focusing on the accumulation of merit and wisdom. By accumulating merit, we purify all the negative karmas. By accumulating wisdom, we purify all the destructive emotions. If we die while practicing these two accumulations, we will have no regret, because we have led a spiritual life and can look forward to a good rebirth in the next life.

Please do not create regret for yourself;
even if blamed by others, there is no regret.

While we are living, we should try our best to do some meditation. Meditation is good for us; but it is also good for everyone around us. Spending time alone in meditation is a very compassionate activity; we practice bringing peace and that calm into our daily lives, which can impact so many other beings. Our practice will help us to stop harming others and to show more compassion toward all creatures, even the smallest insect.

I was recently part of a panel discussion on global warming at Harvard University, at which chaplains from many religions were asked what we should do about global warming. I said that before doing anything else, we should meditate to bring some peace and coolness *inside* ourselves. For some traditions, this may seem inadequate; some may say it is better to take immediate actions out in the world. But from a Buddhist perspective, we should begin by cultivating peace, wisdom, and compassion *inside* ourselves. The more we act from that peace, wisdom, and compassion, the more benefit we will bring. With those qualities inside us, we will be more attuned to the well-being of the earth.

In traditional Tibetan culture, there has long been a deep respect for the natural world and the spirits living there. For instance, Tibetans would not carelessly cut down a tree; there was an understanding that many beings were living there among the roots of the tree and that the underworld spirits—the nagas—would be very angry and disturbed if their home was taken away from them. It would be bad to make the nagas upset with you, and so people were respectful. Buddhist study and practice should increase our awareness of interdependence.

It should make us more aware of the fact that we are deeply connected with others, and that how we treat the earth directly impacts us. If each person were to cultivate that deep sense of interdependence, it would help solve the climate crisis because it would lead to a fundamental change in people's behavior. Inner change leads to outer change.

When we live according to the natural law of karma, we see that we are all connected, that we are all related. It is said that at some point every living being has been our mother. Whatever we put out we will receive back. If we are more aggressive toward the earth, the earth will be more aggressive in return. If we look at all the damage we have done to the earth, it is no surprise that we have an increase in natural disasters. We have disrespected the earth and have created so much imbalance; now, that aggression is returning to us in the form of disasters like hurricanes and wildfires. Out of greed, we have consumed so much of the earth's natural resources. We have clear-cut the forests; we have developed so much of the land; we have destroyed the homes of countless living beings; we have disrespected and disturbed the nagas and other natural spirits. That disturbance will inevitably affect us; the spirits will become angry with us.

We meditate in order to cultivate more positive emotions, like love and compassion—not only for our own survival, but for the survival of all beings and of the earth itself. Some people may not agree that the first step in solving the climate crisis is to meditate in order to transform greed and aggression within us. But the transformation of these negative emotions is the foundational change upon which all of the other positive solutions depend.

We are often told that the best way to solve pressing issues is to become more and more active and busy. We need to protest; we need to express our anger at politicians; we need to motivate others to change. But if we do not make the fundamental changes within ourselves, all of our other actions will have less impact. If we act out of negative emotions rather than out of wisdom, the results will not be as stable or pure. Refraining from regretful activity is sometimes the most important first step in cultivating change.

Reside alone, without attachment to friends;
even if one is without attendants, there is no regret.

The more relationships we develop, the busier we become. If we have many friends, there will be so many demands on our time. Many people enjoy having a busy social life. Some people say that they forget their emotional pain when they are with friends. Many people say that they become depressed when they spend too much time alone. Staying busy is a way to distract ourselves from our suffering—we have become so good at that in our modern society. We are always running from our feelings. We can barely sit down for a meal anymore without looking at our phones. It is increasingly hard for people to be alone with their own thoughts.

Whether or not our activities will be beneficial depends on our motivation. If our motivation is to help others based on wisdom and compassion, then our activities will be part of our spiritual practice. If our relationships and activities are based more on the ego and on negative emotions, then there will be negative consequences. If a relationship is based on desire, there will always be anger when that desire is not fulfilled. If our friendships are rooted in negative emotions, there will also be a lot of conflict.

In our modern society, we are increasingly becoming detached from one another. We are becoming more isolated and losing some of our capacity to navigate conflict; such isolation is very unhealthy. But this is not what Jetsun Rinpoche is referring to here. He is referring to the *intentional* solitude of a spiritual practitioner. If our spiritual practice is strong, then even in solitude we will feel more and more connected to all living beings through love and compassion.

If you have many relationships, there will be no end to your social obligations; it will feel like you are stuck in a giant web! Maybe you enjoy that, but how much time does it leave you to do spiritual practice? Will you have any energy left for the cultivation of your inner life? You may know so many people, but will you reach the end of your life and realize that you do not know yourself?

There is a famous Tibetan poet who wrote a cautionary poem to spiritual leaders. He said that although lamas who are in charge of large monasteries and temples may seem to have renounced the ordinary small family house and obligations, they have come to the monastery and made it into a very large home with all of the same attachments and responsibilities! The great yogi Shantideva said that he prayed that in his next life he would never take on any responsibility or obligation. The moment you have responsibilities it's hard to be free; it's hard to find as much time for practice.

Marriage to a person, or to a role, brings with it so many obligations. We often take on duties and roles due to societal expectations and our own fear and insecurity. We fear being alone; we fear what society will think of us if we do not marry; we fear what will happen when we grow old and have no children to care for us. It takes courage to choose a more solitary spiritual life. It takes courage to make your spiritual practice and the cultivation of wisdom the center of your life.

We tend to esteem very powerful leaders. We recognize the courage of military heroes and see courage as something very active. But the courage to go into solitude for the sake of cultivating wisdom and compassion is one of the bravest things a person can do. The Mongolian ruler Kublai Khan once asked Choegyal Phakpa who the bravest person in Tibet was. Choegyal Phakpa replied that the great yogi Milarepa was the bravest person in Tibet, because he renounced everything, including himself, to achieve buddhahood in order to benefit all sentient beings.

Society will not necessarily understand our priorities if we choose a spiritual life. Giving up worldly attachments may look like failure to some. We may stop pursuing career advancements and may remain very poor. But freeing ourselves from these attachments brings fearlessness. We will no longer be afraid of change; we will no longer be afraid of losing anything; we will no longer be afraid of death.

It is said that when Genghis Khan was dying, he became very fearful. He asked the priests and lamas for advice about how to live forever. He wanted to defeat death like he had defeated all of his other enemies. But nobody can live forever; everyone who is born has to die. In juxtaposition to this, the great yogi Milarepa is said to have died singing his mystical songs. Here we have a great warrior king who killed millions of people yet was terrified of his own death; all his priests and doctors were unable to fulfill his last wish to live forever. On the other hand, we have the example of a solitary yogi without attendants, living alone in a cave eating only nettles, who died peacefully without any regrets. This should tell us something about the kind of fearlessness that comes from spiritual practice, as opposed to that which comes from worldly power.

Look into the mind as the principal realization of view;
even if one's realization is small, there is no regret.

As we have discussed, looking into our own mind can be very painful. We spend a lot of our lives running away from uncomfortable emotions. When we actually sit still and observe our thoughts, so many painful memories and feelings can arise. It often feels like our thoughts are controlling us, that we are not really free. We spend so much effort trying to distract ourselves, thinking that if we fill our lives with work and activities and friends, we will not have to feel this discomfort.

Meditation is about coming home to the mind, rather than running from it. This can be very painful at first—which is why so many people abandon their practice early on. When we finally make the space to get to know our mind, we may experience a torrent of thoughts and may think that we are failing at meditation because we have more thoughts and more suffering than ever before!

If we don't give up and we continue to meditate day after day, eventually the rush of thoughts will begin to slow. We will no longer feel that we have to run away from ourselves; we will begin to see little glimpses of the true nature of the mind that is beyond all of the clouds of emotion and memory. When we see the true nature of clarity and emptiness—which is the realization of the wisdom view—we gain a sense of tremendous freedom. Through this, we learn that we can access this wisdom all the time; we can slow the thoughts and connect with that inner space; we no longer need to try to outrun our thinking.

Meditation is the only way to know our true essence—our true nature. But it takes a lot of practice. At this point, most of us do not know who we really are. Everything we claim as "self" is based on societal conditioning and the projections of others. The only way to truly know ourselves is to go within, and the only way we can truly know others is if we know the nature of our own mind.

Rely on eating food to harmonize disease;
even when one is ill, there is no regret.

We often eat food because we are attracted to the taste and to the smell. If we are health-conscious, maybe we also take into consideration what will be wholesome for our bodies. If we have limited resources, we may not be able to choose what we eat. Food insecurity impacts so many people in the world. Many people do not have access to fresh organic food and have to eat whatever they can find. We usually have a high level of emotional involvement with food. We experience craving for some foods and become attached to them. Ideally, we should eat food that will harmonize our elements and increase our health, not food that will stimulate our desire and craving and other emotions.

In Ayurveda and Tibetan medicine, there is the principle that our humors are affected by the balance of the elements in our body. When the five elements of earth, water, fire, wind, and ether are imbalanced, they become the three *doshas* of *pita*, *vata*, and *kapha*, which are the root cause of all disease. Jetsun Rinpoche is advising us to eat food that harmonizes these doshas, so that we live healthy lives without disease.

**Perform conduct according to your vows;
even if it becomes misconduct, there is no regret.**

Generally, there are three levels of vows: the Hinayana pratimoksha vows, the Mahayana bodhisattva vows, and the Vajrayana samaya vows. Jetsun Rinpoche is clarifying that if we happen to commit misconduct as a result of a conflict between the different vows we have taken, we should not have regret so long as we are practicing according to the importance and priority of our individual level of vows and practice.

For example, many Mahayana practitioners are vegetarian according to their bodhisattva vows. But if we have taken the Vajrayana samaya vow, we need to consume the ritual samaya substances of *bala* (meat) and *nada* (alcohol) during the *ganachakra* practice. This may appear to be misconduct according to the Mahayana vows, but the Vajrayana samaya vow supersedes the Mahayana vow.

**Examine your own faults; do not examine others' faults;
even if there is little affection, there is no regret.**

We often blame others even when something is actually our fault. It is very difficult for us to examine our own flaws. As the Bible verse says, "Why do you see the speck in your neighbor's eye, but do not notice the log in your own eye?" Yogis have a very different orientation; even if someone causes them harm, they do not become angry or blame the other person. Yogis accept whatever happens as due to their own karma.

If we spend our time finding fault in others, we will not experience any spiritual transformation. We have to look very honestly at our own shortcomings and take responsibility for our own reactions. Our ego always wants to believe in its own righteousness. If there is any conflict, we are always sure that we are correct and the other person is wrong.

On the other hand, we should not let such examination and recognition of our flaws make us feel discouraged and apathetic. The most compassionate thing we can do for ourselves is to take an honest inventory of our own faults, then use our spiritual practice to transform those faults in order to gain freedom. Sometimes we have to do things that are very uncomfortable for the ego in order to experience transformation. When Jetsun Rinpoche says, "even if there is little affection," he is saying that sometimes when we challenge ourselves in this way, we may not like what we find. We may be uncomfortable when we acknowledge our own faults; but because it is essential to our transformation, we will have no regrets.

Make the benefit of others your principal consideration;
even if one's own benefit is lost, there is no regret.

Jetsun Rinpoche has reached the stage of irreversible Dharma on the path to achieving full enlightenment. As a bodhisattva, his principle aspiration is to benefit sentient beings. Because bodhisattvas at the irreversible stage have gone beyond self-grasping, our materialistic minds may judge their practice as being without any personal profit or incentive. But yogis at the stage of irreversible Dharma will suddenly achieve full enlightenment; they therefore will have no regret about losing their temporary benefits.

At this stage, although our own benefit is lost—at least in the worldly sense—we will have no regret, because we are benefiting others and moving closer to buddhahood. If we have given up our resources or our home—even if we feel we have lost something—we will have no regret, because we are exchanging our own self-interests for the sake of benefiting others.

Sing a small song agreeing with experience;
even though one may be lost to idle talk, there is no regret.

Although Jetsun Rinpoche is humbly referring to his doha as a "small song," we know this is actually a *great* song of experience that is arising out of his direct realization. Some people may misunderstand this doha to be an ordinary song full of idle talk. Idle talk is considered to be one of the four verbal negativities, which also include lying, harsh words, and divisive speech.

We commit more negative karma through speech than through body and mind. Speech is a critical site of both positive and negative actions. It is said that the Buddha's teachings are his greatest enlightened activities, expressing his compassion and wisdom. Speech can be used for expressing wisdom or it can be misused to express anger, desire, and ignorance. Jetsun Rinpoche's doha is an expression in song of his profound wisdom and compassion; it is part of his irreversible Dharma practice. Thus, because he has not committed any idle talk, he has no regret whatsoever.

Apply the measure of thrift to possessions;
even if celebrations are poor, there is no regret.

Here, Jetsun Rinpoche is advising us on proper conduct regarding offerings and possessions. This is a particularly important instruction for spiritual teachers, who may be tempted to misuse spiritual offerings. My khenpo always instructed us not to be indulgent and decadent and not to misuse donations from the faithful. He said that these faith offerings from devotees are very hard to consume and that we would need iron teeth and jaws to chew and digest those gifts! Faith offerings have very heavy karma because you need to be worthy of the faithful spiritual qualities projected onto you by the devotees.

I cannot imagine Milarepa or Jetsun Rinpoche celebrating elaborate birthdays or New Year's celebrations with lavish meals with dancing and singing. For them, all entertainments were mere distraction. Singing is idle talk; dancing is misconduct. Here, Rinpoche is saying that if we are moderate and thrifty, then we should feel no regret if there are no big celebrations. Instead, we should be glad, knowing that we are protecting ourselves from those negative karmas.

Rinpoche is also reminding us that we should live frugally, not wasting anything. He is cautioning us not to become addicted to material gain, and that we should use only what is necessary. We should live in a way that does not increase our grasping and should avoid any showmanship in our lifestyle or in our celebrations. If we take these measures, it will help to reduce our destructive emotions and help to free us from our addiction to consumption.

Please seek an irreversible Dharma,
like a stone thrown into the ocean.

Jetsun Rinpoche is advising us to seek an irreversible Dharma practice. Irreversible Dharma has a general and a specific meaning. In general, it refers to a Dharma practice that helps us achieve higher spiritual paths without ever reversing to lower levels. Specifically, it means that our bodhisattva practice should help us to achieve complete buddhahood for the sake of all beings, instead of reverting to Hinayana practices that are only focused on achieving nirvana. We should have a practice that always helps us to progress to higher levels. Rinpoche is also referring to the practices free from regret that he has just enumerated in the doha, which will support this irreversible Dharma.

When a stone is thrown deep into the ocean, it sinks to the bottom; it becomes one with that ocean; it is irreversible and irretrievable. Likewise, Rinpoche is saying that we should practice a Dharma that sinks as deeply into our lives as that stone in the ocean. Such Dharma will be irreversible, completely submerged in our mental continuum.

Please seek a non-arising Dharma,
like a banana tree with its top cut off.

There is a relative and an ultimate meaning of "non-arising." Relatively, it refers to Dharma practice that purifies negative karma and destructive emotions. Ultimately, it refers to the wisdom of emptiness, which is free from non-arising and cessation. When we have the realization of this non-arising wisdom of emptiness, we have gone completely beyond active and sleeping defilements and beyond karma. Like cutting off the head of a banana tree, those defilements and karma can never grow again.

**Please seek an antidotal Dharma,
like a light in a mass of darkness.**

Generally, all Dharma practices should be antidotes to our defilements and negative karma. In the *Dhammapada* the Buddha said, "Abandon nonvirtues, cultivate all virtues, tame one's mind; this is what the Buddha has taught." The root of all of our defilements is the darkness of ignorance, which can be removed through the light of wisdom—the ultimate antidote.

**Please seek a scripturally authorized Dharma,
like a disciple of a Vedic brahmin.**

We should practice Dharma that has been transmitted from an unbroken lineage. "Scripturally authorized" means that it has a lineage that can be traced all the way back to the Buddha. The Dharma has been transmitted from the Buddha to the mahasiddhas, taught by the panditas, translated into Tibetan, and practiced by the Tibetan lamas.

Jetsun Rinpoche is comparing that transmission to the lineage of the Vedic brahmins. The brahmins are known to pass the oral tradition of the Vedas down through the generations. Ancient India has a tradition called *gurukula*, which is a spiritual family where the guru is like a father and all the students are like his children, with knowledge being passed from one generation to another in that spiritual family.

**Please seek a conducive Dharma,
like applying vitriol to gold.**

We should seek a Dharma that is conducive to our transformation and purification. In ancient times, a substance called "oil of vitriol" played a very important role in alchemy. It was extremely corrosive and capable of destroying most substances except gold. Similarly, we must seek a conducive Dharma that has the power to burn away all of our impurities.

Conducive conditions are important to a successful Dharma practice, especially when we are first cultivating our practice. Especially in the beginning, having a peaceful space and environment will help us cultivate our meditation. Having spiritual friends who will support and encourage our practice is an important aspect of such a conducive environment. We should avoid friends who engage in negative activities and who distract and discourage us from our practice. In these ways, Jetsun Rinpoche is emphasizing that we should always seek conducive conditions that support our Dharma practice.

12

The Great Differences

Although those door protectors inside the temple
seem to be hitting, hitting, they do not hit.

In many Buddhist temples, there are depictions of four guardian kings who serve as door protectors. Although they may look like fierce warriors, they are actually protectors; they do not hit anyone or cause any harm. The Buddha bound by oath many protectors to protect the Dharma and its practitioners, and it is for this reason that we see many protectors in Buddhist shrines and temples. There are also stories where bodhisattvas, out of wisdom and compassion, subjugated negative beings and helped them to become protectors in order for those beings to benefit themselves and others.

Although those increasingly powerful laypersons
seem happy, happy, they are miserable.

Although those Dharma practitioners facing hardship
seem miserable, miserable, they are happy.

People in positions of power, such as politicians or business leaders, may seem very successful and happy from the outside. But if we could look into their minds, we might see that although they present an *external* image of happiness, they are often quite miserable. Their outer success has not brought them more peace or satisfaction. Often their accomplishments have only served to increase their negative emotions and stress.

If we met Milarepa on the street today, would anyone consider him successful based on his outer appearance? Or if we met the Buddha when he appeared so emaciated after his six years of meditation, would we ever think of him as successful or happy? From the outside, the great yogis may seem very miserable, but if we could get a glimpse into their minds, we would see that they are in a constant state of bliss.

Although that wealth coming from generosity
seems to be dwindling, dwindling, it is increasing.

The more we practice generosity, the more our wealth may appear to be decreasing. But from a karmic perspective, if we are giving with pure motivation, the positive results will always be accumulating more wealth. Even if we appear to be losing all of our wealth, we are gathering so much positive karma. That positive karma will always lead to greater wealth, to greater spiritual abundance and joy.

There is a story of a Tibetan religious king who conducted a test where he distributed wealth equally among his subjects three different times. Each time, the rich became richer and the poor became poorer. In the end, he accepted that it must be the karmic result of past generosity that the rich became richer. After that, he stopped his endeavor to make everyone equal. This story emphasizes that we should focus on cultivating generosity, and that generosity will result in more material and noble wealth. Although we may not see the benefits immediately, or even in this lifetime, our virtue and generosity will be creating karmic conditions for greater abundance and joy.

Sentient beings and buddhas are equal,
yet happiness and sadness create the great difference between them.

Sentient beings have emotions because we have a mind. Due to this mind, we have karma—and we act and react, generating more karma. Buddhas are free from emotions because they have gone beyond the mind and are no longer generating karma. Buddhas have seen the true nature of the mind. By seeing the true nature of the mind, buddhas have gone beyond the mind.

You may be wondering, if buddhas have gone beyond emotion, do they still understand the suffering of sentient beings? The answer is yes. Because buddhas are omniscient, they can still relate to the suffering of all beings. They are not personally experiencing these emotions—they are no longer caught in that cycle of negative karma—but their compassion includes awareness of the suffering of all beings.

Sentient beings have all of these emotions and karma. But if we are on the spiritual path, we recognize that our true nature is buddha nature. The difference is that buddhas have fully realized that nature and have gone beyond all of the defilements, all of the karma, all of the negative emotions. Having not realized that nature, we are still trapped in samsara, caught in the cycle of karma and forced to take rebirth again and again.

Sentient beings and buddhas are equal in the sense that they both have buddha nature. The way they differ is in their level of realization of that nature. Buddhas have gone beyond the mind, gone beyond feelings, and they have stopped generating karma. All beings are, by nature, the Buddha, but due to karma and defilements, their experiences of reality differ: sentient beings are suffering in samsara and buddhas are free from suffering.

Self and others are equal,
yet the reason for grasping creates the great difference between them.

If we are not attached to our self, there will be no difference between self and other. How can we abandon this self-grasping? Why do we have so much attachment to the ego? According to Buddhist understandings, whatever we are attached to becomes part of the ego, and that egoic self becomes the center of the universe for each person and continues to proliferate. The more we grasp onto things, the more our ego grows.

But if we try to find this ego-self, we will not be able to. Although the ego may have grown to identify with all this property, all these accolades, all these surrounding people, and even an entire country, we will not be able to actually find any separate and solid self. Until we understand that there is no such self, we will continue grasping.

When we see that the true nature of the self is selflessness, then we will transcend that ego. When we have gone beyond the self, there will be no more dualism, no difference between self and other. When we realize selflessness, there will be no distinction between self and the universe; they will have become one. We will see that the true nature of the self is the same as the true nature of all beings and all phenomena. We will no longer try to protect and defend the ego, because we will no longer see it as something separate from the world.

As long as we are clinging to this sense of self, we will always be on the defensive; we will feel like there are so many opposing forces, and we have to work so hard to protect our ego. There is so much conflict as a result of this self-clinging. Understanding selflessness brings us so much peace, because we are no longer in opposition to the universe. With the wisdom of selflessness, we see that we are all unified. Having let go of any idea of self and other, there is nothing to defend.

Enemies and children are equal,
yet loving kindness and anger create the great difference between them.

Our beloved children and our worst enemies both have buddha nature. Whether we see that buddha nature or not depends on our emotions. One person's enemy is another person's beloved child. When our anger is projected onto someone, they become our enemy. When our love and attachment are projected onto someone, we will do anything to care for and protect them.

Whether someone becomes a friend or an enemy is not based on the reality of that person. It is based on what we are projecting onto that person. It is based on how their actions affect us. If it was actually in the nature of the person to be an enemy, then they would be universally hated by everyone. If it was in the nature of our child to be beloved, then they would be universally treated the same by everyone. But our own child will grow up to be disliked by some people. Even in our own relationships, sometimes we love our partner and sometimes we argue and we feel hatred.

In our short lives, in the course of seventy or eighty years, look at how our sense of who our loved ones are changes. Today you may be on a honeymoon; in ten years, you may be going through a difficult divorce with that person you once felt you would love forever. There is a very thin line between desire and anger. We see this all the time in our lives. The closer we get to someone, the more desire we have, and the more chance there is that our attachment will also be a source of anger and even hatred when our wishes are not fulfilled. For example, if our partner betrays us, we can move from desire to anger rapidly.

Anger and attachment go together. Wherever there is attachment, there will also be the potential for anger. We create so much discrimination between loved ones and enemies based on how someone makes us feel. So much of this discrimination is based on whether someone is supporting or attacking our ego. If we go beyond self, then there is nothing to defend and we will be much less reactive. We will have nothing to lose and we will not feel threatened when someone criticizes or betrays us.

There is no universal consensus on who is good and who is bad. It is entirely subjective, based on our experience, karma, and projections. According to our karma and emotions, we classify everything around us into categories of agreeable or disagreeable, loved or hated, good or bad. We also have many objects and people that we categorize as neutral:

neither loved nor hated. Often, we ignore the neutral people and objects because they don't trigger our positive or negative emotions.

Someone who has realized buddha nature can see the buddha nature of all beings. They no longer need to sort people into these categories of good, bad, and neutral. They see the ultimate nature of all beings and all phenomena: everyone is the same, and there is nothing to reject or defend.

Everyone obtaining a human body is equal,
yet victory and defeat create the great difference between them.

Our ordinary lives are filled with loss and gain. There is constant tension between success and failure. There are societal forces—class struggles, oppression—that create so much suffering. We are always struggling against all of these external forces. Categories such as class and income level are constructs—they are not innate. If we go beyond the forces of loss and gain, there is no difference between rich and poor—all humans are equal.

Many people think of the United States as a country of equal opportunities, democratic institutions, and more freedom and less oppression relative to many other countries. But in reality, there is still so much suffering, discrimination, and class struggle, even in rich, democratic countries.

Jetsun Rinpoche is saying here that all who obtain a human body are equal. But due to differences in socioeconomic status, race, gender identity, and so many other factors, people are still not treated equally in society. So much is projected onto people and there is so much hatred and oppression arising from desire, anger, and ignorance. Rinpoche is reminding us that, by nature, self and others are the same. By nature, enemies and loved ones are the same. By nature, all human beings are the same. But at the *relative* level, due to various conditions, their circumstances will be different. Rinpoche is helping us to see the difference between the relative world and ultimate reality. At the relative level, we are always discriminating and seeing differences.

When we study human development, we see that a child learns the distinction between itself and the rest of the world at a very young age. Although this is an essential developmental step, most people get stuck in that misconception for their entire lives and never transcend it. In fact, at the time of death, we may become very overwhelmed at the dissolution of our body because we thought we were such a permanent separate self. That feeling of confusion may overwhelm us and may make us very spaced out at the time of death.

When we die without any awareness or spiritual practice, death can be very overwhelming. The process of our consciousness separating from our body is very alarming and overpowering if we have never cultivated our spiritual practice. As a result of that fear at the time of death, we will not awaken, and we will be forced to take rebirth. As long as the underlying dualism of self and other continues, we will take rebirth again and again. This dualistic identification of self and other is compounded life after life, driven by our attachment and aversion.

In the Abhidharma teachings it is said that when the mind is looking to take rebirth, it finds its future parents in union, whereupon it is said that the mind then becomes attached to one parent and averse to the other. That is the beginning of self and other based on attachment and aversion. When our true nature is obscured by ignorance, our self-attachment always wants to win and defeat anything that is in opposition to our ego.

Beings who have obtained a human body,
do not rejoice in sinful activity;
since the duhkha of this life is unbearable, what need is there to mention [the duhkha of lower realms]?

All the virtue you perform,
perform connected with view and dedication;
please do not make it into defiled virtue.

Humans are very intelligent relative to many other living beings. We can use this intelligence for the good of bringing peace to the world, but we can also use it for bad ends like world wars, bringing so much harm and pain to many people.

We can determine whether an action is virtuous or nonvirtuous based on our own experience of the *results*. Nonvirtuous actions are those that cause harm to ourselves and others. We may not recognize those results immediately, but over the course of time we will see that nonvirtue gives rise to further suffering.

The Buddha lived over 2,500 years ago, and since then many things have changed. But as far as the experience of pain and pleasure, happiness and unhappiness, we are all still having these basic experiences in samsara. Circumstances may have changed dramatically from the Buddha's time, but basic human motivation and experience remain unchanged. Although we have all of these modern technologies and scientific discoveries that were unimaginable in the Buddha's time, we still get sick, get old, and die. The basic truth of suffering has not changed—this is the conditioned nature of our lives.

In the 2,500 years since the time of the Buddha, we have not gotten any happier. In spite of all of the comforts of contemporary life, we are not more content or fulfilled. We may live longer and we may survive more diseases than we did, but our root emotions and sufferings are the same as they have always been for humans.

This basic fact of suffering makes the Buddha's teachings as relevant today as they were when they were first taught. Wisdom is timeless; it is not dependent on the material world or on changes in society. As long as we struggle with the same three poisons of desire, anger, and ignorance, we will need the corrective antidotes and spiritual practices in order to realize wisdom. That inherent wisdom, the buddha nature we all have inside our minds, will always be the same.

We need to integrate the Buddha's teachings into our own lives. The three trainings of wisdom, meditation, and discipline can be found across the many different schools of Buddhism. Some traditions emphasize discipline, with very specific restrictions on diet, clothing, and activities. The purpose of discipline is not to repress and control you; its purpose is to bring you more freedom through simplifying your life. Once your life is simplified, you will have more freedom and focus.

With that freedom you will have more time to study and meditate, and with that meditation you will then be able to engage in the training of wisdom.

Some other traditions emphasize meditation. For example, if you visit a Zen center here in the West, you will see that their training involves so much sitting meditation right from the beginning. Through meditation, they try to realize discipline and wisdom. Then there are some traditions that prioritize wisdom training. For example, Tibetan monks and nuns may spend thirty years studying different texts. Completing the foundational study of the five major subjects in Tibetan Buddhism can take twenty years, and it takes another ten to fifteen years of further study to become a scholar of the highest Vajrayana teachings.

Many Tibetan Buddhist centers emphasize teaching and study. The risk with this is that the best scholars may become so preoccupied with study that they do not practice enough meditation. They may miss many opportunities to go on retreat and to gain experiential wisdom instead of just intellectual knowledge. The goal should be to integrate and deepen those wisdom trainings through meditation. Although each tradition may have a different starting point, they need to incorporate all of the three trainings. These three trainings are complementary, and all three are necessary to free ourselves from the three basic defilements.

We often gravitate toward a spiritual practice because we have become exhausted by all our emotions; we are just so tired of suffering. Humans may be more intelligent than other beings but we also have more mental suffering because it is so hard for us to be in the present moment and we have so many mixed emotions inside us. We have pain and we also have pleasure; we have happiness and unhappiness. This combination of emotions creates so much difficulty in our lives, but it also creates the ideal conditions for us to pursue spiritual practice. If we were always in pain and always unhappy, we would be too preoccupied with survival to find and pursue spirituality. For example, if we are starving, the search for food would probably be the singular focus of our lives—any deprivation generally becomes the center of our attention.

Human life is conducive to spiritual practice because we have all of these mixed emotions: we have both pain and pleasure; both happiness and unhappiness. This mixture helps us to become more creative. If we only experienced pain, we would not have the energy or motivation to seek the spiritual life. Due to the fact that we have these glimpses of pleasure and happiness, we strive to attain a more lasting happiness. We will be drawn to spiritual practice not only as a result of suffering but also because we have the experience of happiness and we want to maintain that experience.

Pain and pleasure are very relative. If we have never experienced spiritual peace or joy, we will think that pleasure and happiness are the highest states. But happiness and pleasure are relative states; they are conditional, they are always changing. Although attaining pleasure and happiness may be the initial motivation that helps us to start a spiritual practice, eventually we will realize that happiness and pleasure are empty. In deep meditation, we transcend mere pleasure, mere happiness. Through meditation, we transcend these conditioned experiences and make contact with that inner space in our mind. We begin to see that happiness and pleasure are like clouds that come and go. When we become aware of the spacious quality of our buddha nature, we begin to experience freedom; we experience a peace and bliss that is beyond all feelings.

Now that we have obtained this precious human body, with such potential to become a buddha, we should not waste our life creating more pain and suffering for ourselves and others. In these lines, Jetsun Rinpoche is wondering why, if we cannot bear the pain and suffering of our present life, would we want to create more negative actions and be reborn into the lower realms? Rinpoche is also encouraging us to engage in virtuous behavior with right view, and to properly dedicate the merit, in order to achieve full enlightenment for the benefit of all sentient beings. Through the integration of right view and perfect dedication, defiled virtue can be transformed into pure and perfect virtue.

"There is no happiness for samsaric beings";
if that meaning does not exist for oneself,
what is the benefit of giving teachings?

Without turning away from thoughts of this life,
what is the benefit of engaging with the Dharma?
Without fear of birth and death,
what is the benefit of teaching the oral instructions?

Jetsun Rinpoche is emphasizing the importance of knowing the nature of samsara through one's own personal experience, rather than just talking abstractly about the nature of samsara. In other words, we should seek to validate the teachings and the scriptures through personal experience.

These lines in the doha are questioning what motivates our spiritual practice. As we have discussed, meditation has become popular in the West as a form of stress reduction and relaxation. As part of this process, its focus on wisdom has been lost; for many people, meditation is just about feeling better in this life. People equate Buddhism with meditation, but they do not understand the deeper dimensions of Buddhist philosophy and practice.

It is said that if we have attachment to this life, we are not a spiritual practitioner. Rinpoche is expressing a similar idea here: the perfect spiritual practice is done with renunciation. Renunciation, in this sense, means that we have grown tired of living in this vicious cycle of samsara, we understand the nature of this cycle, and we begin to focus on liberation. We realize that all emotions, even pleasurable emotions, are a form of suffering. Even good emotions give rise to more pain because that is the nature of impermanence; nothing pleasurable can stay the same.

With renunciation, we shift our focus from wanting to attain happiness in this lifetime to wanting to experience freedom and wisdom. When we understand that all emotions are a form of suffering and that they are always changing, we gain the insight necessary to begin detaching from emotions. Having developed renunciation, we no longer want to meditate in order to feel happiness. Instead, we are drawn to spiritual practice in order to be liberated from life itself, from this cycle of samsara. We understand that life itself is suffering, and when we realize that wisdom, we go beyond all craving; we experience a spiritual bliss and freedom that is beyond all feeling, beyond mind itself.

We should not misunderstand this nonattachment to life as a form of nihilism. From a Buddhist perspective, death is not the end of the mind. Having nonattachment, therefore, is not about being careless about life or about hastening our death. Rather, we are trying to free ourselves from the cycle of samsara through the realization of our inherent wisdom.

We are practicing to go beyond the mind itself, not with the goal of acquiring happiness, material gain, or pleasure in this lifetime. This shift in focus away from worldly concerns should not be misunderstood as meaning that we should disregard our physical well-being. We need to eat; we need to care for our body. But the goal of our practice extends beyond this lifetime and this physical body. We practice in order to attain enlightenment for the sake of all sentient beings.

As long as we remain attached to this life, we are limiting the power of our spiritual practice. If practice is done only for this life, there is a risk of spiritual materialism. Such a materialistic attitude might involve practicing with the goal of improving our conditions, making offerings to a teacher or temple with the hope of increasing our wealth or healing our body, and so forth. But if we are attached to an outcome in this lifetime, we are not perfecting our practice.

The more that we recognize the suffering of life in the relative world, the more we will cultivate renunciation. Renunciation is based on understanding how our lives actually function. If we understand our life as merely our physical body with no mental continuum, then we will not see any purpose in practicing for any benefit beyond this lifetime. We may only meditate because we think it will clarify and sharpen our brain and improve our performance.

Neuroscience has become very interested in how meditation changes the brain. The data is very compelling, proving how meditation can alter both the structure and the function of the brain, with significant implications for behavioral and societal concerns as well. It is wonderful that this data is helping prove the value of teaching people meditation, and it is wonderful that we are becoming more aware of the transformative power of meditation and compassion.

However, there is a risk that this fixation on the therapeutic benefits of meditation will make us focus too much on the material benefits of meditation in this one lifetime, obscuring the greater purpose of meditation. We are not meditating in order to change our brain; we are meditating in order to uncover the inherent wisdom of the immaterial mind that goes with us from life to life. It is impossible for science to measure that wisdom! But we can experience these changes directly through years of practice.

When we practice with the belief that we will be reborn again and again, we become much more focused on cultivating the mind rather than simply improving brain health or reducing stress and reactivity. Improvements in performance and physical health are useful side effects of meditation but they are not the goal from a Buddhist understanding.

When we believe in rebirth we can renounce our attachment to this body and we can recognize the impermanence of material gain. The only things that can go with us at the time of death are the qualities we have cultivated in our mindstream. We cannot keep anything we have cultivated at the physical level. Our brain structure and function may be improved but our brain will die along with the rest of our physical body.

Rebirth is not as commonly accepted in the West. We can see how that lack of belief in the immaterial mind is affecting so many aspects of our lives. It affects our priorities, our goals, our reasons for practice. If we think there is only one life and nothing continues, we may find it useless to spend so much time in spiritual practice and contemplation. Many people think that Buddhism is too focused on suffering. They may say, "Life is short, I want to enjoy it!" They may think the purpose of life is to have as many experiences as possible. As we have discussed, many people even think that being driven by emotion is a sign of vitality.

But life is very uncertain. We could die at any time. Some people use this impermanence as a reason to focus on chasing pleasure and happiness in this life. Spiritual people use this impermanence to focus their lives on spiritual practice. Faith in rebirth gives us confidence that we are investing in our spiritual practice for something much greater than this one short life.

But even among practitioners who believe in rebirth, some may still carry a materialist goal. Many people direct their practice toward attaining a higher rebirth. They accumulate merit through so many offerings to the temple, to the Buddha, to the Sangha. Accumulation of merit is very important. But if there is no emphasis on the accumulation of wisdom, then the motivation is still materialistic and, therefore, it is not a complete practice.

The accumulation of merit is based on the first five paramitas, which comprise the practices of giving, ethics, diligence, patience, and meditation. But if we accumulate merit with the goal of increasing pleasure and happiness in the next lifetime, then we are still trapped in the emotions that perpetuate our suffering.

According to teachings, such as those given in *Parting from the Four Attachments*,[38] all spiritual practice should be based on renunciation—not only of this life, but of future lifetimes. The purpose of spiritual practice is to go beyond samsara entirely. Even if we are reborn in a god realm surrounded by luxury and comfort, if we are attached to pleasure and happiness then we are still trapped in samsara. Even if we take birth in the god realm, we will eventually die and fall into a lower realm. We must therefore cultivate right view and right motivation in our practice. Without right view, we will merely be chasing after material benefit and there will be no liberation.

38. *Zhen pa bzhi bral*, by Jetsun Rinpoche Dragpa Gyaltsen.

Without cutting the hairy leaves of conceptuality,
what is the benefit of shaving one's head?
Without bringing change to ordinary perception,
what is the benefit of changing the color of one's clothes?

In this verse, Jetsun Rinpoche is referring to monastics who shave their heads and wear robes of a particular color as a sign of renouncing their home and family. Rinpoche is asking what benefit will they gain from making these changes to their outward appearance, if they are still inwardly attached to the "hairy leaves" of conceptuality? Rinpoche is reminding us here that mental transformation is far more important than any changes to our outer appearance. He is emphasizing that there is no benefit in changing one's uniform if one has not changed one's perception toward the ordinary world. If one is still attached to the impure appearances of samsara, changing one's outer appearance is not spiritually beneficial.

Without relying on the sacred guru,
what is the benefit of abandoning one's country?

As we have discussed, historically, students in India and Tibet often traveled far from their home and country to study with teachers or gurus. Some found a root guru and relied wholeheartedly on that teacher and devoted themselves to a single practice. But some spiritual seekers kept on searching and could not settle on any teacher or practice.

We see this so often these days in the West, where students keep shopping around at various Dharma centers and never settle on one community or practice. Many of these seekers have already left their churches or synagogues and are looking for an alternative religion or spiritual practice to follow. They continue shopping and searching in so many meditation centers and ashrams but many never commit to one center or teacher. Without receiving instruction and empowerment from a qualified guru, one cannot receive much benefit from study and practice.

Without actually practicing the oral instructions,
what is the benefit of hearing and contemplation?

When the time of death arrives,
nothing helps aside from Dharma.

According to Buddhist tradition, the purpose of hearing and contemplation is to enable us to practice. In Vajrayana, first we receive the empowerment, and then we receive the transmission and oral instructions. Many students busy themselves collecting empowerments as a way of receiving blessings, only occasionally receiving oral instructions and—even more rarely—actually applying those instructions to a particular practice. Students may have long lists of empowerments they've received, but without practice they will not experience much inner transformation or spiritual benefit. Jetsun Rinpoche is reminding us that at the time of death, only that which we have cultivated spiritually in the mind will be beneficial and continue with us beyond death.

Generally, a greedy and deceitful guru
has no time to bestow the profound oral instructions.
A big liar misleading others with provisional meanings
has no time to meet with the definitive meaning.

A great magnifier of samsara's duhkha
has no time to obtain nirvana.

Jetsun Rinpoche is pointing out the potential faults of the guru. Religion and spirituality can be used very easily to con other people. Throughout the centuries, there have been many charlatans pretending to be gurus. As long as these false gurus are craving something for themselves, like power, wealth, or attention, they will try to profit off of innocent and faithful people.

In ancient India following the life of Buddha Shakyamuni, the eighty-four mahasiddhas and many panditas served the Dharma with pure teachings and practice. They proved themselves to be great teachers and gurus without the support and promotion of the tulku systems or any family lineage systems, which are widely prevalent and promoted in Tibet.

When any tradition becomes organized into a system that has fame, power and wealth, there is always the possibility of the tradition being misused by some greedy and deceptive people, to protect and promote their own personal power and fame at the expense of pure Dharma. This is also one of the reasons why different contenders to the throne have had power struggles throughout Tibetan Buddhist history.

In contemporary society, we can see how the capitalist mindset has had a negative impact on Dharma organizations. We can see spiritual centers that prioritize fundraising and expansion. Some centers may even become more like profitable businesses rather than places of learning and practice. Capitalism cultivates greed and deception.

In ancient times, there were no advertisements or promotions regarding spiritual teachers. Teachers would not make their qualifications public. Many of the best teachers tried to avoid being well known. It was far more important to impart the teachings to a very small number of qualified students rather than to speak to large audiences. Shyness and humility are important qualities for all practitioners—but they are especially important qualities in a teacher. Humility is not valued as much in the West. If a student asks a question about a teacher's level of spiritual realization, and the teacher doesn't reply with an answer, the student may view this as a weakness.

Traditionally, teachers would never claim to have experienced high realization. They would be very careful not to use their role to increase their ego. They would be more focused on the spiritual development of their students than on their own identification as a spiritual leader. They would be satisfied with a very small group of practitioners and they would not be focused on growing the temple or competing with other centers for fundraising support.

It is very challenging here in the West to keep the capitalist mentality from increasing greed and deception in spiritual communities. Capitalism teaches us to "sell" ourselves and to exaggerate our experience or accolades. According to Buddhist teachings, claiming you have some realization that you have not attained produces very negative karma. Claiming oneself as the reincarnation of "such and such buddha" or claiming that you have high realization without any concrete proof can become a big lie that misleads others.

If marketing and fundraising helps to establish a center that can flourish for generations, then of course this is beneficial. Although these efforts may be too focused on outer growth, there will still be some lasting benefit for later generations. The motivation to develop a center for the sake of practitioners is certainly a better incentive than growing a center in order to further the promotion and power of a teacher. But all of this focus on fundraising and worldly activities can come at the expense of focusing on practice. There is a risk that such a center will become more like a business than a place of devotion, contemplation, and meditation practice.

If you visit some temples in remote areas, they may be very poor and small, but there is much more peace. At these smaller establishments, there is not as much to distract the sangha and they have more time to be in retreat. You will often find the best practitioners out in these remote areas, at temples and retreat communities that are not well known.

When Jetsun Rinpoche refers to "a big liar misleading others with provisional meanings," he is talking about the guru who speaks only at the relative level without teaching the profound meanings. If a teacher is not providing teachings on the ultimate reality, then he is a "big liar." Provisional meaning refers to the relative world of conditioned things. The definitive meaning refers to ultimate reality and to seeing the empty nature of all things.

Provisional meaning refers to the accumulation of merit. As we have discussed, the accumulation of merit is very good, but it remains at the relative level. It is not a perfect practice at the ultimate level. Accumulation of merit only becomes perfect when it is joined with the ultimate awareness of wisdom.

People often only go to a temple for worldly reasons. If they are sick or having financial trouble, they may go and make offerings and pray. The rituals and ceremonies they participate in are beneficial, but they are all still relative activities. If we get too attached to these outer rituals and ceremonies and if we pray only when we have worldly troubles, we will not get any closer to realizing ultimate wisdom, the clarity and emptiness of our own minds. Rinpoche is reminding us as teachers and as practitioners not to get too focused on outer activities at the expense of cultivating inner wisdom.

Deception can proliferate when there is no awareness of ultimate reality. Some teachers may teach in order to meet the emotional needs of their students. They may serve more as therapists or friends to their students. While this may bring some temporary comfort to students, it will not help them realize emptiness. It may actually just increase their attachments, making them cling to that teacher as a parental figure. They may become jealous if that teacher pays more attention to a different student. All of these family dynamics can play out in spiritual communities when the teacher is fueling the student's emotions, even if it is through positive attention.

Teachers that provide instruction from an authentic lineage and from their own realization of wisdom are very rare. These teachers are focused on liberating the student rather than on having followers. They do not want the student to become attached to the relative guru. They want to spark inner wisdom in their students. Students who can awaken to their inherent wisdom through hearing these profound teachings are also very rare.

Meeting a truly qualified teacher may initially be a very uncomfortable experience for the student. The student may be accustomed to receiving special attention when they excel in school or business. They may be looking for the teacher to support their ego and recognize their accomplishments and their service to the Dharma. An authentic teacher will be very skillful in helping the student reduce that ego involvement by not reinforcing it. The student may feel like the teacher doesn't care about them or that the teacher is too challenging.

Good teachers use skillful means to help students cut through their habitual patterns. Although this can be alarming and disorienting to the student's ego, if it is done with wisdom and compassion, it can create the conditions for great awakening and awareness in the student. Many students drop out of a spiritual community if their emotional needs are not being met. This is unfortunate because these may actually be optimal conditions for very important transformation to take place. Such transformation, however, can only occur within a setting where there is mutual respect and consideration between the teacher and student.

The authentic Buddhist teachings are based on the ultimate truth. But the truth can be very painful! We often don't want to hear the truth. We usually seek conditions that will reinforce the ego rather than uncover the truth of things. The truth of emptiness can be very frightening to people. The truth of impermanence can be upsetting. The knowledge that we are aging and that each day we are moving closer to our own death is very disturbing. Most people try not to think of death. Most people prefer to remain distracted by worldly activities.

But if we insist on avoiding the truth, how much spiritual transformation can there really be? How much transcendence of the ego is really possible if we are mostly concerned with seeking affirmation from the guru? We are often motivated to seek a teacher and spiritual community when we are suffering, hoping that a teacher will validate our thoughts and feelings. But if, for example, the teacher speaks about forgiveness instead of providing emotional support when we share a traumatic memory, we may feel very angry. If we are very devoted to a teacher and the teacher never seems to recognize our efforts, we may feel very disrespected. It is important to remember that a truly qualified guru will always have your spiritual realization as the priority, not your ego development. This may be very uncomfortable. In the presence of an unqualified guru, this can lead to tolerating abuse. Because of this, the student and the teacher must both examine each other's motivations and actions. They must also examine whether the relationship is cultivating more dependence or more liberation in the student.

One in the great black darkness of ignorance
has no time for the dawn of the sun of wisdom.

Some time ago, one of my well-known khenpos was invited to perform a funeral service. He recited the root text of a shastra and then he left. Although he did a perfect dedication to benefit the deceased person, the family was not happy with the khenpo and asked the monastery to send other lamas who could perform "real" funeral services that include musical instruments, tonal chanting, and setting the shrine with *tormas*. But although the ritual lamas who can perform these elaborate rituals are more popular with the families, and they are better in social skills because they have learned from regular interactions with families, they are not learned in the meanings like my khenpo was. These ritual lamas earn more offerings and are popular, and so they feel that they don't need to study hard to learn the meanings. Because they don't know the meanings, they cannot become great teachers like my khenpo. As a result, they will not be able to help others to cultivate wisdom through explaining the profound meanings of the Dharma.

13

Searching and Uncovering

**If the meaning of "illusion-like" is realized,
one's search has uncovered words of truth.**

**If the meaning of non-arising is realized,
one's search has uncovered delusion.**

THIS IS A VERY profound statement. To realize the meaning of illusion, first we have to realize that we are the creators of our own universe. We hear sounds because we have ears. We see objects because we have eyes. We smell things because we have a nose. If our sense organs are not functioning, we cannot generate our experience of the universe. If we are blind, we lose our ability to experience visual objects. If we are deaf, our universe is quiet.

We experience the universe through these dualistic interactions with the outer world. Are these experiences universal? Do they represent ultimate reality? As we have discussed, if these experiences were universal, then all beings would experience the world in the same way. But that is not the case; each being perceives phenomena according to their own sense organs and consciousness. So what we see cannot be ultimate reality. Someone standing right next to you may perceive the same object in a completely different way. Is what we see real? Is what we hear real?

All of our sensory experiences are merely a projection of our own mind. Until we see the empty nature of the mind, we cannot see the ultimate reality of all of the sense objects we perceive: that the whole universe is a projection of our own consciousness. Your universe is different from every other being's universe. This is because "your" universe is inside your own mind.

Apparent objects are only there because of the mind that is perceiving them. The mind is not only perceiving them, it is evaluating, judging, reacting, and quantifying that experience of the object. *We* determine whether the objects we perceive are beautiful or ugly. We determine based on our individual experience whether objects we perceive are valuable. We project so many emotions onto the world, but these qualities are not inherent to the objects in the world. If they were, there would be universal agreement about what is ugly and what is beautiful, what is valuable and what is not. But as the saying goes, "beauty lies in the eyes of the beholder."

If we understand that all of these judgments and evaluations are projections of our own mind, then we need to ask, "what is it in our mind that is projecting?" Is it our desire that is perceiving the object as beautiful? Is it our jealousy or our anger that is projecting aversion onto an object? Is it our ignorance that experiences all of the neutral objects without much awareness? We go through so much of the day on autopilot, bringing so little awareness to objects. We generally only focus on objects when we feel very strong emotions toward those objects.

If our passion is strong, we may project desire onto an apparently unattractive person. If we don't have passion, we may experience only neutral feelings even in the company of a very beautiful person. This is the same with food; if we are starving, we may find even something very disgusting desirable; the hungrier we become, the more attractive and delicious food becomes.

We can see from this examination that the qualities of an object are entirely based on the conditions in our own mind, and the conditions in our mind are dependent on our emotions. When we reflect on this, we begin to realize that we cannot find anything that exists independently, either in the outer world or in our own mind. In essence, our experience of the world is an illusion—it is like a mirage or a hologram. Without the coming together of the sense object, the sense organ, and the sense consciousness, we would not experience anything in the phenomenal world. Our experience of the universe is entirely based on these conditions.

If we are successful in dream yoga and can see the clear light dreams, going beyond both the dreamer and the dreams, we can experience this illusory nature in all of our interactions during the day. When we realize the empty nature of illusion, which is non-arising, we are free from delusion and ignorance.

If the meaning of cause and result is realized,
one's search has uncovered provisional meaning.

If the meaning of "space-like" is realized,
one's search has uncovered definitive meaning.

If the meaning of emptiness is realized,
one's search has uncovered conceptuality.

Buddha Shakyamuni taught both provisional meanings and definitive meanings. The essence of provisional meaning is knowing the relative truth and realizing the cause and result (karma.) The essence of definitive meaning of the ultimate truth is knowing and realizing emptiness through the simile of space, which is free from concepts.

After the Buddha attained enlightenment in Bodhgaya, he remained silent for forty-nine days. He was silent because he did not think anyone would be ready to receive his teachings on the ultimate truth. Eventually, after his disciples repeatedly requested teachings, he turned the first dharma wheel starting with the four noble truths at Sarnath, near Varanasi. As his students became more prepared, he shared many more teachings.

If you examine the Buddha's teachings in depth, you will find that there are sometimes contradictions. For example, sometimes the Buddha said that the self exists and in other teachings he said the self doesn't exist. These contradictions are not a result of the Buddha being confused about the ultimate truth—he was enlightened and he had directly experienced the ultimate wisdom of clarity and emptiness. The contradictions we find in the teachings are a result of the Buddha's wisdom and compassion in teaching according to the capacity of his students. Because he always considered what would most benefit his disciples and other yogis at any given time, the Buddha knew not to overwhelm someone who was not ready to hear about selflessness or emptiness. It would be useless to give a profound teaching on emptiness to someone with the mind of a child. The teachings would need to be skillfully revealed in order to benefit people of different abilities and aptitudes. In this way, the Buddha knew how to avoid harming someone if they were not ready for the ultimate truth.

It is said that the Buddha gave eighty-four thousand different teachings. He gave so many Theravada teachings, so many Mahayana teachings, and so many Vajrayana teachings. If you read the sutras, you can see that the Buddha gave teachings gradually so that disciples could move step-by-step toward a deeper understanding. It is said that the Buddha "turned the wheel of Dharma" three times. The Buddha gave so many teachings in those turnings of the wheel, including the tantric teachings. Tantric teachings were only given to a chosen few who had a very high level of intelligence.

Jetsun Rinpoche is reminding us that there is provisional meaning and there is definitive meaning. When the Buddha says in some sutras that the self exists, this is only a provisional meaning. He is not speaking of the definitive truth. The Buddha knew that if he told certain audiences that the self does not exist, they would be unable to relate to anything he was saying. They might never be inspired to follow the Dharma and may have just walked out of the teachings, never to return.

With his skillful means, the Buddha knew he had to meet the students wherever they were in their comprehension. Sometimes that meant using the provisional truth in order to help the students make a connection to the Dharma. The Buddha knew how to provide this graduated path so that his students could slowly arrive at a deeper understanding without being so confused or shocked by emptiness that they stopped listening or practicing.

The definitive teachings are those related to the experience of the ultimate truth. The provisional teachings are teachings on relative truths. Rinpoche is saying that if the meaning of cause and result is realized, one's search has found provisional meaning. The purpose of the Buddha teaching all the provisional teachings is to at least bring on some kind of understanding and some kind of belief in the law of karma. We can understand the relative world better the more we comprehend the natural law of karma. The better we understand the relative world, the more we will be prepared to hear profound teachings on ultimate reality.

As we have discussed, our current civilization has achieved such extraordinary technological progress and economic abundance. From one perspective, we have reached a pinnacle of progress. But our understanding of the natural law of karma is still very limited such that much of our "progress" and "development" is bringing more harm than good to sentient beings and to the planet. If we truly understood karma, all of our development would be rooted in compassion and a deep understanding of interdependence. We would recognize that harming someone else for our own gain will never bring us happiness. If we lived according to the natural law of karma, all of our economic systems and our political decisions would be based on the well-being of everyone, not on greed and privilege.

Capitalism is inherently unfair. We are told that the "American dream" is possible for anyone. We have this motto, "pull yourself up by your bootstraps," and we promote the myth that anyone can succeed if they have strong willpower and a good work ethic. But this is simply not true; it is not a level playing field. There are so many negative forces that continue to widen the gap between the rich and the poor. If we incorporated teachings on karma into our education system, we would impact how we design all of the other systems and developments in our societies. Without a deep understanding of cause and effect, we will continue causing harm, depleting our natural resources and polluting the planet and becoming more and more divisive in our political dialogue.

Capitalism also promotes hoarding. We are taught to pursue way more wealth and property than is necessary for our survival. Ours is a culture of overconsumption, and this overconsumption drives this gap between the rich and the poor. If consumption made us happier, we would see a much higher level of peace and well-being in rich countries like the United States. We are not happy, though—we are running around like chickens with our heads cut off! We are never settled, never content. We have lost the basic sanity that comes from having a peaceful mind. We have no rest and no understanding of the causes of our suffering.

People who believe in the law of karma often have a greater sense of peace and acceptance. Although many of us learn about karma, it is much harder to actually integrate that understanding into our lives and to have faith in karma as the natural law. Karma is hard to understand because its scope is so extensive, unfolding across countless lifetimes. If we look only at this one life, the workings of karma may not make any sense to us. For example, something terrible may happen in our lives that we feel can't possibly be in accordance with cause and effect. Maybe we have always been kind, loving, and generous toward others, yet we may still lose everything we have. This lack of obvious cause and effect may make us doubt karma, and even become angry at the injustice of it.

In capitalist systems, the bad guys often seem to win. Many big corporations are built on so many lies and inflict so much suffering on others. In *this* lifetime, liars and cheats often appear to be the winners of abundance and financial security. Lying and cheating can bring someone temporary benefit. In the short term, violence may appear to triumph over peace. If you are a pacifist and a very bad person attacks you with a gun, the person with the gun will appear to have won that conflict. They may even take your life. In the eyes of the world, that violent person may have appeared to win the fight. But from the perspective of karma, nonviolence wins over the course of many lifetimes.

In capitalism there is so much emphasis on climbing the corporate ladder and being promoted. Being promoted isn't always related to the quality of your work. It is often about how well you can "play the game." This may mean supporting your boss even when you disagree. It may mean projecting a certain image even if it is incompatible with your values. It may mean attending all of the staff parties and building your social network even if they are not people you actually want to spend time with. People often betray their own values in order to succeed financially.

When we see people succeeding who are being unethical and unkind, it can shake our faith in karma. Our faith can be shaken when we are always diligent and compassionate yet terrible things keep happening to us. Many terrible misfortunes happen to very loving and spiritual people. How do we handle these tragedies, especially when we feel they are unjust? If the negative forces seem to be winning and the positive forces seem to be losing in our world, what do we do? Do we allow this to make us negative also? Do we lose faith in positive behaviors and outcomes? This is the choice and the challenge we have in our lives.

If someone can maintain faith in karma in spite of terrible challenges, they will develop a deep inner strength. They will have the capacity to transform suffering into compassion for others. As we have discussed, some of the people who have suffered the most have become our greatest spiritual leaders. But if someone allows these challenges to destroy their faith, then the negativity has won.

We have to remember that karma extends across so many lifetimes. We should not be looking for the result only in this immediate life. Because we cannot remember what we have done in previous lifetimes, we usually focus our understanding of karma on this one life alone. This can make us feel that karma is random and unfair. If we could remember everything that we have done in past lifetimes, karma would make more sense to us. We cannot control what we have done in the past, but we do have the freedom and the agency to respond to our current challenges with awareness and wisdom. We can plant the seeds for future positive results by approaching our challenges with compassion and understanding.

The Buddha had a deep understanding of past, present, and future when he taught about karma. He understood that although you may appear to be losing in the short term, if your actions are taken with wisdom and compassion, you will be sowing the seeds for future positive results.

If we don't have a solid understanding of the natural law of karma, we will not gain much from the teachings. We may retain a lot of information and knowledge, but without faith in karma, that knowledge will not be very transformative for us. We might study so many texts, we might have read the whole *Abhidharmakosa*, and we might be able to recite profound teachings, but we won't have integrated that wisdom into our lives if we do not have faith in karma.

The whole purpose of the Buddha's provisional teachings is to communicate the law of cause and result and to generate faith in it. Faith is magical. Faith can sustain us even when karma is unfolding in ways we cannot understand. If challenges shake our faith in karma to the point where we stop believing and abandon our practice, we will have abandoned the most important opportunity to cultivate our spiritual practice in this precious human lifetime.

Without understanding karma, how can we hope to accumulate merit? Understanding karma is a profound and very internal experience. We cannot gain this understanding of karma simply by observing the outer world. Understanding karma is about knowing that all of our outer activities start in our own mind. The potential for both positive and negative actions are inside us. The more we understand karma, the more we will choose to cultivate the positive qualities inside us.

If we act like detectives and try to catalog and understand the manifestations of karma in this one lifetime, we will only get lost and confused. Our relative mind and our memory are too limited. We cannot see all of the clues and all of the evidence. We cannot understand why something happened in this life, because we do not have enough data. It is important to study teachings on karma, but it is also important to place our faith in it. Faith will give us so much strength and integrity through life's challenges. If we put our faith in karma, we will be able to use that faith to cultivate more positive thoughts and activities.

Having even a very simplistic understanding of karma can be tremendously transformative. If we understand that positive thoughts and actions bring positive results, we will likely see positive changes in our lives. If we understand that negative thoughts and actions bring negative results, we will become less driven by negative emotions, and we will learn to stop and reflect before we react. We will begin to see how negative thoughts cause us so much harm.

If we live according to this basic understanding of cause and result, we will see a transformation in our lives—even if we don't yet comprehend the deeper complexities of natural law. Based on that experience, we will gradually gain a more profound understanding of karma.

Understanding karma at a deeper level can prepare the mind for encountering definitive meaning and for eventually understanding the empty nature of the mind itself. It is like laying a solid foundation: the more positive karma we create, the more we will be able to support an understanding of ultimate reality.

Meditation is so challenging because the mind is used to having a rushing torrent of thoughts. We usually feel more comfortable when we are preoccupied and busy. Why is it so hard for us to just sit and do nothing? When we meditate, instead of emptying our mind of thoughts and finding that inner space, we often become more and more involved with conceptual thinking. The longer we try to meditate, the more the thoughts proliferate. Many of us have had the experience of sitting for an hour-long meditation and realizing we have not had any gaps of awareness between the rushing thoughts.

The more thoughts we have, the more we react to them, producing even more thoughts and emotions. Instead of stepping back and observing the conceptual thinking, we become completely immersed in it, identifying entirely with the thinking mind and losing the capacity to become a witness. In these situations, we have no sense that there is a greater awareness. Our whole world becomes ruled by our thoughts and concepts and we don't have any realization of empty space in our lives. This is why meditation is very challenging.

Without cultivating that awareness of spacious calm, so much of what we think and do in our lives brings more stress and more suffering. The Buddha's gift to humanity is the opportunity to awaken to that greater awareness. Through understanding the relative world, we can awaken to the ultimate and unconditioned state of clarity and emptiness. We can use the relative world as a means for growing our awareness of the ultimate. We can bring awareness to all of our basic activities of daily life.

Most of the time, we use the relative world to increase our conceptual thinking. Instead of using our ordinary experiences to deepen our awareness, we are increasing our emotions; we are becoming more lost. The mind becomes more and more cluttered until we have lost all contact with the spaciousness that we were born with.

If one is connected to the mind of the sacred guru,
one's search has uncovered the oral instructions.

This does not mean that if you make a connection with a relative guru you will automatically receive the guru's realization without any practice of your own. As we have discussed before, the relative guru is the relative guru; the ultimate guru is the innate wisdom of the mind of the guru and students. The guru helps us with oral instructions to make that connection to the inherent clarity and emptiness of our own mind.

All of our spiritual practices are an effort to realize the inherent buddha nature within us. If a practice is not awakening that inner nature, then it will not be very effective. It may be a ritual that calms the mind and helps us to relax, but it will not be a practice that brings any deeper realization. If we are practicing a Vajrayogini sadhana, for example, we should be using that generation and completion practice to access the clarity and emptiness of our own mind. If we see the deity as an object of worship, if we become attached to the outer representations of the deity, then our practice will not be very beneficial in helping us see the Buddha within.

The purpose of whatever practices we receive, and whatever connection we make with a guru, is to reveal the true nature of our own mind. All of the Buddha's teachings are intended to help us see the nature of our own mind. If we receive teachings without engaging in any investigation of our own mind, if we accumulate information without doing any meditation, it will not be very beneficial on a deeper level. It will be similar to taking a class on Buddhism at a university: we will gain knowledge, but we will not gain any experience of our true nature.

The difference between receiving Dharma teachings from a qualified guru and studying Buddhism academically has to do with experience and integration. The difference is not just about the teacher's own spiritual understanding; it is also about whether the students practice and incorporate what they learn. The Dharma is intended to be deeply integrated into our own life and practice, not just stored as knowledge.

We may feel drawn to study Buddhism academically because it is presented using a method of study that is familiar to us. Professors can present Buddhism in a much more organized way—that is their skill. They can design a very accessible and enjoyable class experience that includes clear powerpoint presentations and so forth. But the wisdom of the Buddha, the very essence of Buddhism, is often missing in this education. The professor's goal is not to awaken you and cultivate your inner realization. Professors are equipping you with knowledge so that you can get a degree, find a good job, teach, translate, or publish important papers. But for all these practical goals, the essence of what is being taught is lost in the process. The deeper wisdom is not being transmitted.

Although the teachings presented at Dharma centers may be much less organized and much more spontaneous than those taught in an academic setting, the purpose is to awaken you. Rather than simply transmitting knowledge, the goal of Dharma teachings is to transmit the wisdom of the lineage from a qualified guru to students who are ready to receive it. For that transmission to occur there must be some connection to the teacher. The goal of our study is not to receive a PhD with honors or find a good job. The goal of our study and practice is enlightenment for the sake of all beings.

Furthermore, however much of the Dharma is understood,
If one is not a suitable recipient of instructions,
the view will not be realized.

As we have discussed, the Buddha created the three trainings—discipline, meditation, and wisdom—as antidotes to the three root afflictive emotions of desire, anger, and ignorance. Among these three trainings, the training of wisdom is the most important. Cultivating the wisdom view impacts how we perceive everything in our world. Whether we will realize this wisdom view depends on our training and practice, and on whether we are a suitable recipient of instruction.

The right view is important because it can help us to transform our worldly life into a spiritual life. With the right view, all our worldly activities can be incorporated into our spiritual practice. Practitioners have different strengths and weaknesses. Some students have very good discipline but maybe they don't spend as much time in meditation. Some students have a daily meditation practice but they don't cultivate wisdom. Other students cultivate right view but they may not be diligent in their meditation and discipline.

The doorway into the spiritual path is different for everyone. According to our personality, our conditioning, and our karma, we will have different levels of integration—we will be at different places on the Vajrayana path. Someone who has cultivated right view may experience wisdom in their daily activities even if they are not as diligent about their formal practice. Someone with right view may be able to better use all of the challenges and circumstances in daily life to deepen their spiritual realization.

Right view is more important than meditation and discipline because it has the power to extend into every aspect of our lives. There are many great yogis who lived very ordinary lives as laypeople. Marpa, for example, was a farmer. He lived with a wife and family and even drank alcohol. When his soon-to-be student Milarepa met him for the first time, Marpa was out plowing his fields. But in the midst of that ordinary family life, Marpa somehow had the capacity to transform his daily life into spiritual practice and realization.

On the other hand, the Buddha was born as a prince. He was being groomed to become king and was given everything he desired so that he never had to leave the palace walls. Although he was surrounded by all of the luxury and pleasure imaginable, he still felt compelled to venture out of the castle gates. On his journeys into town he successively encountered an old person, a sick person, a dead person, and a renunciant dedicated to the spiritual life. Due to his intelligence, these experiences of suffering and impermanence were enough to make him renounce his kingdom and leave everything behind to pursue a spiritual life. He meditated by himself for many years, finally achieving full enlightenment under the Bodhi Tree.

In Milarepa's case, we know that he was raised in a very difficult family situation. It was a very unstable and traumatic environment with so much killing and stealing. This violence and misery also sparked some renunciation in Milarepa, impelling him to leave his family and pursue a spiritual life.

We can see from these three examples how wisdom can arise in dramatically different circumstances. The Buddha renounced his kingdom, Milarepa renounced this family life of anger and violence, and Marpa awakened to deeper wisdom even as he plowed the fields and raised a family.

We may be able to see a reflection of ourselves in these examples. Some of us are drawn to spiritual life because we have achieved fame and wealth and yet we still feel dissatisfied. We begin to realize that no amount of recognition or pleasure will bring us satisfaction. Others come from circumstances more like Milarepa's family. Maybe we experienced emotional or physical abuse. Maybe we grew up in very violent circumstances. Eventually we reached a point where we could not bear that suffering any longer and have become determined to find some mental peace.

For many people, our lives are more like Marpa's. We have been living an ordinary life with a family and work. Then, often around the middle of our lives, we develop a longing for a deeper experience. Maybe we have become very weary or dulled by the same routine year after year. Maybe we feel ourselves aging and this impermanence makes us realize how brief and precious this life is. Regardless of our background, we all have the ability to use our particular experiences to awaken some wisdom and transformation.

If we do not cultivate any spiritual awakening in our lives, we will continue to search for satisfaction in worldly pursuits. But no matter how many external changes we make, we will continue to experience the same conflicts, the same boredom, the same disgust and unhappiness. We may attempt to resolve these feelings by leaving a job, leaving a relationship, leaving a town. We will keep making outer changes in an effort to bring inner peace.

But there is no end to this cycle. There are always conflicts, always challenges. No matter how many changes we make, we will keep repeating the same emotional experiences if, whenever things are not working out for us, we solve it by leaving. It has become easier and easier in our modern world to keep running away from our unhappiness. We just keep changing our situation thinking that something better will happen. But usually we are only changing the outer objects, not the underlying habitual patterns.

If we are not treating the underlying negative emotions, we will continue to be caught in this cycle of swapping out objects whenever we are dissatisfied. As long as we are being driven by our negative emotions, we will not be ready for inner transformation. That is why most of us need to come to some sort of breaking point in order to want freedom from that cycle. For some of us that breaking point is illness or tragedy.

For some it is boredom in a routine. For others it is disillusionment or addiction in spite of fame or power.

We generally approach our problems by doing whatever we can to feel relief. We try to solve our material problems with material solutions. Maybe we become workaholics, or we try to solve our ideological problems with more ideas, more theories, more evidence to prove our views. We often try to solve our emotional problems by distracting ourselves with activities, entertainment, food, or exercise.

It is helpful to take an honest inventory of our strengths and our weaknesses. It is helpful to understand whether we are someone who is most driven by ideas, by emotions, or by actions. It is helpful to observe what our dominant negative emotions are. Are we driven most by desire, or by anger? Or is ignorance the dominant emotion, making us feel very dull and spaced out and unaware in our lives? Understanding what motivates us and what our dominant negative emotions are can help us understand the best spiritual antidotes.

What can we do if we lack discipline, cannot keep a meditation practice, and also do not cultivate right view? The Buddha offered a fourth doorway into the practice for those who are very active or who struggle to connect with the other trainings. He said that the best thing to do in that case is to serve the Dharma through devotional service. Through service to the guru, the Dharma, and the sangha community, we can subdue the ego and cultivate some merit.

In short, Jetsun Rinpoche is reminding us that right view is necessary for transformation. If we have right view, our mind is always protected. Right view is essential to awakening. But how can we cultivate right view? In the end, with the study and practice of Dharma, what matters is how much we are transformed rather than how much we have learned intellectually.

Do not be diverted by the worldly distractions
of not cutting off conventional proliferations.
If one is not able to live in solitude,

one will not obtain siddhis;
give up and leave your circle of people and things.

Jetsun Rinpoche is advising us how to practice in solitude, without depending on other people or things. First, he says, we need to overcome the distractions that arise due to conventional proliferation of thoughts. Second, we need to learn how to practice alone and independently; the more we depend on our circle of family and friends, as well as other things, the more lonely and restless we will become and we will not be able to practice properly or achieve any siddhis. All meditation practices are designed to help us to live independently and become more free. We were born alone and we will die alone.

As we have discussed, we are all connected to so many different circles of people and objects. We have family, friends, colleagues, and sangha members, and we are part of a larger society. We also come to identify with so many worldly possessions. Whether all of this will become part of our spiritual practice or remain a distraction depends on our attitude and whether we have cultivated right view.

If we have right view, then even if we are surrounded by family or friends—if we are plowing the fields like Marpa—we may still be able to experience some transformation and inner freedom. On the other hand, if we do not cultivate any right view, we may force discipline on ourselves, but we may still not feel any transformation. We may go off and meditate in a cave for years, but our mind may remain obsessed with ideas, objects, and comforts that we miss. Although we may be physically in solitude, we have not found any mental solitude.

It is very common to get obsessed with whatever we don't have. If someone is very poor, they may become obsessed with getting rich. If someone is very weak, they may become obsessed with power. Forcing spiritual discipline upon ourselves may only increase these cravings and obsessions. With the right view, it is possible to find solitude and liberation in the midst of a busy marketplace. With the wrong view, one can remain completely crowded with emotions and relational problems even while sitting in solitary retreat on a remote mountain for years.

The solitude that Rinpoche is recommending has more to do with whether we have cultivated right view than what our outer circumstances are. Right view allows us to properly diagnose our afflictions and treat them accordingly. Without that awareness, we may be treating our afflictions in ways that further increase our negative emotions and entanglements.

If we do not have right view, then family and friends can become a distraction from spiritual life. If we have a good family, then maybe these distractions will be very enjoyable, but they won't be helping us to awaken. If we have a negative family situation, that may increase our anger and further obscure our view. We may react to that negativity with increasingly negative emotions, becoming more and more trapped emotionally in that web of dysfunction. Strong emotions can preoccupy and overtake the mind. Emotions can be so powerful that we may lose any capacity for manifesting the wisdom view. The key thing is to pursue our spiritual life in accord with whatever our personal situation is.

As we have discussed, many of the great yogis seemed, from the outside, to be living ordinary lives. Simply avoiding worldly life will not necessarily allow us to overcome distraction. Our mind is capable of being completely distracted and conflicted even in isolation. What is most important is that we allow our present situation to become a catalyst for transformation. There are so many doorways into the Dharma. We can use whatever our own experience is, whether it is one of luxury, of trauma, or of mundane daily life, as a means for transcendence. This transcendence only happens when we have some wisdom about the true nature of our mind. Without right view, we will just keep going from object to object in the hope of finding some relief from suffering. We will just keep changing our home, our partner, our environment, our interests, but we will not find any liberation from this vicious cycle.

This obsessive moving from one object of desire to another is what keeps us caught in the cycle of samsara. This is why we are reborn again and again. Although we keep changing our outer circumstances, we are not addressing our deeply ingrained emotional patterns—we are not healing our root afflictions. Instead, we just generate more and more karma, causing us to cycle again and again through samsara impelled by our karma and emotions. Because we have not attained the wisdom view, we continue to suffer the same pain caused by desire, anger, and ignorance across so many lifetimes.

For a yogi who has attained right view, outer objects are secondary, the environment is secondary, and relationships are secondary. These circumstances will still be conditional and will constantly be changing, but they will have much less power over the mind. We will have the wisdom to see that swapping out one object for another does not solve our underlying affliction. This will help us to focus instead on our own spiritual transformation and to use all of our worldly challenges as opportunities for spiritual growth.

Realizing right view provides the mind with much more stability and protection, regardless of the challenges and struggles we all experience in life. Of course, this does not mean that we should remain in abusive relationships or situations. But it means that those situations will have less power to harm the mind, and we will have more clarity in making boundaries and removing ourselves from situations that cannot be repaired externally. We will recognize that we are capable of tremendous inner healing regardless of what is happening around us.

If the germ of the ultimate is not realized,
there is no essence in the husk of convention.

In this context, "germ of the ultimate" refers to the right view of ultimate truth, and "husk of convention" refers to the relative truth. Ordinarily we place so much importance on the relative world. We are conditioned into relativity from such a young age. Our priorities are often very focused on external progress and on our relationship with others and with the material world.

It is common for people to live their entire life completely overtaken by mundane activities in the relative world. We have lost contact with the deeper essence. We have not gained any understanding of ultimate reality. Many people do not consider these deeper questions until they are dying. But at that time, they may no longer have the energy or clarity to explore these spiritual dimensions.

As we have discussed, people can experience fear and existential dread when they reach the end of their lives. They may wonder what the purpose has been of all of that activity. Many people have strong regret that they remained so distracted and so consumed by the outer world. Many people are fearful of where they will be going spiritually after death. Some people are very frightened because they believe death is the end of everything and they wonder what the point of life has been.

When we remain focused on the relative world, we don't experience much freedom. We may become completely overtaken by strong emotions. But if someone experiences the ultimate realization of right view, then all worldly activities lose their grip on the mind. For someone with the awareness of right view, life unfolds like a dream or a play; the mind can bear witness and it can engage, but it is not overwhelmed by the relative world. When the mind remains in contact with that ultimate reality, the illusory nature of conditioned existence becomes very clear.

Of course, this is not easy to realize. We are so deeply invested in the relative world. We have been conditioned across countless lifetimes to experience the relative world as the true reality. These are very difficult patterns and habits to break. Sometimes it takes something very dramatic occurring in our lives to wake us up to the deeper questions of meaning and reality.

Not carried away by the distractions of the eight worldly dharmas, abandon activities and take up practice.

The "eight worldly dharmas" refers to the following concerns in our life: gain and loss, fame and infamy, praise and blame, and pleasure and pain. Although these concerns are very important to worldly people, yogis see them as distractions and obstacles to spiritual practice. For those without any spiritual practice, the purpose of life is to pursue and get attached to gain, fame, praise, and pleasure, and to be averse to loss, infamy, blame, and pain. Jetsun Rinpoche is encouraging us to abandon those activities related to the distractions of the eight worldly dharmas and to commit to our spiritual practice.

Realization of right view is the most important opportunity of this precious human lifetime. It is very rare to have a spontaneous awakening. We need to rely on all of these skillful methods and trainings to gradually realize the right view. Discipline and meditation provide a graduated path through which we come to experience wisdom.

Someone who is highly evolved, who has done so much spiritual practice in previous lifetimes, may be able to experience right view without that same graduated path. In that case, the result becomes the path. These practitioners can integrate right view into everything they do in the relative world. Whether this is possible will depend on the individual karma and experience of the practitioner.

There are many examples of great Zen practitioners and great yogis and mahasiddhas who have had this direct experience of right view. These spiritual masters cut through all dualism and can bring that wisdom into everything they do. As we have discussed, such highly realized masters can even seem outrageous and shocking in their "crazy wisdom" to those who are still caught in dualism. These yogis have gone beyond right and wrong, beautiful or ugly, attachment and aversion. They have gone beyond karma.

As long as our mind is trapped in the relative world, we will continue generating karma. But when our mind has the realization of ultimate reality, then we have gone beyond karma. The awakened yogis have gone beyond the afflictive emotions. The negative emotions are no longer the cause of volition in their minds. Without that defiled volition, their activities are not a cause for the proliferation of karma. Their worldly activities are all just an illusion, like a mirage or a dream. For these yogis, the result and the method have become one. The result has become the path.

We do not have that realization of reality. At our level, our thoughts and actions start with volition in the mind. That volition generates karma and all of the afflictive emotions. We cannot cut through dualism; we cannot go beyond right and wrong. We therefore still need to rely on the natural law of karma, on meditation and discipline, to free ourselves from negative emotions and to generate positive karma.

As we've discussed, solitude doesn't necessarily mean renouncing our lives, leaving all of our family and commitments, and going into solitary retreat. Solitude has more to do with how much freedom we can cultivate in our own mind. The more we can integrate right view into our daily lives, the more freedom and spaciousness we will experience in the mind. We will be able to stand in a busy marketplace and have the inner freedom of a yogi on retreat in the mountains.

For most of us, life is a series of thoughts. We identify so deeply with our thoughts that we mistake them for a self. We cannot imagine a consciousness that could exist beyond thought. We cannot conceive of an awareness that is nonconceptual. As we have discussed, our thoughts and emotions create our entire experience of the universe. If we decide that someone is an enemy, then we can see everything about that person as ugly and negative. If we fall in love with someone, for a period of time we will see everything they do as beautiful, desirable, and good. That's what we do in life. Our entire lives are based on our dualistic perceptions and not on any ultimate reality.

We decide whether something is right or wrong based on our emotions and on our conditioning. Discipline is based on this dualism and on trying to do what is right and good. However, as we can see in life, what is good and ethical to one person is completely unethical and bad from someone else's perspective.

With right view, we can transcend this dualism. This may seem so paradoxical because everything we do right now is based on discriminating and judging. But the more we cultivate right view, the more we may have these little glimpses of wisdom. Our awareness will become much more expansive and we will not be defending an ego anymore. Without that ego to defend, we become much less concerned with attachment and aversion. We stop needing to judge and discriminate. To cultivate right view, we have to see our mind and its true nature. Once we have seen that true nature, we can be in the busiest place and experience no distraction from ultimate reality. If we have not seen the true nature of the mind, then we need to try to free ourselves from our dependence on the relative world and from all of our mundane activities. Through discipline and practice, we can begin to limit the distractions.

The greatest distraction of all is our addiction to thinking. We don't even recognize thinking as an addiction. Thinking is rewarded by our society, by our family, and by our education system. Conceptual thinking is a habit that is incredibly hard to break. Through abandoning activities and practicing meditation we can begin to slow the thoughts and become aware of the spaciousness and freedom in the mind.

14

See the Connections

See the connection between view and meditation;
see the connection between conduct and time;
see the connection between oral instruction and scripture;
see the connection between the person and Dharma practice;
see the connection between meditation and post-meditation;
see the connection between lineage and guru.

JETSUN RINPOCHE IS EMPHASIZING the importance of six connections: between view and meditation, conduct and time, oral instruction and scripture, person and practice, meditation and post-meditation, lineage and guru. As we have discussed, meditation without wisdom is just relaxation. It may be comforting and help with sleep and stress reduction, but it will not be very transformative on a deeper level. Because of the rapid pace of modern life, we have become very impatient mentally and physically. Due to that constant activity and instant gratification, sitting still in meditation has become even more challenging.

In the old days, although people may not have practiced meditation, they spent more time sitting quietly around a fire or observing the natural world. With the development of cell phones and computers, people are losing the ability to even find space in the day for contemplation. We used to have to wait quietly at a stoplight, or in line at a store. Now we have lost even these quiet moments because we automatically look at our phones for some distraction.

The more we condition the mind to be constantly active, the more challenging it is to sit still. Sitting still and reflecting used to be as much a part of life as sleeping, walking, or eating. But with the pace of modern life accelerating, sitting still and finding some mental solitude is very hard. We barely sit still to eat meals. People often eat while driving or working. Even when we are alone, we are constantly on social media, so we are not really getting to know our own mind. If we look at older generations, they knew how to sit outside after a day of work, relaxing the mind and just reflecting on the sky or the trees and birds. We can still see this in other cultures, but it has become increasingly rare in America. People may travel to a beautiful place for vacation, and then they will just sit on the beach or in the mountains looking at their phones.

We may get some physical rest when we start a meditation practice, but that doesn't mean we will get any mental rest. As I have mentioned, the thoughts may increase when we sit down and start to pay attention to mental activity. Our age of multitasking may have some benefits in our lives. Maybe it helps us to become financially stable, or maybe it helps us accomplish dreams of parenthood and career simultaneously. But it has also given rise to many negative habitual patterns in the mind. We have become habituated to feeling that we have to constantly be doing something. We feel that if we are not constantly productive, we will fall behind. For some people, productivity is directly linked to survival. Some people have to work three jobs just to survive in this country due to this increasing gap between the rich and the poor. But for many people, the need to be busy comes more from some emotional insecurity or restlessness. People have the sense that if they just do a little bit more, they will feel happier, more financially secure, or more satisfied.

Due to this habit of constant activity, we may feel very disoriented and uncomfortable when we try to sit still for meditation. The mind may feel very restless and insecure. We don't want to experience all of the feelings and thoughts we have been running from. This is how life is for so many people. No one wants to get to know their own mind. People are chasing fulfillment in ways that will never ultimately be satisfying.

It is quite remarkable how we can go through many years of education without ever gaining insight into what will actually make us feel more at ease in our own mind and body. We are actually being trained to ignore the body in order to be productive. We are trained to run away from the nature of the mind by filling it full of information. We have forgotten the art of relaxing and truly resting.

Meditation is becoming more popular in this country because people are reaching a breaking point with stress and exhaustion. They are taking yoga and meditation classes in the hope of feeling better. Often, these activities are done without any awareness. People may sit in meditation and plan their shopping list. People may do yoga as if it were any other kind of exercise class. Often, we see people even forgetting to breathe deeply while they are practicing. They may become very flexible and physically strong, but spiritually the yoga has not been transformative at all. Our body may feel more rested but there has been no rest on the mental level.

We have all had the experience of waking up from a night of sleep feeling physically rested but mentally exhausted from our dreams. The body may be lying still, but the mind and emotions are manifesting terrifying nightmares. When meditation is not done with wisdom, it may be a lot like dreaming: we are sitting still, but all of our desires, fears, and anger are playing out in the mind, completely overwhelming us with thoughts and emotions.

That kind of meditation will not liberate us. As long as meditation and view are two separate things, we will not experience any mental freedom. We may feel more relaxed and peaceful, we may find some health benefits, but we will not experience liberation and spiritual transformation. We need to combine our meditation with right view in order to experience any mental rest.

Once we have joined meditation with right view, then we can be in meditation even while we are doing activities. When you are in the presence of a great meditation master, you can sense that everything they do is an extension of their meditation. There is no distinction between their awareness when in formal meditation and their awareness in worldly activities. This is what we refer to as "meditation in action."

The challenge for us is that our meditation has not joined with the wisdom view. It is difficult for us to have awareness even in *formal* meditation practice. And it is nearly impossible for us to maintain meditative awareness while stuck in traffic or dealing with conflict.

That is why it is important to first learn how to ground ourselves in sitting meditation. Some people are naturally more physically grounded. You can sense that when you are sitting next to someone. Even if that person is a stranger, you can sense that they have some elemental chemistry that makes them more rooted. Just by sitting next to them you may also feel more grounded.

Other people are very action-oriented. They seem to be buzzing with mental and physical activity. Even if you are sitting still beside them, you can feel their restless energy. We can even experience this around different cities. If we go to New York City, we may be able to feel the energy of that whole area. If we go to a holy place like Bodhgaya in India, where Buddha became enlightened, we may feel a very different spiritual energy. Although, on one hand, New York may be much cleaner, more structured and efficient, we may not feel much peace there, because the collective energy is very fast-paced.

If we walk around Cambridge in the middle of night, the energy in Harvard Square is very different than it is during the day. But if everyone sat down and began to meditate there in the middle of day, the energy of the whole area would shift. It may feel much more peaceful than it does even at night. Even though most people sleep at night, their minds are still so active. All of that mental activity is still creating some energy field. If those same people were awake but meditating, we might feel a much greater sense of calm in the city.

The purpose of meditation is to stop all of that thinking in order to make contact with that deeper awareness and, ultimately, with the clarity and empty nature of the mind. If all human beings could simultaneously stop thinking and rest in that meditative awareness, there would be an extraordinary shift in the energy on this earth.

There have been studies that show how crime rates go down when meditation is introduced to an area. There have been very good results when meditation is brought into schools or prisons that are experiencing violence. We have good scientific evidence that meditation can have such a positive impact on society. But in spite of that, our society has not learned to value meditation. We have not learned to teach it as part of our core curriculum in schools.

We are still under the impression that a productive society must be constantly active. Capitalism doesn't understand what meditation produces, and it therefore does not place any value on it. The more time we spend in meditation practice, the less interested we may become in pursuing wealth. We may become less greedy and consume fewer goods. This may hurt our gross domestic product, but it may increase our gross national happiness and well-being. Maybe this approach is a threat to capitalism, but we can see how much benefit it brings to countries like Bhutan that have formally instituted this focus on gross national happiness and well-being over profit.

Technology has become so central to our lives that we almost begin to treat ourselves as machines. But we are not computers! We are human beings! We need some balance in our lives in order to be healthy. We can see how much this frantic pace of modern life has impacted our health. People may feel too busy to even breathe mindfully.

When everyone is rushing around us, we can get swept up into that frenzy of activity. The only way to counter this is to slowly train ourselves to sit in meditation daily. We have to start very gradually. It is very hard to break the habitual patterns, so we need to be patient with our mind and body. We need to be patient with our restlessness and know that it is a normal part of building a daily practice. Over time, meditation will become more and more comfortable.

First, we just have to learn how to sit still and do nothing. Gradually, we will begin to experience some relaxation benefits from meditation. As we become more relaxed and comfortable sitting still, then we can begin to integrate some shamatha meditation. We can meditate on an object like the breath or a blue flower. As we begin to be able to bring some concentration to our meditation, we can begin to integrate insight into our meditation practice.

When Jetsun Rinpoche says, "see the connection between view and meditation," "view" refers to insight meditation, and "meditation" in this context refers to shamatha practice. Shamatha and insight have to go together. Shamatha meditation without any wisdom or insight will relax us but it will never liberate us. There will be no transcendence.

It is said that in the form realm and even in the formless realm, beings can do shamatha concentration meditation for eons but they will never be liberated from samsara because they don't have insight meditation. Meditation and view need to be integrated so that we will be liberated. Peace and relaxation are not synonymous. Relaxation can occur without any underlying experience of peace. We may feel relaxed when we are watching a movie. We may feel relaxed when we drink alcohol or do drugs. We can achieve relaxation artificially through changing our brain chemistry. But this type of relaxation will not bring us any lasting peace.

Early in our meditation practice, we may actually feel *less* relaxed. Some people may prefer to have a glass of wine after a long day, because that feels like instant relief. But as we know, using any substance to achieve relaxation has the potential to become addictive. The more accustomed we become to drinking at the end of the day, the more we will develop dependency on it. Maybe we will need *two* glasses of wine to achieve the same relaxation. Maybe we will begin to want a drink earlier in the day. The more we depend on that substance for relief, the more we will crave it. Meditation is more reliable because there is no potential for addiction. We are not creating a chemical dependency. We are revealing the mind and the body's own ability to balance itself.

When Rinpoche says to observe the connection between conduct and time, he is referring more to the developed discipline of body and speech regarding how to refrain from harming others. There is a general saying: "The Vinaya disciplines should be observed according to the time and place where you reside." This is similar to the expression, "When in Rome, do as the Romans do."

Jetsun Rinpoche is also asking us to pay attention to the connection between oral instruction and scripture. "Scripture" refers to the Buddha's words in both the sutras and the tantras. Rinpoche is reminding us to always look for the connection between the oral instructions and the scripture. If a guru gives the oral instructions that differ from Buddha's teachings, then instruction and scripture are not meeting. In order to validate the teachings that we receive, we must be able to measure them according to the Buddha's original words.

Rinpoche then asks us to appreciate how Dharma practice is connected with "the person." What he is saying is that our Dharma practice should be in accord with our particular intelligence, personality, and afflictions. In order to apply the correct antidote, we have to understand which poison we are treating. What are the negative emotions that are dominant in our life? Are we more prone to the dullness and confusion of ignorance? Are we more prone to reactivity and anger? Are we controlled by desire? What type of intelligence do we have? According to that, we have to diagnose and choose the best practices.

As we know, the mind is very complex. Circumstances and emotions are always changing. Our attitude is always changing. If it is unclear what our main practice should be, or if we have not yet met a spiritual guru, then we should focus on generating positive karma through the accumulation of merit. This is a good general practice for everyone, no matter what type of intelligence and dominant afflictions they may have. The common foundation practices are suitable for all practitioners. These common foundation practices include contemplating the preciousness of human life, impermanence and death, the nature of life in samsara, the law of karma, and practicing shamatha meditation.

Foundation practice—or *ngöndro*—is the perfect method for transforming our negative karma and afflictions. The ngöndro practices are the same for everyone regardless of whether they are an angry person, a passionate person, or a confused and sleepy person.

In Vajrayana, we can see three different manifestations of buddhas. Some deities are depicted as being very peaceful, some as wrathful and frightening, and some deities, representing desire, are depicted joined in sexual union. These are the three manifestations of deities that we encounter in tantric practice, which relate to the negative emotions. It is easy to misunderstand the true meaning of these images.

When buddhas are depicted in a wrathful form, this does not mean that the buddhas are angry and full of hatred. When buddhas are depicted in a passionate form with the mother and father deity in union, this doesn't mean that these buddhas are experiencing desire or attachment. When buddhas are depicted with rich ornaments, this doesn't mean that the buddhas are showing ignorance. These manifestations are actually skillful means for transforming our own root afflictive emotions. If we are an angry person, we may make a very strong connection with a wrathful deity. That connection will bring us into the spiritual path and transform our anger. If we have so much desire, we may be drawn to the passionate images of deities, which will help us transform our desire. If we have confusion and ignorance, elaborate, wealthy looking buddhas may be more suitable to transform our ignorance.

Dharma is for everyone. Dharma does not discriminate against the angry person or the passionate person or the confused person. Dharma has many skillful antidotes to the root poisons of desire, anger, and ignorance. There is so much power in the negative emotions. But instead of renouncing those emotions, we can harness that energy and experience very powerful transformation. Vajrayana is very skillful, because it shows us how to use negative emotions to transcend negative emotion. For many people, this can be more effective than renunciation because we are not spending all this energy trying to refrain from anger or desire. Instead, we are bringing all of our energy into the spiritual path and allowing it to transform us.

As we strengthen our habit of daily meditation, we will begin to notice some changes. Even if we can only meditate for ten minutes a day in the beginning, we may slowly begin to notice some differences in our mind and physical body during the rest of the day. The effects of meditation can even begin to change our dreams and allow our sleep to become more peaceful.

As Jetsun Rinpoche is pointing out, our meditation is not separate from the rest of our lives. His Holiness the Dalai Lama always says that he does his meditation in the early morning hours, but it recharges and energizes his mind throughout the rest of the day. The more we practice, the more we will also begin to notice how we can remain connected to that awareness throughout our other daily activities. Our formal session of meditation practice and our post-meditation should connect.

The guru can be perceived differently by different students, according to the student's family history or current needs in their life. For some, the guru is like a friend. For some, the guru is like a father figure. For some, the guru is just an ordinary teacher. For others, the guru is perceived as a therapist or counselor. Some people may see the guru as a healer. There are as many perceptions of the guru as there are students!

According to the traditional guru yoga practice, "the relative guru is perceived as the embodiment of all the buddhas; the ultimate guru pervades all samsara and nirvana; the guru of intrinsic cognizance is the nature of one's mind, the original protector." The student will receive the benefit of blessings according to how they perceive the guru.

The Vajrayana practice of guru yoga can be very transformative because it helps us to see the purity within us and within all things. It is much harder to discover this purity through ordinary relationships. Our ordinary relationships are very complex and filled with mixed emotions. We may have glimpses of this purity in how we love a baby, for example, but that purity always changes. Ordinary relationships are very challenging because they are based on so much desire and anger. Our circumstances are always changing. Our feelings are easily hurt. Our regrets and resentments build up through the years. There are inevitable issues within a family. Although we feel so much love for our family, it is usually not an effective method for realizing any purity within us; it is very conditioned. The same person that brings us so much happiness can also bring us so much pain.

Guru yoga is a way to see that purity within us. We are not relating to the guru out of desire or anger. We are not trying to satisfy our own needs. The relationship to the guru is more reliable than ordinary relationships. The guru is there to awaken the student to their own true nature. The guru is the key to liberating us from that subjective conditioning of our emotions.

Normally in our relationships, when we feel happy, we feel connected to friends or family. When there is a conflict, though, we disconnect from these same people. So many families have members who are estranged from one another because their disconnection and their differences in experience seem irreparable. Someone's ego is too hurt, and it is easier to just cut that family member out of their lives.

Guru yoga can seem very strange at first, especially in cultures like America where it is not as common. People may feel very uncomfortable doing prostrations and expressing this kind of reverence and devotion. People may misinterpret this as subservience or attachment to another person. But guru yoga helps us to subdue our own ego. Until the ego is subdued, it will be very hard for us to see the purity within our own mind. The expectation is not that we see the human teacher as entirely perfect; the practice is to put our faith in that teacher to reveal the purity within us. The more devotion and connection we generate toward the guru, the more we are cultivating the wisdom and purity within us. When we experience that purity, we can see the purity in everyone.

Guru yoga is very powerful because it is based on faith. Faith can be incredibly transformative. Faith is much more powerful than ordinary love and has more potential to bring us deep inner peace. Guru yoga is the key to seeing the purity in the world. It is often too challenging to see that purity subjectively because our own emotions and conditioning cloud everything we experience. But through devotion to the guru, we can glimpse the purity in the world. We can experience this purity in the presence of a great teacher. Everything around us may seem purer and more radiant when we are near them. This can give us a glimpse of what is possible. Guru yoga is an accelerated path because it works so skillfully to help us recognize the nature of the mind.

Seeing the connection between lineage and guru also helps us to not become mistakenly attached to one guru. When we have faith in our guru, we are having faith in the entire lineage, from the Buddha all the way down to our root guru. This faith is a reminder that we all have buddha nature. We should feel very encouraged by the lineage. We should also be reminded by the lineage not to become attached to our own guru in an ordinary way, as we would become attached to a parent or a friend. We are connecting with the wisdom of the *guru*, not with an ordinary human being. We should not expect that guru to fulfill our emotional needs like a parent or a friend would.

If we can reveal the purity within us, we can begin to see the buddha nature in everyone. We can see the Buddha in our partner, in our children, and even in our enemies. Eventually, we can see the buddha nature in all sentient beings and we can see our universe as a pure realm.

Guru yoga can be more challenging than doing practices like Tara puja or other rituals because we are trying to see buddha nature within a living human being. It is more challenging, and yet, it is the best way to begin to see the buddha nature within ourselves and within all beings.

Generally, there is no end to the words of sutras and tantras;
right now, the important thing is to stop words.

Jetsun Rinpoche is cautioning us here not to get caught up in intellectual pursuits. He is reminding us, once again, that there is no end to academic study. The more the mind pursues knowledge, the more appetite it will have for more knowledge. The mind is very entertained by intellectual study. If we are studying the Dharma for the sake of getting a degree or a job, then once we reach that goal we may lose interest.

As we have discussed, if we want to awaken to our buddha nature, we need to do more than intellectual study. The purpose of studying all of the Buddhist texts should be to help our practice. If studying the Dharma is not helping our practice, then it is not transforming us.

Some traditions place too much emphasis on intellectual study; other traditions place too much emphasis on sitting meditation alone. It is important for us to have a balance. If we only study and never practice, we may not have any personal experience of wisdom. If we practice without any instruction, we may not understand the purpose of our practice and may become discouraged when we have obstacles.

It is important to know what the most suitable practice is for us. It is important to receive proper instruction. If we practice without any study or understanding, it will be just a physical practice. Sakya Pandita said that if we want to climb a mountain, we first need to learn all of the proper techniques of mountaineering. Without that preparation, we will not know how to handle the many challenges that will arise: when the weather changes, we will not know what to do; if we have not studied maps drawn by others who have traveled those paths, we may easily get lost; and we will not be successful in reaching the summit.

The Sakya tradition emphasizes a balance of study and practice. There are many accounts of Sakya lamas who remained in a meditative state for days or weeks after clinical death. This is evidence of very high realization. It shows us that these masters had developed their practice on a very deep level, even while being great scholars and teachers. My own late guru, His Eminence Chogye Trichen Rinpoche, stayed in a meditative state for two weeks after his death. During that time his body did not change or show signs of deterioration.

Jetsun Rinpoche is reminding us to let go of our addiction to words and ideas. The more words we have, the more thoughts we will generate; the more thoughts we generate, the more words we will have. There will be no end to that proliferation of conceptual thinking. All of that thinking does not necessarily support our faith or our practice if we are not using the Buddha's words to reveal our inherent wisdom. Instead, we are reducing the Buddha's words to philosophical study, and we are generating personal opinions and gathering evidence to prove our conclusions.

If we lose touch with the ultimate goal of our study, then all of our intelligence will not be revealing any innate wisdom. Instead, all of these words and ideas will obscure that spaciousness. Not only that, but our academic pursuits will generate more words and concepts in those around us who may agree with or refute our opinions.

We often reduce the wisdom found in these profound texts to mere ideas, our conclusions being based on our particular conditioning and type of intelligence. This type of research is more like an archeological excavation. We look very closely at objects. Perhaps we discover new historical facts, find errors in translation, or argue about the meaning of a certain term, but we will not find any wisdom that way. Even if we agree with the Buddha's words, if we do not have any personal realization, we are merely reciting something—we are not experiencing it. The purpose of studying Buddhism is to reveal our inherent wisdom. It is not to reach intellectual conclusions based on our limited understanding.

Having cut doubt in the meaning,
now, the important thing is to stop looking.

The traditional purpose of studying and contemplating the Dharma is to help our meditation practice. In order to practice, we need to have some engagement with the practice manuals in order to overcome our doubts. If there is doubt and we keep on looking, we cannot start our practice properly. Yogis, therefore, having cut doubt regarding their practice manuals, then focus on the sadhana of their yidam instead of looking and window shopping here and there without committing to their yidam practice.

If we rely too much on intellectual pursuits, there will be no end to our study. Our mind is so hungry for information. We find intellectual study so entertaining. It comes much more naturally to us than sitting still. Meditation practice takes time. We often find it so boring in the early years of our practice, and we may begin to think we are wasting our time. We may think it would be much more valuable if we were producing something instead of sitting still.

When we have a restless mind, we usually search for entertainment and distraction. We want to feel comfortable, to forget our problems, to strengthen our ego. We search and search for a place for the mind to rest. But the more we search, the more restless we become. Even Dharma talks and discussions of karma may make us very uncomfortable. We may sit through a whole Dharma talk while daydreaming about a vacation or planning what we will order for dinner.

There are so many options for quick distraction in our modern culture. It is easy to check our social media and feel satisfaction that someone liked an image we posted. But then we may look further and see that someone else wrote a negative comment. Now we are even more restless, and we look somewhere else to be distracted from that initial distraction. The choices are overwhelming. We have access to thousands of films and hundreds of channels. We have limitless access to information on the internet. All of the choices we have can make it even more difficult to find mental ease and rest.

We are under the false impression that if we search hard enough, something will satisfy us. We will find the perfect house. We will order the perfect shoes. We will find the best job. The problem is that we fill all of our time with searching, thinking that it will satisfy us. Sitting quietly in meditation has a much greater chance of bringing some ease to the mind and increasing our well-being and satisfaction in life. But we use all of the time in which we could be meditating to search the external world for some sense of relaxation and fulfillment.

Jetsun Rinpoche is reminding us that we have to stop our endless searching. We need to practice, relying on study and faith. If all of our intellectual study has increased our doubt, we will never meditate and we will never experience transformation.

[There is] no purpose in doing worldly activities;
now, the important thing is to abandon distractions.

Traditionally, there are four common purposes and one ultimate purpose to our spiritual practice. The ultimate purpose of our practice is to achieve enlightenment for the benefit of all sentient beings. But on the way to achieving that ultimate purpose, in the course of our spiritual practice, we will encounter many needs and challenges. To overcome them, we rely on what we call the four common purposes: pacifying negativities, increasing positivities, empowering confidence and diligence, and subduing opposing forces. Jetsun Rinpoche is advising us that there is no purpose in doing worldly activities driven by negative emotions, which will only distract us from our spiritual purposes.

When meditation and spiritual practice are the most important things in our lives, everything else will be secondary. We may still need to work and make money so that we can eat and have shelter, but that will no longer be the primary focus of our lives. We will only be doing those activities in order to support our spiritual practice.

We often reverse these priorities. We make our worldly activities the most important thing in our lives and use spiritual practice in the hope that it will make us more successful. As we have discussed, it is very common for people to do spiritual practice and make offerings because they want to have a prosperous business or improve their health. These people come to the temple for divination and do certain practices and pujas according to the advice of lamas. Many people even use spiritual practice to try to enhance their athletic performance. Many athletes have adopted some mindfulness practice in order to perform better under stress.

While this type of spiritual practice may be better than doing nothing, it is still transactional rather than transformative. We are using it to try to increase our power, strength, or focus. There is so much ego involvement. The goal remains very superficial, and there is no cultivation of wisdom and compassion.

The best thing we can do is to make our spiritual study and practice the primary focus of our lives. All of our other worldly activities should be conducted in a way that will support our practice. If we use spiritual practice merely to achieve worldly things, we limit the transformative power of these practices.

One cannot depend on Yama, the lord of death;
now, the important thing is to practice.

The time of death is uncertain; develop diligence.

If we watch the daily news we will constantly be reminded of how death can happen at any time. We are reminded of how many people die in terrible accidents or in war. Many people die tragically at a young age from illness. We do not contemplate the possibility of our own death very often. We may think, "I'm still healthy and I have many more years to live. I will begin my spiritual practice once my children grow up, or once I am retired and have more time." But death can be so sudden and surprising. Death can happen at any moment, so we should not wait to begin our practice.

If we don't believe in anything continuing beyond this one lifetime, then maybe the thought of dying young actually discourages us from practice. We may think, "If I only have forty years on this earth, I want to enjoy myself; I don't want to stay at home quietly meditating. I want to experience all the pleasure I can in this world!" Or maybe we use our spiritual practice merely to improve our happiness in this one lifetime and we don't care about anything beyond this life.

From a Buddhist perspective, our mind will continue even after death. That is why it makes sense to prioritize our spiritual practice. We cannot bring anything with us from this life except what we have cultivated in the mind. Death is a great teacher. If we remain mindful of death, we will not place so much importance on accumulating material things. We cannot bring our house, our car, our savings, or our body with us after death—only the mind will continue. The best investment of our time is to focus on training the mind and realizing our inherent wisdom. Jetsun Rinpoche is encouraging us to develop diligence in our spiritual practices.

If one is happy, it is the kindness of the guru;
if one is sad, it emanates from previous karma.

If we have faith and devotion toward the guru, it will inspire many good qualities to develop in our lives. People with more faith and devotion generally experience more peaceful lives, even when they face difficult challenges. If someone is very smart but they do not have any faith or devotion, they may have trouble trusting anyone. They cannot place their trust in the guru. They can never relax, because they are always preparing to defend their ego. They may not even trust their family or friends and remain suspicious of others.

The more mantra we recite, the more protection we will have in the mind. The more practice we do, the more spacious our mind will become. The more spacious our mind, the more freedom we will have from negative emotions. The more purity we have in the mind, the more we will experience the purity of the world around us. That purity is the basis for all positive emotions and actions.

People who have more faith are usually more joyful and peaceful. They are naturally more diligent in their spiritual practice because they are experiencing all of the benefits of that practice. They have so much trust in the process, and that trust in the spiritual path brings them a sense of deep calm.

Even in our ordinary relationships, the more trust we have in someone, the more peace and calm we will experience in that relationship. On the other hand, if people do not trust each other in a relationship, they will remain vigilant and cautious. They will have doubt in the other person's loyalty or motivation and will be cautious of being hurt emotionally. Many people experience this kind of anxiety, even within a marriage where there should ideally be trust and peace. All of those doubts can torment people, even within the most intimate relationships in their lives. There is no guarantee that someone we have faith in will remain kind to us or faithful to us. But the experience of faith itself will bring us more peace. With this increased peace and stability, we can better navigate any obstacles and disappointments.

Those who have different levels of faith in the refuge objects of the Guru, Buddha, Dharma, and Sangha will have different levels of peace and joy in their lives. When we witness qualities such as love and compassion, knowledge and wisdom, and power and abilities in our refuge objects, it will kindle the clear faith that helps to bring the peace and joy that arise from witnessing those qualities. If this clear faith strengthens in the "wishing faith"—the wish to achieve enlightenment—our joy and peace will become even more long lasting. If wishing faith becomes "unshakable faith"—the complete and total trust in the refuge objects that comes from realizing the profundity of interdependent origination and the ultimate nature in the refuge objects—we will experience joy and peace unconditionally all the time.

When Jetsun Rinpoche says, "If one is happy, it is the kindness of the guru," we should not misunderstand this as saying that our happiness has nothing to do with karma. In fact, it is primarily due to our faith in the refuge objects that we generate merit and experience joy and peace. The refuge objects are a powerful factor in helping us to kindle that faith. There is a saying that the faith of devotees is like a ring, and the blessing of the guru and refuge objects are like a hook. To receive the hook-like blessings from the guru and refuge objects, the students need to generate that ring-like faith.

From a Buddhist perspective, all of our feelings of happiness as well as sadness, pain, and suffering, are a result of past karma. When we are experiencing extreme suffering, we can even rejoice, knowing that we are now exhausting that negative karma. This may seem very contradictory—to rejoice when we are suffering—but while we are suffering, we are also purifying that past karma. When we realize this, it may help us to be more accepting of our pain and unhappiness.

As we have discussed, acceptance helps to preserve our energy. Being outraged by the injustice of what is happening to us will increase our anger and negativity and cause us to expend so much energy, feeling that life is not treating us fairly. Acceptance, on the other hand, can bring stability to the mind. Acceptance preserves the energy that we need to navigate the obstacle we are facing.

And as we have already emphasized, acceptance does not mean that we should remain in an abusive situation. We can accept suffering while still removing ourselves from a situation that is causing harm. Acceptance also does not mean blaming a victim. We should not treat someone who is suffering with disregard. We should not assume that they "deserve" what is happening to them. That is a misunderstanding of karma. If we use karma to decrease our compassion for others, then we are not living a Buddhist life, and we are not cultivating any wisdom or compassion.

If you suffer loss, don't be discouraged;
if you experience gain, don't be arrogant.

Loss and gain are a constant in our lives. Without a spiritual foundation, we may become very depressed or discouraged when we lose something or someone. At the other end of the spectrum, when we have more success, we may become very arrogant or self-righteous. The teaching is saying here that no matter what happens in our lives, we should maintain some equilibrium, some equanimity. If we recognize that there will always be ups and downs, we can stop identifying so completely with loss or gain. When we have some success, we should keep in mind that everything is always changing and that loss is also inevitable. This will keep us from becoming arrogant. When we experience hardship, we should take comfort in impermanence, knowing that everything is always changing and that there will be other gains. This can help us survive very difficult losses.

Ultimately, as we have discussed, we will lose everything except what has been cultivated in the mind. Even if we are a billionaire, we cannot take any of that wealth with us after death. In fact, death may be even more challenging for the wealthy, because of their identification with their wealth. On the other hand, if our lives have been filled with loss and challenge, and we have used those losses to cultivate a very strong and balanced mind, at the time of death we may be very calm. From one perspective, the billionaire may look like the successful one. But from a spiritual perspective, someone who has nothing, but who has cultivated spiritual qualities, has gained something of much greater value.

So, how we respond to loss and gain depends on our spiritual perspective. There is an upside and a downside to everything in the conditioned world. There is a hill on every side of a valley. No one has a life that is flat all of the time without any loss or gain. The nature of conditioned existence is that we cycle through happiness and unhappiness, pain and pleasure, because things are always changing. We cannot pause our lives at a moment of happiness and expect that it will stay the same.

How we live our lives should not be determined by the ups and downs, the gains and losses. If we allow our mind to be disturbed by all of the ups and downs, we will remain stuck on an emotional roller coaster. Through engaging in spiritual practice, and just through the passage of time, we can gain a steadier response to all of the ups and downs. We can often see this in older people who, even if they are not spiritual, have survived enough ups and downs to realize that it is not worth getting too upset over things. Because they no longer identify as much with all of the gains and losses, people are often much more at peace in their old age.

We can observe that people who get very excited and happy when something goes well are often more prone to get very discouraged and demoralized when things go wrong in their lives. They do not have as much tolerance for those changes, because they do not have a wider perspective that would give them equanimity.

15

Leave Dharma and Go!

The person of faith
in the eighty-four thousand gates of Dharma
may turn away from sinful actions.
One must engage in virtuous activity;

The Buddha's teachings are categorized into eighty-four thousand different subjects, or "gates of dharma." The essence of the Buddha's teachings on all of the eighty-four thousand Dharma subjects fall into the three trainings we have been discussing: the training of wisdom, of discipline, and of meditation. The Dharma teachings help our mind become more liberated from the core afflictions of ignorance, desire, and anger. The more faith we cultivate in the Dharma, the more we will stay away from negative actions and engage in positive activities.

The Buddha's teachings are like medicine; there are so many teachings because there are so many afflictions. When we are sick with afflictions, we need to diagnose and treat those imbalances with the correct Dharma medicine. Nothing else can take away our mental and emotional pain and suffering. We have to use the Dharma to train the mind and to experience freedom. The way that we face our current pain and suffering is a good indication of how we will face our own death.

Understanding the essence of the Dharma will depend on whether we believe in karma. If we believe in karma, we will change how we are living. We may have to make some sacrifices. We may feel very uncomfortable as we begin to recognize the ways in which we are producing more negative karma.

People often come to Dharma centers with the hope that they will do some meditation and light some candles and feel some increased happiness and peace. But as they meditate, they may confront some very ugly truths about how they have been living and how they have been treating others. They may find the teachings on karma very challenging. It may be very hard to take accountability for our own negative actions and the resulting consequences.

It is important for us as spiritual practitioners to understand which activities are harmful and which activities are virtuous. We have done so much out of ignorance in the past; because we were ignorant of karma, we did not even understand the results of our actions. We may have acted out of desire and anger countless times, feeling certain that our actions were justified. We may never have realized how much harm these actions actually bring to others, or how much they have been poisoning our own mind. We may be angry at someone else, but as long as we are angry we remain connected with that enemy, carrying the poison of that anger with us everywhere we go.

Through understanding karma, we have the opportunity to make corrections. We can hold ourselves accountable. We can take inventory of our lives and confess our negative thoughts and actions. We can accept responsibility for actions that have caused harm to others and to ourselves. We should try to learn from these negative actions and their results.

In ordinary life, we become so focused on pursuing our goals that we do not consider how this pursuit negatively impacts those around us or the earth. We approach so many things in our lives as if they were wars. We go to the battlefield determined to win, regardless of how much pain and suffering we have to inflict on our enemies. On a smaller scale, we do this when we approach any conflict with anger and determination to win or profit from the situation.

If we want to live that kind of life, then maybe we will win many wars. Maybe we will be incredibly successful and build an empire. But eventually, in this lifetime or a future life, we will face the karmic consequences of how we have lived. This is simple cause and result. We will have to experience the consequences of our nonvirtuous actions.

We can see how this is happening at the collective level in our world. We go into everything with this warlike mentality. No one is at peace; everyone is restless. Even if we are not actively engaging in nonvirtuous activity, we sense the collective restlessness and unhappiness, and that has a negative impact on us. Human beings are creating collective karma, which is also impacting us at the individual level. Human beings are harming the earth, and that harm is then causing us illness and suffering.

Even our entertainment is conducted like a battle! All of our reality TV shows and our sports are based on a winner and a loser. We get so much excitement out of watching these competitions. We play video games and watch movies that increase our negative emotions. The more we fuel this aggression within us, the more aggressive our whole society becomes.

Why is our society so violent? Why do we support all of these violent games? Why do we have so many shootings? Business leaders want profit more than they want to have a peaceful or safe country. People support these outer expressions of their afflictive emotions because it temporarily brings some relief. Although it is increasing their negative emotions, it can temporarily feel like a good outlet for all of that anger and desire. But ultimately it is increasing their mental suffering.

The teachings help us become more aware of how our own aggression causes pain to ourselves and others. They encourage us to engage in more virtuous activities. According to Buddhism, if we cannot help others, then at the very least we should refrain from causing any harm. This may seem so simple to us, but it is actually very hard to implement in our lives. We aren't even aware of the harm we cause others through lack of awareness. We may underestimate the harm that verbal aggression or even gossip can cause others. The more mindful we become of even the small ways in which our negative emotions harm others, the more we will refrain from that harm and the more peace we will feel.

The more faith we have in the Dharma, the more it will transform our actions into virtuous activities. We will act with loving-kindness and compassion to help others. If we cannot help others, at least we should try our best not to harm others. That is how we can live according to the natural law of karma and according to the essence of Buddhism. These are the two essential practices we can integrate into every aspect of our lives.

Even within a twenty-four-hour period, we face so many choices and challenges. We have so many ethical dilemmas where we are unsure of what is the right thing to do. There are so many opportunities for us to commit negative verbal activities. We are so conditioned to be judgmental of others and to criticize them behind their backs. We are very prone to reactivity when someone says something unkind to us. We become angry when someone takes out their aggression by driving aggressively and honking at us.

If we remember the simple discipline of doing virtuous activities and refraining from harming others, we will know how to respond. If we have very negative thoughts, even if we do not act, we are committing harm to ourselves by allowing that negativity to poison us. We should bring awareness to that negativity and allow it to dissolve. The more negative thoughts we have, the more likely it is that we will engage in negative verbal conduct or action. Just this simple guidance can help us navigate any challenge that arises. We can see such positive transformation if we live according to this conduct. We can become free of that vicious cycle of negative emotions and reactions.

it is necessary to possess a mind without [mundane] activity.
Further, give up Dharma activities and go!

Jetsun Rinpoche is advising us to abandon all eight worldly dharmas related to the mundane activities and to leave our mind alone in its original natural state. If these mundane activities obscure and distract the mind further away from the original pure natural state instead of helping us to see that original state, then it is better to abandon even what appear to be Dharma activities.

Rinpoche is pointing out how the practice and the practitioner can be mismatched, and how practitioners can use practices incorrectly. In the following lines, he illustrates the potential shortcomings of the practitioner and the faults and spiritual deviations of these thirteen Dharma activities that were prevalent in Tibet at the time he was composing this doha.

Do not slander the Dharma
and do not abuse the person.
Perceiving a confusion between Dharma and person,
one may then ask how that is perceived;
a person is perceived to be misled with Dharma
because of [their] inferior intelligence and small learning.
Without possessing the goal of realization,
greatly exaggerating and disparaging Dharma teachings and persons,
covered by the worm spittle of conceptuality,[39]
grabbed by the hook of the Mara of conceit,
without the key point of many being of one taste;
leave also Kadampa dharma and go!

Sometimes we experience the slander of Dharma and the scolding of practitioners within different Buddhist traditions. For several years, I was conducting my classes at the Cambridge Buddhist Association in Cambridge, Massachusetts. It was one of the oldest Zen centers in the

39. This metaphor refers to speaking about Dharma practices from a purely conceptual point of view, one that is not integrated with personal experience.

United States, founded by a member of one of the most prominent Boston families. During those years, I had meetings and discussions with two other resident teachers. One teacher was a Theravadin monk, and the other was a Mahayana Zen priest. Neither of these teachers accepted Tantra as Buddhist practice.

The Theravadin monk challenged me on many aspects of Vajrayana practice. He asked, "Why do Tibetan sanghas have to do prostrations and respect those married lamas?" According to Theravada tradition, monks don't prostrate to lay teachers, and also no one sits higher than the fully ordained monks. Theravadin monks don't accept the Mahayana sutras, including the *Heart Sutra*, which was one of the main practices of the Zen priest. Theravadins only accept the suttas collected in the Pali Tripitaka as the words of the Buddha.

On the other hand, the Zen priest accepted the Theravada Pali Tripitaka and the Sanskrit Mahayana sutras. But neither the monk nor the priest accepted the tantras as the Buddha's teachings. Instead, they shared their belief that tantra is a Hindu tradition. I told them that I accepted Theravada, Mahayana, as well as Tantra, as the Buddha's teachings. I invited them to study all of these traditions with an open mind instead of drawing conclusions without deepening their knowledge.

Each spiritual tradition has its own way of searching. We have so many different methods. We have developed so many spiritual languages. What has led us to the spiritual path? What are we searching for? What are our methods for exploring the ultimate truth? It is very positive for spiritual communities if we can stay open and curious about other traditions.

It is important to know the essence of what we are trying to realize in our Buddhist practice. Not all Buddhists would agree on why they are practicing. Our spiritual goals are in accordance with our level of understanding; with the school of Buddhism we are studying; and with our own intelligence, curiosity, and awareness. Jetsun Rinpoche is reminding us not to get trapped within a certain school. He has enumerated thirteen different risks or missteps that we can take if we do not have a clear understanding of why we are doing our spiritual practices.

Rinpoche is saying that even the Kadampa teaching of mind-training, although it is especially good for people whose minds are more wild, should not become a dogma. There is a risk in all of the traditions that someone may become self-righteous, feeling that they somehow are more pure or moral than others, due to their spiritual practice. This is a dangerous pitfall if we use our practice to inflate our ego.

Sometimes monastics will have good discipline but will become rigid and biased and discriminating toward others. They may look down on people who are not on the spiritual path and they may esteem their own moral conduct. This may increase their pride and their ego.

In a similar way, Buddhist scholars can become very attached to their point of view. They may lose the skill of listening to others. They may stop being open to different perspectives. They may become very obsessed with their own theories and conclusions. If they are esteeming their own ideas to the point where they feel superior, then this is also a dangerous fault. They are using the Dharma to increase their pride and their arrogance.

There is also a risk that meditators will become very biased against scholars and scholarship. They may treat Buddhist study as worthless compared to meditation. They may think that scholars can write about spiritual experience but have no personal realization of the truth. Meditators may also be building up their own egos through esteeming their path and judging other Buddhists. Rinpoche is warning us not to get attached to one method, one school, or one way of connecting with the Dharma and practice. Instead, while committing to one's personal practice, method, tradition or school, one should still respect others with an open mind.

Not making a distinction between the acceptance and rejection of virtue and nonvirtue,
pretending to be knowledgeable without having understanding,
performing wild conduct without heat,
creating deceptions and filling the country with lies;
leave also yogin dharma and go!

Jetsun Rinpoche is referring here to those yogins who pretend to be learned without having much understanding of karma. They don't even know what to reject or accept regarding virtues and nonvirtues. They also perform wild conduct without achieving the heat on the first level of the path of application. With such pretentious lies, they deceive the faithful country folk.

Rinpoche is referring to meditators who think they have had some spiritual realization, and then become teachers or gurus who use their power to mislead people. Although Dharma practice and study should be done for the right reasons, Rinpoche is cautioning us about how easily spiritual practice can be abused, increasing our negative emotions and causing harm to others.

Having accepted secret mantra as Dharma
without possessing the ripening path of abhisheka,
separated from the key points of the method of the path of liberation
because of not having met a lord of secret mantra;[40]
leave also Mahamudra dharma and go!

Jetsun Rinpoche is referring to those tantric practitioners who accept mahamudra—realized through the practice of the two stages of anuttarayoga tantra—but then try to practice mahamudra without receiving the ripening empowerment and the methods of the liberating path. It is better to abandon such mahamudra practice that is not connected with any tantric deity—a "lord of secret mantra"—such as Vajrayogini.

Having accepted Mahayana as Dharma,
separated from compassion and bodhichitta,
action, dharma, and person are not connected

40. Here, "having met a lord of secret mantra" refers to realizing a deity, for example, Vajrayogini, as the union of clarity and emptiness—that is, mahamudra.

in the dharma of the effortless basis;[41]
leave also Dzogchen dharma and go!

Jetsun Rinpoche is continuing to warn us about the spiritual traps and deviations and how to abandon the common faults on the spiritual path. There is a danger that we will begin to identify too strongly with a certain practice. We may actually use that identification to increase our ego or to reject other traditions. We may identify ourselves by our religion, saying, "I'm a Buddhist," or "I'm a Christian." If we are identifying with a theistic religion, then first we need to have some understanding of what God is. If we understand God as love and compassion, then we can try to transform ourselves so that we can embody those qualities. That identification can help us to increase our virtue and positive qualities and to benefit others.

On the other hand, if we bring God down to our level, if we use God to bolster our own ego, and claim that our religious views are the only truth, then there is a danger that we can become extremists or fanatics. In that case, our religion may actually increase our anger. We may feel hatred toward those who do not share our views of God. This is true in all traditions. We can use our spirituality as a basis for personal transformation and the benefit of others, or we can use our spirituality to increase our ego and our extremism.

As we've discussed, Rinpoche is warning us regarding the Buddhist traditions that were prevalent in Tibet at the time when he was writing this doha. We may identify ourselves as Dzogchen practitioners. Dzogchen is a very high practice. But if we are not at that level yet, then what happens is we bring Dzogchen down to our level and use it to increase our own pride and ego. Instead of transforming, we may actually increase our negative qualities! There are many ancient Dzogchen stories that illustrate this danger.

---

41. The "dharma of the effortless basis" refers to the nature of the mind, the union of clarity and emptiness.

Once there was a Dzogchen master who had two disciples. The master was introducing the disciples to *rigpa*, the nature of the mind. One disciple concluded, "Oh, now that the master has taught me about ultimate reality and liberation, I can freely do whatever I want to do!" Instead of transforming, that disciple committed many unvirtuous activities and increased his negative karma. The other disciple practiced in a graduated way and slowly progressed along the path. His practice became stronger and his understanding grew more profound.

A practitioner needs to start where they are. Dzogchen is the "great perfection"; it is the pinnacle of realization in the Nyingma tradition. We need to be realistic about our personal practice, understanding that, at our level, it is still imperfect. We need to bring that humility and that dedication to our practice.

If we merely adopt Dzogchen practices as an identity and believe that we have immediately realized that great perfection, and if we suddenly think we can do whatever we feel like doing because we have achieved liberation, then we are doomed. Our negative qualities will only increase if we have this misunderstanding.

The Mahayana practice of cultivating compassion and bodhichitta is at the heart of Dzogchen practice. The purpose of that practice is to achieve enlightenment in order to help sentient beings. But if we misunderstand and think that now we have realized freedom and can do whatever we please, then action, dharma, and person are not connected.

We should not be mistaken and think that Rinpoche is denigrating any of these thirteen traditions he is warning us about. On the contrary, he is warning about the pitfalls for the practitioner if they misunderstand, misuse, or misidentify with any tradition or teachings. These warnings are for the practitioner, not a rejection of the practice itself.

Like a rabbit with horns, the aggregates are without a basis—
in particular, counting mouths, eyes, and wrinkles,
searching for a characteristic without a basis of a characteristic;
leave also Abhidharma and go!

The purpose of studying the Abhidharma is to cultivate wisdom. "Abhidharma," means "seeing the Dharma." But if we do not see the Dharma properly, if our study is only increasing our concepts and thoughts, then it is not helping us to achieve liberation. We all know that rabbits do not possess horns! In the same way, the aggregates are without a basis. If our study of the Abhidharma only increases our identification with characteristics instead of purifying the characteristics, then the Abhidharma is not helping us to transform. "Mouths, eyes, and wrinkles," refers to the physical *ayatanas*.[42] If we do not understand the nature of emptiness, then our "counting of mouths, eyes, and wrinkles"—that is, the five aggregates, the twelve ayatanas, and the eighteen *dhatus*—is no different from counting the horns of a rabbit. Rinpoche is warning us that if we study the Abhidharma without cultivating wisdom, then it will be about as useful as counting the horns of a rabbit.

A reckoning that connects contradiction with contradiction
to deceptive, unreal, deluded appearances is meaningless
and, not benefiting the mind, one is deceived at the time of death;
leave also logic dharma and go!

We should use logic in order to validate the ultimate truth in the mind. In Buddhist philosophy, there are three types of logic: direct logic, inferential logic, and scriptural logic. But if we learn logic and apply it with ego, becoming a contrarian who debates everyone and gets caught in ideas, then we are not benefiting our own spiritual growth or anyone around us. If our study of logic is not benefiting the mind, then we will even be deceived at the point of death, and all our debating will not result in any transformation. Logicians may appear very smart and skillful—they may have a very rational and calculating brain—but if they don't gain any insight into the ultimate truth, then all of that debating will not be very helpful.

Jetsun Rinpoche is reminding us that all of this logic is only based on

42. Tib. *skye mched*; often translated as "sense bases."

relative truth; it is not ultimate. A "reckoning that connects contradiction with contradiction" is only able to prove the relative truth. It does not help us to realize the ultimate truth; it does not help us to achieve buddhahood. That is why Rinpoche is instructing us to "leave also logic dharma and go!"

Possessing an internal tumor of grasping truth in deluded appearances,
holding the acceptance of emptiness as the essence;
with the effort of establishing the pervasion of the minor premise;[43]
leave also Madhyamaka dharma and go!

Madhyamaka teachings, like those in the *Heart Sutra*, are always talking about emptiness. We are taught, "Form (matter) is emptiness. Emptiness is form. Form is not other than emptiness, nor is emptiness other than form." But if we are merely expressing emptiness through speech while our mind is still clinging and grasping onto the apparent objects, then all of these verbal expressions of emptiness will be of no help!

There are many syllogisms in Madhyamaka: the syllogism of neither one nor many to investigate the nature of emptiness, the syllogism of vajra fragments to investigate causality, the syllogism of refuting the arising of existence and nonexistence to investigate the result, the syllogism of refuting the four possibilities of arising to investigate both cause and result, the syllogism of dependent arising to investigate the lack of true existence of all phenomena, and so forth. There is also the famous Chandrakirti's sevenfold reasons of the chariot, used to investigate the nonexistence of a permanent self within a person.

If these methods help us to realize the empty nature of the mind, then they are useful and transformative. But if they remain at the level of speech, and the mind is still filled with grasping, then they will not be of much benefit.

43. "Minor premise" is a term used in a logical syllogism.

Spending life pursuing conventional words,
having no understanding of the meaning of mind, however knowledgeable,
when death comes, one dies in a body of delusion;
leave also dialectical dharma and go!

Jetsun Rinpoche is referring to the dialectical dharma of those who pursue knowledge based on words and definitions of characteristics for how to impute and identify dharmas (phenomenal objects). The purpose of learning in Buddhism is to help us achieve liberation *from* these imputable objects. The purpose is to realize the wisdom that helps us to see the empty nature of the objects instead of remaining attached to these imputable objects. This is the reason why we have three gateways to liberation. The three gateways are (1) all phenomena have the nature of emptiness beyond conceptual reference, (2) all phenomena have the nature of characterlessness beyond conceptual thought, and (3) all phenomena have the nature of wishlessness beyond acceptance and rejection.

"Dialectical dharma" defines each and every object based on characteristics—unique characteristics, general characteristics, and contrary characteristics. Dialectical dharma may help us to increase our conventional knowledge, but if this dialectical dharma is not helping transform the mind, then, at the time of death, we may still die with ignorance and delusion.

The master, not possessing qualifications,
makes dharma connections[44] with the following three:
greedily charging prices for Dharma,
enjoying the consort of the guru without samaya,
and being attached to both union and liberation without the method;
leave also Vajrayana dharma and go!

44. "Makes dharma connections" means creating disciples.

Jetsun Rinpoche is referring here to those tantric ritual masters who go around to the families in the villages in Tibet performing unsolicited initiations and rituals for destruction and liberation, and then implying that the families need to make offerings. Many ritual masters can perform different pujas, but they don't have any knowledge of the meanings of the rituals—they merely recite the words like a parrot. There are many stories where such "masters" drink Tibetan beer, called *chang*, and, at the end of the day, they become very drunk and engage in wild conduct without honoring the tantric samaya. Rinpoche is warning us about such tantric practitioners.

"Union" refers to the yoga of sexual union with a qualified consort. "Liberation" refers to the destructive rituals that annihilate evil sentient beings. "Method" refers to proper compassion and motivation.

Held in the prison of misconduct of body and speech,
mind itself is without the view and meaning of meditation.
Duplicitous hardship is purposeless;
leave also ordained dharma and go!

Generally, fully ordained monks are supposed to keep more than 253 precepts, and fully ordained nuns are supposed to keep more than 364 precepts. All those precepts are related to the physical and verbal conduct of the pratimoksha vows. When any of those precepts are broken, they become "misconduct of body and speech." My khenpo used to remark that "sometimes one may feel that one has taken those precepts in order to break them, because no one is perfect and precepts are very easy to break." Many of these monastics don't even know all of the rules they are supposed to keep!

Generally, one becomes Buddhist by taking refuge vows. By taking refuge in the Dharma, no Buddhist should harm others. From refuge vows, all Buddhists take some form of the pratimoksha vows, up to and including the bhikshu and bhikshuni vows of full ordination. Then, after taking bodhisattva vows, one has to keep eighteen root vows, forty-six secondary vows, and eight vows of ritually maintaining bodhichitta. After taking tantric samayas, one has to keep fourteen root vows, fourteen branch commitments, and the gross vows. Those who practice mother tantra also need to keep eight left-side mother tantra commitments. Since we are not perfect, we may break those vows, and that is the reason why confession practices, like reciting the mantra of Vajrasattva, are incorporated into our daily sadhana to renew the vows. When we make mistakes, it is better to have received the vows and then do the required confession than to have not taken the vows at all. Some masters say that if one has taken all three levels of vows, it is most important to protect the highest tantric samaya—even if keeping samaya means breaking one's pratimoksha vows, that is justified.

I've heard stories of ordained monks joining the army to fight against their enemies, and then being praised by the community as a hero. Many monastics travel by plane these days, and they go through customs without declaring the value of the goods they are carrying, avoiding paying whatever taxes are due. Many don't even care to file income taxes. There are also religious figures claiming themselves as emanations of such and such enlightened buddha without any proof. Can these misdeeds break their precepts? Followers generally overlook such misconduct, except the misconduct occurs between opposite genders.

Jetsun Rinpoche is cautioning that ordained sangha members should not become prisoners of their own precepts. Sometimes, in temples and monasteries there is a misunderstanding that Buddhism is only about observing the precepts. Sanghas may become very extreme about these precepts. They may think that you are only a Buddhist if you are correctly observing all of these rules, and if you are breaking any of these rules, you are not a Buddhist. For example, according to some traditions, if you eat meat you are breaking a precept. Whatever precepts we take, if this discipline is not integrated with view and meditation, then we will not experience much inner transformation. If we esteem our precepts and practices as the best and the only correct way to practice Buddhism, then we can easily fall into wrong views.

Ignorantly meditating without hearing and contemplation,
doing construction or sewing when sitting,
behaving with misconduct if one goes to the village,
ending meditation sessions in foggy and sluggish sleep;
if one looks, one looks for gifts,
permitting those with gifts into the retreat boundary,
leaving those without gifts outside;
supporting their relatives by feeding them with devotional offerings;
leave also great meditator's dharma and go!

Even if we appear to be on retreat and doing meditation, if we are actually still focused on these worldly things, then it will not be very beneficial. If we meditate without receiving instruction or engaging in any contemplation on the teachings, then our meditation practice will not be very good. Or maybe we think that we can multitask, we can meditate while doing some simple activity like sewing or constructing something. Unless we have a high level of realization, we will not actually be in a meditative state while engaging in those activities. Maybe we appear to be deep in meditation but internally our mind is actually very sleepy and sluggish. Or maybe we meditate all day but then go down to the village and engage in misconduct.

If a meditator only permits the wealthy benefactors to go inside retreat houses and stops others outside the gates, then the retreat boundary is loose and not properly sealed. If the meditators use the devotional offerings to benefit their relatives, then they may become sinful. That is why Jetsun Rinpoche warns us that one should leave the great meditator's dharma if one has fallen into these faults.

Not understanding if the profound Dharma is explained;
enjoying jokes, pointless idle talk,
seductive dances, and song;
the dharma and view of these deceitful ones is merely "in the mouth."
Creating calumny and disputes here and there;
if they can, robbing wealth from the neighbor's home;

disregarding family responsibilities and remaining idle;
leave also housewife dharma and go!

Jetsun Rinpoche is advising housewives not to use the Dharma as an excuse to engage in these non-Dharmic activities. Rinpoche is warning that those who do not understand the profound Dharma should not use Dharma as an excuse to throw away one's family responsibilities and engage in idle talk, entertaining by singing songs and making jokes, misusing Dharma to deceive others, creating calumny and disharmony among the sangha, or robbing wealth from others—which refers to cheating others including one's friends and neighbors in the name of the Dharma.

Profit, fame, conflicts, arguments,
livelihood, frustration, dissatisfaction:
a source of misfortune and suffering opposed to virtuous dharmas;
spending life in misery without any purpose,
there is nowhere to go but down into the three lower realms;
leave also householder dharma and go!

Jetsun Rinpoche is referring to the spiritual deviations of householder Dharma. They misuse Dharma for the sake of the eight worldly dharmas like profit, fame, and so forth. While engaging in the eight worldly dharmas, they face many conflicts, arguments, struggles, and discontent. They experience so much misery in their present lives due to the karmic results of committing those nonvirtues. In the next life, they may be reborn in the lower realms with lots of suffering. Rinpoche is advising us to leave such householder's dharma.

In all of these thirteen examples, Rinpoche is not saying that we should stop practicing! He is saying that we should stop identifying with a Dharma practice and tradition if it is causing us to not engage in proper practice. If we are using any Dharma practice or tradition as a facade, not really practicing or experiencing any real transformation, then we need to leave all of that identification behind. We must leave anything that is not conducive to our practice and transformation.

First, leave nonvirtuous activities;
in the middle, leave mundane activities;
finally, leave Dharma activities.

The mind of the yogin who has relinquished activities is happy;
the great meditator who gathers wealth is a layperson;
meditating with characteristics is conceptuality;
the virtuous actions of body and speech are misconduct.

First, we should try to purify all of our negative karma, all of the nonvirtuous activities. Next, we should leave the mundane activities. These are the neutral activities that are merely wasting our time, like watching television for hours or going to watch sports instead of practicing. If there is some spiritual benefit in activities, then that is fine, but otherwise, if entertainment is merely making us lazier and more distracted from our spiritual path, then we should abandon those neutral activities. "Finally, leave Dharma activities," refers to those preceding thirteen worldly dharma activities.

If we are in the state of mahamudra, if we are in the state of awakening, then there is nothing left to practice. The final result is to remain in the state of mahamudra, free from all proliferations, free from all of the extremes. As we have discussed, all activities start with volition in the mind. First, there is the mental karma, then the verbal and physical actions arise as a result of that volition. If the mind is in the state that is free from all karma, then the body and speech are also naturally free from activities. When the mind of the yogi relinquishes all activities, there is an experience of profound peace and joy. When we are no longer chasing after worldly things, no longer accumulating wealth or chasing after fame, then we can experience this deep peace.

Meditation should help us to overcome all of the characteristics, all of the conceptuality. If, instead, our meditation increases our conceptual thinking based on the characteristics, then it's not beneficial. If the activities of our body and speech are not conducive to remaining in the state of mahamudra, then we have to consider them misconduct. Even if they appear positive and virtuous, if they are disturbing our state of mahamudra, then they are not helping and we should leave these activities.

Without activity, leave the six consciousnesses relaxed.

Leaving the six consciousnesses relaxed without activity refers to how we can become a witness to everything happening around us related to the six sense objects. Usually we react with desire if objects are agreeable and react with anger if objects are disagreeable. Those two reactions happen if we have not discovered the nature of the mind. As a consequence, all objects of the six consciousnesses become conceptual, emotional, and karmic objects. But if we remain in the deep experience of the meditative state of rigpa—basic awareness—we will have the experience of relaxation due to the self-liberated six consciousnesses. We can witness all objects without any reaction because we can see the empty nature of all objects.

If attached, even attachment to the deity is bondage.
If desirous, even desire for buddhahood is deluded.
If grasping, even grasping at Dharma is deceived.
Dissolve awareness into the natural state.

There is no way to experience ultimate reality without knowing the nature of the mind. If we use our practice to increase our attachment to the Buddha, or to whatever deity we are practicing in our sadhana, then we remain in bondage. If our practice is increasing our desire to attain buddhahood, then we are also not having any true experience of the spaciousness of our own mind. If we don't experience clarity and emptiness within us, we will never be able to see the true nature of reality.

Spiritual study and practice are like a bridge that we must use to go beyond the river of samsara. But it is easy to become attached to the bridge instead. Maybe we write books about the bridge. Maybe we sit on the bridge and meditate for many hours. But if we do not understand that the bridge is only there to help us cross the river, we may lose perspective and remain attached to the bridge forever.

If we can see our own true nature, we can be liberated from samsara. We can go beyond the bridge, beyond the river of suffering, beyond all of our attachments to the practices or to the result. Jetsun Rinpoche is reminding us to "leave the six consciousnesses relaxed." As long as there is some strain and some effort in our activities and Dharma practices, then our consciousness and our sense organs are not relaxed. We become preoccupied with the Dharma objects, whether they are ideas or statues or teachers. The attachment to the objects keeps our mind in bondage, even to the Dharma.

We cannot experience spiritual bliss without some level of relaxation of all of the senses, of all of the grasping after objects. Yogis who have used their practice to see the true nature of their own minds can relax into a blissful state. Understanding that clarity and emptiness allows them to let go of all of the grasping. Once they have crossed that river, they let go of the bridge itself.

The Heart Sutra mantra—*Tadyatha om gate gate paragate parasamgate bodhi svaha*—also has the same meaning of going beyond. We are going to the next level on the five paths and ten stages of Mahayana or on the thirteen stages of Vajrayana. The practitioner leaves and goes to the next level, and finally goes completely beyond into the awakened state of enlightenment, which is *bodhi*.

16

The Oral Instruction for Those Who Understand

This is the oral instruction for those who understand:

Awareness flows into the emptiness of mind;
characteristics of grasping and grasper are liberated at
their own place;
even the term "biased opinion" does not exist;
the mind realized in the view is blissful.

JETSUN RINPOCHE IS INSTRUCTING us that the purpose of all of the traditions and practices is to go beyond, to see the true nature of the mind. Once we have seen the true nature of the mind, that truth is blissful. We should not misunderstand bliss as meaning simply feelings of pleasure or happiness. Bliss in this context is a state of peace and awareness that transcends all emotion. Bliss is beyond the five aggregates of form, feeling, ideation, formation, and consciousness. Bliss is not a personal experience; when we experience the true nature of our own mind we also experience the bliss of the universe. We can think of this as a cosmic experience, not a personal feeling.

When we realize the nature of the mind as the union of clarity and emptiness, we have the experience of the great bliss of wisdom. This bliss is free from the characteristics of grasping to both subject and object as well as free from any extremes or biased opinions. This wisdom causes the characteristics of grasping and grasper to simply disappear—to be "liberated at their own place." Rongton Sheja Kunrig taught that by abandoning the perception of the basis as real, the gateway to emptiness will be opened. By meditating on the path as lacking true characteristics, the gateway to the absence of characteristics will be opened. By abandoning the hope of gaining results through realizing emptiness, the gateway to wishlessness will be opened. When we have gained confidence in the view, meditation, conduct, and result, through realizing the nature of the mind, we will always be in a blissful state.

Non-distraction flows into non-meditation;
the characteristics of conceptuality are liberated at their own place;
even the terms "sluggishness" and "agitation" do not exist;
the mind realized in meditation is blissful.

When we no longer have any distractions in the mind, then we can experience the bliss of meditation. We need to practice meditation because we have so many distractions. Meditation is like taking medicine. If we have cured the disease, we no longer need to take the medicine. If we no longer have any distraction, then there is no need for meditation.

For a yogi whose mind is very present, all the characteristics of concepts and distractions are already purified. In that state, there is no sluggishness and agitation—the two main obstacles to meditation. We no longer have these faults within our meditation because our mind is always awake; it is always present. In tantric meditation, when you have realized mahamudra, then you are experiencing bliss all the time. This bliss is the union of clarity and emptiness, and of wisdom and compassion.

Naturally occurring [conduct] flows into ceaselessness;
the characteristics of misconduct are liberated at their own place;
even the terms "acceptance" and "rejection" do not exist;
the mind realized in conduct is blissful.

If we are experiencing this blissful state of mind, then we don't need to make any effort. There is no karma and there is no stress. Everything is just naturally occurring; it is ceaselessly flowing. For example, the enlightened activities of the bodhisattvas and the nirmanakaya forms of the buddhas are unfolding spontaneously due to their bodhichitta. They are also free from the characteristics of misconduct. Since their conduct is based on ultimate wisdom, there is nothing to accept or reject. Someone who has achieved buddhahood no longer has any defilements. Everything for them is in that state of wisdom.

Deathlessness flows into the state of non-arising,
the characteristics of hope and fear are liberated at their own place,
even the terms "present" and "future" do not exist;
the mind realized in the result is blissful.

The state of mahamudra, the mind experiencing the wisdom of great bliss, is free from arising and non-arising. One is free from the characteristics of hope and fear in that resultant state. The mind has gone beyond time, it has gone beyond karma, it has gone beyond the cycle of the wheel of life and nirvana. This mahamudra is an unconditioned state.

The view is produced without being eclipsed;
if delusion is destroyed, it is destroyed by this;
having no opinionated bias,
the absence of the harm of grasper and grasped is amazing!

Jetsun Rinpoche is saying that when the nature of the mind and perfect view are integrated, the experience that results is amazing: we are free from the subject (the grasper) and the object (the grasped). We are also free from all bias and extremes. This integration has destroyed all delusions and ignorance. Perfect view is the antidote to all the root defilements.

Unfabricated meditation occurs naturally;
if the paths and stages are reached, they are reached by this;
not having the cause of focusing on objects,
the absence of the harm of sluggishness and agitation is amazing!

When the nature of the mind and perfect meditation are integrated, that experience is amazing: we are freed from all of the faults of meditation, such as sluggishness and agitation. We are also in a meditative state all the time, without needing to make any effort in trying to focus on objects of meditation. With such meditation, we will accomplish the paths and the stages very quickly.

Ceaseless conduct naturally occurs;
if grasping is turned away, it is turned away by this;
not having the thought of refutation and establishment,
the absence of the harm of acceptance and rejection is amazing!

When the nature of the mind and perfect conduct are integrated, that experience is amazing: ceaseless, perfect conduct occurs naturally without any harmful actions. There is no acceptance or rejection. This perfect conduct helps us to turn away from all grasping. Due to this, any thoughts or concepts that would refute or establish any conclusion—due to aversion and attachment—are also freed.

Not seeking the effortlessly produced result,
conventionally, dharmakaya is obtained by this;
not having the thought of abandonment and achievement,
the absence of the harm of hope and fear is amazing!

Jetsun Rinpoche is referring to the amazing experience that occurs when the nature of the mind and the result are integrated as one, and we are free from both hope and fear. We are also free from any thoughts of abandonment and achievement. What conventionally is called "dharmakaya" is obtained spontaneously without effort.

Sometimes there is bliss in the space of the sky;
there is bliss in the state without extremes or center.

Sometimes there is bliss in the depths of the ocean;
there is bliss in the state without movement or agitation.

Sometimes there is bliss in the sun and moon;
there is bliss in the state of unobscured clarity.

Sometimes there is bliss in the middle of a river;
there is bliss in the unceasing state.

Mahamudra is free from all extremes. The "bliss in the space of the sky" describes the realization of the ultimate view. "Bliss in the depths of the ocean" describes the perfection of meditation that is beyond all distraction. "Bliss in the sun and the moon" describes the clear-light nature of the mind. In that clarity, we are aware of everything just as it is, without any obscurations. "Bliss in the middle of a river" describes the ceaseless quality of the awakened state. In that experience of awakening, we cannot say that there is any beginning or end. We have become aware of an unceasing state that has always been there and will always be there because it is the unconditioned, true nature of the mind.

In the experience of bliss, there is no dualism of self and other; there are no opposing forces. We no longer experience ourselves as separate from the universe. We are the bliss of the sky, the bliss of the depths of the ocean. We experience the bliss of the sunlight, the bliss of the moon. We are one with the clarity and emptiness of space.

It is impossible to express this subtle experience of ecstasy through any language. It arises in that state of highest meditation. It is a transcendent experience beyond all of our senses. It is a joy beyond all emotion and circumstances. Because it is not related to objects or external situations, this transcendent joy can be experienced regardless of outer challenges. Highly realized meditators can experience that joy in spite of physical pain or hardship.

This bliss and joy arises from a state of complete equanimity. We can experience that equanimity only when we know the true empty nature of our own mind and of all phenomena. With this knowledge, we will experience freedom from all attachment and aversion and freedom from all dualism. Whatever might happen to us, it will not impact that inner clarity and equanimity.

We can only experience this bliss when we gain an understanding of ultimate reality through seeing the true nature of the mind. Jetsun Rinpoche is cautioning us to leave behind all constructs, all traditions, all philosophy. The purpose of all of our spiritual practice is to realize that true nature of clarity and emptiness of the mind. Once this clarity and emptiness is realized, we can abandon all of these bridges that have helped us to cross the river of samsara.

This state of unceasing clarity and emptiness is unconditioned. Whatever path we may follow, the purpose is to awaken to that bliss of the union of clarity and emptiness. All of our methods are merely paths to the same truth. As we have discussed, they are like a staircase; the goal is to eventually go beyond the staircase itself. Rinpoche is cautioning us not to get attached to our own method. If we see the method as being the result, then we will never be liberated. Instead, we will remain stuck on that staircase or standing on that bridge, unable to go beyond it. Rinpoche is urging us to leave these traditions and go cross that bridge!

This need to eventually transcend every method is why we have the completion practices in all our sadhanas. If we are practicing an Istadevata sadhana, we need to go *beyond* devata. We cannot become attached to the deity. This is why there is a dissolution practice in our guru yoga and completion practices. All of the higher Vajrayana practices include this training in transcendence. If we are practicing correctly, we will not become attached to the bridge or to the stairs. We will not become attached to the deity or to the guru. We will understand that all of our methods are intended to help us go beyond, to experience the ultimate liberation, the ultimate awakening to our true nature.

Sometimes there is bliss in the presence of the guru;
there is bliss in the oral instructions for cutting proliferation.

Sometimes there is bliss residing in retreat;
there is bliss in practicing in solitude.

Sometimes there is bliss in the middle of the market;
there is bliss in carrying appearances into the path.

Sometimes there is bliss in a row of yogins;
there is bliss in comparing experiential realization.

Sometimes there is bliss in the midst of begging lepers;
there is bliss in performing the conduct of equal taste.

Sometimes there is bliss in the wide-open country;
there is bliss in wandering aimless and alone.

There is bliss when permanently abiding in reality;
there is bliss in the state without bias or partiality.

The conduct of "equal taste" means that wherever we are, whatever is happening around us, it is all the same; there is no good or bad, no attachment or aversion, no hope or fear. Equal taste means that regardless of where we are and what is happening around us, we are always in that awakened state beyond all dualism, beyond all disturbance.

Jetsun Rinpoche is advising us here how to enhance our practices according to the seven equalizing-taste practices of bliss, which are ordered as follows: (1) One starts by receiving oral instructions on listening and contemplating in order to begin one's practice with certainty and confidence on the path. (2) After receiving all necessary instructions, one practices alone in solitude until one's meditation is stabilized. (3) After stable meditation has been accomplished, one then practices in the middle of the market in order to develop the ability to carry all the distracting appearances into the path and to strengthen one's practice and realization. (4) One then exchanges accounts of one's realization with other yogins, which helps to validate and increase one's realization. (4) One challenges one's conduct by practicing "one taste" among lepers in order to experience equalizing bliss. (6) In order to heighten the realization, one practices the conduct of a wandering yogi[45] traveling alone without any goal or expectation. (7) One remains in the resulting state of ultimate reality without any conditions, in the great bliss of wisdom.

At this level of highest realization, we are always in a state of bliss. The authentic guru has the qualifications and blessings to help that state of great bliss arise in our mind. Through the guru's blessings—in the form of oral instructions, empowerments, transmissions, and so forth—the guru can help us to cut through all the proliferations, including our ego.

Rinpoche is saying here that wherever we are, the mind will experience bliss if we are in that awakened state. We will experience bliss residing in retreat. We will experience bliss even in the midst of a busy, loud market. Whatever may be happening around us will not interfere with our equanimity, with our blissful awareness. If we are with other yogis, we can help to increase each other's realization through validating each other's spiritual experiences.

In the awakened state there is nothing to reject and nothing to accept. We can be in the midst of begging lepers, or surrounded by a contagious disease, and yet we will remain in that state of bliss, without aversion or fear. If we have very strong faith, like Mother Teresa, we may be fearless. Mother Teresa did everything for those with leprosy—

45. Skt. *charyagate*; Tib. *spyod pa la gshegs pa*.

bathing, feeding, treating, and caring for them. She said that she was doing all of this in service to God. Because of this devotion, she was able to serve others selflessly and without any aversion.

When we see the true nature of reality, it doesn't matter where we are—even if we are wandering aimless and alone, we will always be at ease, we will always be at home in the mind. When we are in this state of ultimate reality, we are always in a state of bliss.

In the beginning, a good consultation arose;
in the middle, enjoyment arose;
finally, mental bliss arose.

Early in our spiritual path, we need a "good consultation" to arise. This means we need to study, we need to contemplate, and we need to receive instructions from the guru. "In the middle, enjoyment arose" means that then we have to practice. Enjoyment, here, is not ordinary pleasure; it refers to tasting that experience of meditation, that deepening awareness of meditative stability. "Finally, mental bliss arose" refers to the result, the ultimate awakening to the true nature of the mind—which, once it has been realized, results in an unceasing state of bliss.

By leaving activities, one is connected to the beginning of the path;

Here, when Jetsun Rinpoche says that "one is connected to the beginning of the path," he is referring to entering the noble path of seeing—the third of the five paths of a bodhisattva. This path of seeing is achieved only when the practitioner has gone beyond the first two worldly paths, wherein they accumulate virtue and merit while also purifying nonvirtue. "Leaving activities" refers to renouncing and abandoning nonvirtuous activities and going beyond the activities of accumulating merit in order to enter the path of seeing.

by relaxing, the paths and stages are reached;

When Jetsun Rinpoche says, "by relaxing," he is referring to the fourth path, the path of meditation. On the path of meditation, one repeatedly meditates on the realization of selflessness that one has gained on the third path, the path of seeing. The first path—the path of accumulation—and the second path—the path of application—are classified as worldly paths, as one on these paths has still to realize selflessness. Once one is on the fourth path (of meditation), focusing on the selflessness that has been realized on the third path (of seeing), one enters a supremely relaxed state, and can accomplish the remaining paths and stages very quickly.

by covering the head, the distance is clearly seen.

The phrase that Jetsun Rinpoche uses here—"covering the head"—carries the meaning of shading one's eyes. The eye that is to be shaded here is not the ordinary human eye, but the eye of wisdom. And when Rinpoche says, "the distance is clearly seen" he is referring to seeing beyond both time and space, seeing the past and future in the present moment. Thus, when we have completed all the paths and stages of meditation—when we have shaded our eyes (or "covered the head")—we are able to see very far into the distance. When we have realized the wisdom eye, we are able to see beyond all obscurations, beyond time and space; we can see the past, the present, and the future.

Even the deepest hell of sentient beings
is the Dharma palace of Akanishtha.
Even the suffering of both hot and cold [hells]
is the dharmakaya free from proliferation.

Even philosophical conclusions of non-Buddhists
are the essential meaning of Madhyamaka.
Even the oral instructions of the holy gurus
are illusions deceived by illusions.

Even one's own experience of realization
is a picture drawn on water.
Even the arising of the five paths and ten stages
is like counting the number of horns on a rabbit.

Even the accomplished Buddha
is just a name without ultimate existence.
Even dharmata established by awareness
is a banana tree without a heartwood.[46]

Jetsun Rinpoche is speaking of the eight different experiences of equalizing taste. These eight experiences involve going beyond, or equalizing into one taste, all likes and dislikes regarding suffering and happiness, gain and loss, the pleasant (fame) and the unpleasant (infamy), praise and blame. Other texts speak of a variant set of seven experiences of equalizing taste: (1) all appearances are equalized into mind, (2) all mind and mental activities are equalized into illusion, (3) all illusions are equalized into dependent origination, (4) all dependent originations are equalized into emptiness, (5) all emptiness is equalized into union, (6) all union is equalized into nonduality, and finally (7) all nonduality is equalized into all-pervasive space.

When we have become an enlightened buddha, then everything is a pure realm. Even hell is perceived as Akanishtha—the highest of the pure realms. At this level of realization, all the philosophical conclusions—whether Buddhist or non-Buddhist—are the same in the sense that they are, by nature, free from all four extremes. This is the realization of Madhyamaka.

Rinpoche goes on to say that "even the oral instructions of the holy gurus" are relative. This is because the guru cannot transfer their realization to you. For someone who is practicing but doesn't yet have any realization, the instructions are only relative—they are not ultimate.

---

46. In the same way that a banana tree has no heartwood, or center, dharmata, too, has no substantiality.

This is what Rinpoche means by "illusion." Furthermore, any realization we may have will only be like "drawing on water," the experience of realization itself being empty by nature. The five paths and ten stages "are like counting the number of horns on a rabbit," in the sense that these stages are all still relative rather than ultimate.

Even the achievement of buddhahood is only a name without any ultimate existence. Only the experience of clarity and emptiness, of wisdom and compassion, is ultimate. When the dharmata—the empty nature of all phenomena—becomes established by our awareness, it is without essence. In this awareness of emptiness, we see that all phenomena do not inherently exist. Ultimately, we cannot say whether something is existent, nonexistent, both, or neither. The true awareness of emptiness is free from all extremes.

Because the realization of reality without activities
and the verbal view without certain knowledge
resemble one another, there is a danger of error.

In the following lines, Jetsun Rinpoche highlights four powerful modes of practice and the potential errors and deviations that sometimes accompany each of them.

The first of these verses warns of the danger of confusing a perfect view of the ultimate reality of dharmata with an imperfect, merely verbal view without any actual realization. As we have discussed, if we put too much emphasis on the view, there is a danger that our practice will become imbalanced and we will disregard our meditation practice. As we have discussed, some Tibetan Dzogchen masters have said that if you are in the state of rigpa, if you are in the state of wisdom, then you don't need to do any practice. Now, if you *are* truly in that experience of ultimate reality, then this is true. But many practitioners may use this to become lazy in their practice. They may claim to have a perfected wisdom view and may therefore disregard their practice, feeling that they do not need to do any ngöndro or meditation. It is easy to deceive ourselves in this way.

Rinpoche is trying to help those who don't have the true realization of wisdom. He is cautioning them not to make the error of deceiving themselves that they have experienced wisdom and using that to avoid practice. Those meditators who have genuine realization may appear similar to those who do not because they are both not doing any formal practice. But of course there is a big difference between them.

Making the assumption that the fact that everything is empty means that we don't have to do any practice may lead us to rely on a mere verbal expression of the wisdom view—one that is unsupported by any true experience. Before we use emptiness as a reason not to do any practice, we first need to *actually realize* clarity and emptiness! If we have not yet realized emptiness, we need to rely on methods, and we need to do spiritual practice.

This does *not* mean that there is no value in expressing the view verbally—there is. It can be helpful in our training. It can help to give us a map and a guidebook. It can help us to recognize experiences we may have along the path. But verbal expressions of the view cannot give us the direct experience of the view itself. Many great masters have cautioned scholars to not get attached to the verbal view without experience or transformation. As we have discussed, if our understanding of wisdom is merely intellectual, then we will still die a very ordinary death.

Realization of the truth is a direct awakening in the mind. It cannot be experienced through speech. Tibetans have an old saying: "If you are good at talking, then you are also good at misleading people!" We can see how this often happens among politicians and other leaders. We can also see how many scholars become so eloquent and spend their lives trying to convey truth through dry speech and impressive philosophical language. Their downfall is that they may spend their entire lives talking and proliferating ideas instead of doing any spiritual practice. View cannot be realized on the tongue! It must be experienced in the mind.

Because the oral instruction of relaxing the sense organs and losing the six sense consciousnesses to distraction resemble one another, there is a danger of error.

Jetsun Rinpoche is referring here to the second deviation: the danger of confusing perfect meditation—performed with self-liberated sense consciousnesses and organs—and imperfect meditation—in which the sense consciousnesses are lost to distraction and faults in meditation.

Meditation can be very relaxing. All of our sense organs and our entire body can be at ease. But, as we have discussed, other worldly activities can produce this same physical relaxation. Distraction through entertainment and other passive activities can also relax the body. Watching a movie can be very relaxing because our eye consciousness is completely lost in all the images and we stop worrying about our problems for a little while. Music can be very relaxing; our ears are completely absorbed in the beautiful sounds and we may stop thinking about our anxiety for a while. Food can completely relax us as our consciousness related to smell and taste becomes consumed by pleasurable experience. Massage can be very relaxing to the body. Drugs and alcohol can be very relaxing. Anything agreeable that the six sense organs can consume may provide some level of temporary relaxation and pleasure.

What is the difference between relaxation based on distracting or satisfying the senses and relaxation based on meditation? The difference is that relaxation based on engaging the sense organs can only produce more dullness, more craving, or more restlessness. Spending an entire night watching movies may temporarily distract us, but afterward we may feel very dull and sleepy or our problems may resurface and our anxiety may increase.

On the other hand, practicing meditation *sharpens* the awareness. As we know, this sharpening of the senses can be painful at first. Our increased awareness tends to shine light on what we are trying to run away from emotionally, and we generally don't want to sit with that awareness of suffering. But doing so will bring us a much deeper experience of peace, a peace that will not have any addictive quality. As we practice sitting with this sharper awareness, our consciousness will no longer be controlled by our emotions. We will no longer be losing our consciousness to sensory objects.

Meditation is the opposite of indulging the sense organs and sense consciousness. When we meditate, we are freeing our consciousness from getting lost in this addiction to the sense objects. Our eye consciousness becomes liberated and no longer seeks stimulation through visual objects. Our eye consciousness can be totally at peace staring into space. Our ear consciousness becomes liberated and no longer seeks pleasurable sounds. Our ear consciousness can feel deeply at peace in total silence. Through meditation, we can gain independence from all of our craving and addiction to sensory pleasure and distraction. When we are meditating, we are no longer letting our emotions pursue these sense objects. We can become free of that vicious cycle where our consciousness is completely addicted to consumption.

All that consumption makes us so dependent, not allowing us to experience any mental freedom or agency. Our emotions propel us to chase after the sense objects in search of satisfaction. Meditation is the method for freeing ourselves from that dependency, from that addiction. Through practice, we begin to have some freedom in where we place our consciousness. We no longer chase after every pleasurable object. In short, meditation gives us independence.

Because intensely produced renunciation
and the coarse behavior of a madman
resemble one another, there is a danger of error.

Jetsun Rinpoche is referring to the third deviation: the danger of confusing perfect conduct—that based on renunciation—and imperfect conduct—in which one behaves wildly due to destructive emotions without any renunciation. Someone who realizes ultimate reality can easily renounce ordinary life. If they are a wandering yogi, they may appear to others to be an ordinary beggar. They may have very shabby clothing and they may sleep on the street. They may appear no different from someone who is without resources due to serious mental illness, trauma, or addiction. As we have discussed, some of these great masters even acted out of "crazy wisdom," doing many things that seemed to be misconduct. But they were manifesting out of the experience of the ultimate reality of wisdom free from destructive emotions. These yogis had transcended the dualism of good and bad, attachment and aversion.

There is a big difference between someone with direct experience of ultimate reality and an insane person. But from the outside, they may appear the same. Those yogis who have realized wisdom may seem like "madmen," but having the awareness of ultimate reality, they are actually more sane than ordinary people.

Because the complete exhaustion of hope and fear
and the aversion of one who has an inner grudge
resemble one another, there is a danger of error.

Jetsun Rinpoche is referring to the fourth deviation: the danger of confusing the achievement of the perfect result that has gone beyond hope and fear with the aversion of one who has an inner grudge. In ordinary life, we try to avoid people and experiences that we don't like. We have grudges and aversions. Our anger makes us ignore people or become estranged from family. People can make the mistake of thinking that avoidance is the same as nonattachment or liberation. They may think, "I have separated myself from those bad people or bad things, and now I am free." But aversion and avoidance are not based on wisdom.

Someone who is truly at peace has gone beyond attachment and aversion, beyond hope and fear. There is no longer anything to wish for or anything to oppose. This is a state of very profound inner peace. This experience of transformation has the power to transform anyone who comes in contact with that peaceful person.

On the other hand, those who don't do any meditation may talk about love and compassion; they may protest war and injustice. But internally they may still be operating based on afflictive emotions. Whenever we have attachment—even attachment to a certain positive outcome—then it will naturally bring with it more expectations, more fears, and those expectations and fears will increase our anxiety and insecurity.

Someone who has gone beyond attachment and aversion no longer has any expectations of a certain outcome. They no longer have any fears about something going wrong. They can remain at peace regardless of the situation. They no longer label something as good or bad. Without expectations of a certain outcome, there is no fear.

Yogis who have gone beyond both hope and fear will have an unshakable peace and equilibrium. That liberation is the true sign that we have been engaged in right view, right conduct, and right meditation.

Authorship Statement

The upasaka Dragpa Gyaltsen
sang this song of experience
in reliance upon both sutra and tantra,
the words composed in verse
and beautified by poetic ornamentation
to decrease the arrogance of scholars
and increase the enthusiasm of the faithful.
Thus, the teaching of the song is complete.

JETSUN RINPOCHE CLOSES HIS *Great Song of Experience* with a brief authorship statement, which is a standard feature of Tibetan literature. In this statement, Rinpoche says that there are two purposes of this song. One purpose is to bring more enthusiasm and inspiration to the faithful, so that we, too, will experience inner transformation. The other purpose is to decrease the arrogance of scholars. Rinpoche's words can be sharp when he speaks of scholars. He does not want this mystical song to become mere intellectual property. His song is arising out of the direct experience of awakening which, as he says, is also validated by being based on the teachings in the sutras and tantras. His song expresses the mystical experience of a highly realized meditator, so it is very different from many of the philosophical texts we study. He mentions that the doha is composed in metric verse, using poetic ornamentation.

Rinpoche's words are an inspiration for our own inner journey of realization. His experience can give us confidence in cultivating these same inner qualities within ourselves. Through his experience, we can get a glimpse of where our training in wisdom, meditation, and conduct can lead. His verses give us faith that it is possible for all of us to realize the true nature of our own mind and, as a result, to realize the dharmata, the empty nature of all things. This is how we will achieve enlightenment for the sake of all sentient beings.

Appendices

༄༅། །ཉམས་དབྱངས་ཆེན་མོ་བཞུགས།།

[1.]

༄༅། །ན་མོ་གུ་རུ་ཧྲྀ་དྷ་ཡ།

ཡོན་ཏན་མཐའ་དག་རྒྱུད་ལ་སྦྱོར་[1]མཛད་པའི།།
བླ་མ་ལྷ་དང་དབྱེར་མེད་བཞུགས་རྣམས་ལ།།
ལུས་ངག་ཡིད་གསུམ་དང་བས་ཕྱག་ཀྱང་འཚལ།།
གཟུང་འཛིན་གཉིས་དང་བྲལ་བའི་མཆོད་པ་འབུལ།།
སྤྲོས་བྲལ་ངག་གི་ལས་འདས་ཡིད་ཀྱིས་བསྟོད།།
དུས་གསུམ་སྡིག་གིས་མི་གོས་བཤགས་པ་བྱེད།།
དམིགས་མེད་འཇིགས་དང་བྲལ་བའི་སྐྱབས་སུ་འགྲོ།།
ཚད་བྲལ་དམིགས་ཡུལ་སྤངས་པའི་སེམས་བསྐྱེད་བྱེད།།
དེ་ཡི་ཆོས་ཉིད་རང་བཞིན་ནམ་མཁའ་འདྲ།།
བསགས་པ་མེད་པའི་དགེ་རྩ་བྱང་ཆུབ་བསྔོ།།
སྣང་སྲིད་སྟོང་པའི་མཎྜལ་འདི་བཞེས་ལ།།
སྐལ་ལྡན་བདག་ལ་བྱིན་གྱིས་བརླབ་ཏུ་གསོལ།།

1. Some versions of this text have སྦྱུར་ here instead.

APPENDIX I

Complete Translation of Jetsun Rinpoche Dragpa Gyaltsen's *Great Song of Experience*

1. Homage

Namo gurubhadraya.

To the gurus and personal deities residing inseparably,
who join all qualities to the mindstream,
I prostrate with pure body, speech, and mind;
I make an offering free from both grasper and grasped;
I offer praise with my mind, beyond the activity of speech, free from proliferation;
I make a confession untouched by the sins of the three times;
I go for refuge without an object, free from fear;
I generate limitless *bodhichitta* without objects,
the nature of which is the space-like *dharmata*;
I dedicate the root of virtue not gathered to enlightenment;
Please accept this mandala of empty phenomena
and bestow blessings upon me, the fortunate one.

[2.]

ལྟ་བ་གཏན་ལ་འབེབས་ཙམ་ན།།
རྒྱལ་བ་རྣམས་ཀྱི་སྟོང་པ་ཉིད།།
ལྟ་ཀུན་ཉེས་པ་འབྱུང་བར་གསུངས།།
དེ་ཕྱིར་ལྟ་བ་ལྟ་རྒྱུ་མེད།།

ཤེས་རབ་ཅན་ལ་ལྟ་བ་མེད།།
བློ་རྟོན་པོ་ལ་ཚིག་ལས་འདས།།
བརྩོན་འགྲུས་ཅན་ལ་བསྒོམ་རྒྱུ་མེད།།
དད་པ་ཅན་ལ་རྒྱུ་འབྲས་མེད།།
སྙིང་རྗེ་ཅན་ལ་སེམས་ཅན་མེད།།
ཚོགས་བསགས་པ་ལ་སངས་རྒྱས་མེད།།

མཐའ་བྲལ་ཤེས་བརྗོད་ཡུལ་ལས་འདས།།
དབུ་མ་སེམས་ཙམ་ལ་སོགས་པ།།
ཚིག་ཏུ་བརྗོད་པ་སྤྲོས་པ་ཡིན།།
ཡིད་ལ་སེམས་པ་རྣམ་རྟོག་ཡིན།།
རང་བཞིན་བརྗོད་མེད་བསམ་མེད་ཡིན།།

ཇི་སྲིད་ལྟ་བ་ཡོད་རིང་ལ།།
སྡུག་བསྔལ་ཀུན་ལས་མི་གྲོལ་ཏེ།།
རྣམ་རྟོག་མ་རིག་ཆེན་པོ་སྟེ།།
འཁོར་བའི་རྒྱ་མཚོར་ལྟུང་བྱེད་གསུངས།།

ཐོས་པས་ཤེས་རྒྱུད་མ་གྲོལ་བར།།
ལྟ་བ་ཚིག་ཏུ་མ་བཏང་ཞིག།
ལུང་དང་རིགས་པ་མན་ངག་གི།
ལྟ་བ་ཐག་ཆོད་བློ་རེ་བདེ།།

སྒོམ་པ་ཉམས་ལེན་བྱེད་ཙམ་ན།།
སྒོམ་མེད་སྒོམ་པ་པོ་ཡང་མེད།།
ཡུལ་མེད་མཐའ་བྲལ་སྒོམ་པ་དེ།།
བྱ་བ་ཐོང་ལ་ཉམས་སུ་ལོང་།།

2. View, Meditation, Conduct, and Result

When only the view is established,
it has been said by the buddhas
"All views of emptiness are a source of faults."
Therefore, the view cannot be viewed.

For one with wisdom, there is no view;
for one with sharp intelligence, it is beyond words;
for one with diligence, nothing is to be meditated on;
for one with faith, there is no cause and result;
for one with compassion, there are no sentient beings;
for the gatherer of the accumulations, there is no buddhahood.

Freedom from extremes is beyond knowledge, expressions, and objects;
Madhyamaka, Chittamatra, and so on
are expressions in words, proliferations.
Thoughts in the mind are concepts;
the nature is inexpressible and unthinkable.

For as long as views continue to exist,
there will be no liberation from all suffering.
Conceptuality is great ignorance,
[from which] it is said one sinks into the ocean of samsara.

Without the mindstream being liberated by hearing,
do not express the view in words.
With scripture, reason, and *upadesha*,
the view is determined, mind is at ease.

When only meditation is practiced,
there is no meditation and no meditator.
That meditation, free from extremes, is without an object;
leave aside activities, and practice!

སེམས་མེད་སེམས་ཀྱིས་སེམས་ལ་ལྟོས།།
མཐོང་རྒྱུ་བྱུང་ན་སེམས་ཉིད་མིན།།

མཐོང་མེད་མཐོང་བས་སེམས་ཉིད་མཐོང་།།
མཐོང་མེད་སེམས་ལ་མ་ཡེངས་ཞོག།

ཆགས་ན་གསལ་བས་ཟིན་པར་མཛོད།།
རྒོད་ན་དྲན་པའི་ལྷུགས་ཀྱིས་ཟུང་།།

གསལ་ལ་མི་རྟོག་སྒོམ་པ་ཡིན།།

ཉམས་ཀྱི་སྐྱེ་ཡིས་མ་ཟིན་པར།།
སྒོམ་པ་ཚིག་ཏུ་མ་བཏང་ཅིག།

སྙིང་རྗེ་སེམས་བསྐྱེད་སྔོན་དུ་བཏང་།།
མཇུག་ཏུ་དགེ་བ་བྱང་ཆུབ་བསྔོ།།

སྤྱོད་པ་ཉམས་སུ་ལེན་ཙམ་ན།།
ལྟ་སྒོམ་ཉམས་སུ་སྐྱོང་བ་ཡིན།།
སྣང་བའི་དངོས་པོ་རྒྱུས་བཏབ་ནས།།
བླང་དོར་མེད་པའི་སྤྱོད་པ་མཛོད།།

མ་བཅོས་ཤུགས་འབྱུང་སྤྱོད་པ་དེ།།
ཚུལ་འཆོས་ཕྱོགས་སུ་མ་བཏང་ཅིག།

གྲོགས་སུ་འགྲོ་བའི་སྤྱོད་པ་དེ།།
ཐོ་ཅོའི་ཕྱོགས་སུ་མ་བཏང་ཅིག།

འཛིན་མེད་རོ་སྙོམས་སྤྱོད་པ་དེ།།
ཆགས་སྡང་ཕྱོགས་སུ་མ་བཏང་ཅིག།

བྱར་མེད་ལྷུག་པའི་སྤྱོད་པ་དེ།།
ཐེག་པའི་ཕྱོགས་སུ་མ་བཏང་ཅིག།

With the mind without mind, look into the mind;
if seen, that is not mind itself.

With seeing without seeing, mind itself is seen;
remain undistracted in unseeing mind.

If attached, make a connection with clarity;
if scattered, hold with the iron hook of recollection.

Meditation is clarity without concepts.

Without being connected with the nectar of experience,
do not express meditation in words.

Begin with developing compassion and bodhichitta;
at the end, dedicate the merit to enlightenment.

When only conduct is practiced,
view and meditation are experienced.
Having sealed the appealing things,
perform conduct without accepting and rejecting.

Do not throw away such naturally unfabricated conduct
by siding with misconduct.

Do not throw away friendly conduct
by siding with wild behavior.

Do not throw away the conduct of non-grasping one taste
by siding with desire and anger.

Do not throw away the conduct of relaxing without activity
by siding with nonvirtue.

འཁོར་གསུམ་ཡང་དག་སྤྱོད་པ་དེ།།
ཟག་བཅས་དགེ་བར་མ་བཏང་ཅིག།

དགེ་མེད་སྡིག་མེད་སྤྱོད་པ་དེ།།
ལུང་མ་བསྟན་དུ་མ་བཏང་ཅིག།

[3.]

སངས་རྒྱས་གཏན་ལ་འབེབས་ཙམ་ན།།
སེམས་ལས་མ་གཏོགས་ཆོས་རྣམས་མེད།།
སེམས་ཉིད་རྟོགས་ན་སངས་རྒྱས་ཡིན།།
སངས་རྒྱས་གཞན་དུ་མ་བཙལ་ཞིག།

ཆོས་སྐུ་དག་པ་གཉིས་ལྡན་དེ།།
གཞི་ཡི་ཕྱོགས་སུ་མི་གཏང་འཚལ།།
གཟུགས་སྐུ་གདུལ་བྱའི་སྣང་བ་ལ།།
སངས་རྒྱས་ངོ་བོར་མ་འཛིན་ཅིག།

གཞི་ལ་སངས་རྒྱས་མེད་པ་ལ།།
ཐོབ་ཏུ་རེ་བ་མི་བགྱིད་འཚལ།།
དོན་ལ་སེམས་ཅན་མེད་པ་ལ།།
སྡུག་གི་དོགས་པ་མི་བགྱིད་འཚལ།།

ལྟ་བ་བསམ་བརྗོད་མེད་པ་ལ།།
མདོ་རྒྱུད་ཐོས་བསམ་བྱས་པས་འགྲུབ།།
སྒོམ་པ་མཐའ་དང་བྲལ་བ་ལ།།
ལུས་སེམས་རྩོལ་བ་བྱས་པས་འགྲུབ།།

སྤྱོད་པ་ཤུགས་འབྱུང་འགག་མེད་དེ།།
ཚུལ་འཆོས་ཕྲོ་ཅོར་ཤོར་བས་འགྲུབ།།
འབྲས་བུ་འཁོར་འདས་དབྱེར་མེད་དེ།།
རེ་དོགས་ཕྱོགས་སུ་ཤོར་བས་འགྲུབ།།

Do not throw away the conduct of completely purifying the three wheels
by siding with defiled virtue.

Do not throw away the conduct without virtue and nonvirtue
by siding with neutrality.

3. Do Not Seek Elsewhere for Buddha

Once buddhahood is established,
there are no dharmas aside from mind.
When mind itself is comprehended, *that* is Buddha;
do not seek elsewhere for Buddha.

Please do not throw away the *dharmakaya* possessing two purities,
by siding with the basis.
Do not grasp the essence of the Buddha
in the *rupakaya*, which appears to those [sentient beings] to be tamed.

In the basis, there is no Buddha;
do not hope for attainment.
In the ultimate, there are no sentient beings;
do not fear suffering.

In the view without thought or expressions,
one is deluded by the activity of hearing and contemplating sutras and tantras.
In the meditation free from extremes,
one is deluded by making physical and mental effort.

In the ceaseless natural activity of conduct,
one is deluded by becoming lost in misconduct and wild behavior.
In the result, the inseparability of samsara and nirvana,
one is deluded by becoming lost in siding with hope and fear.

[4.]

ལྟ་བ་དབུ་མ་ཆེན་པོ་དེ༎
ཁས་ལེན་མེད་དེ་མ་འཁྲུལ་བདེ༎

སྒོམ་པ་ལུས་སེམས་ལྷུག་པ་དེ༎
རྩོལ་སྒྲུབ་མེད་དེ་མ་འཁྲུལ་བདེ༎

སྤྱོད་པ་ཆགས་སྡང་རྒྱུ་གཞི་དེ༎
བླང་དོར་མེད་དེ་མ་འཁྲུལ་བདེ༎

འབྲས་བུ་ཕྱག་རྒྱ་ཆེན་པོ་དེ༎
རེ་དོགས་མེད་པས་མ་འཁྲུལ་བདེ༎

ལྟ་བ་སྤྲོས་པ་མེད་ན་ཡིན༎
སྒོམ་པ་ཡེངས་པ་མེད་ན་ཡིན༎
སྤྱོད་པ་བྱ་བ་ཐོང་ན་ཡིན༎
འབྲས་བུ་སེམས་ཉིད་རྟོགས་ན་ཡིན༎

སྒྲོ་འདོགས་ཆོད་ན་ལྟ་བ་ཡིན༎
ཡེངས་པ་མེད་ན་སྒོམ་པ་ཡིན༎
ཞེན་ཆགས་མེད་ན་སྤྱོད་པ་ཡིན༎
ཡོན་ཏན་རྫོགས་ན་འབྲས་བུ་ཡིན༎

ལར་ལྟ་བ་རྟོགས་པའི་སྐྱེས་བུ་ལ༎
སྒོམ་དུ་ཅི་ཡང་མི་གདའ་ན༎
ཉམས་ལེན་མེད་པའི་སྒོམ་ཆེན་དེ༎
སྤྱོད་པ་སྤྱོད་རྒྱུ་མི་གདའ་ན༎
སྤྱོད་དང་བྲལ་བའི་རྣལ་འབྱོར་ལ༎
འབྲས་བུ་ཅི་ཡང་མི་གདའ་ན༎

ལྟ་བ་མེད་པ་ལྟ་བའི་མཆོག།
གྲུབ་མཐའ་འདི་ལ་དགོས་པ་མེད༎

4. Bliss without Delusion

The view of great Madhyamaka,
being without definitive propositions, is bliss without delusion.

The meditation relaxing body and mind,
being without effort, is bliss without delusion.

The conduct, the causal ground of desire and anger,
being without accepting and rejecting, is bliss without delusion.

The result, *mahamudra*,
being without hope and fear, is bliss without delusion.

If there is no proliferation, that is the view.
If there is no distraction, that is meditation.
If activity is abandoned, that is conduct.
If mind itself is comprehended, that is the result.

If doubt is cut, that is view.
If there is no distraction, that is meditation.
If there is no clinging and attachment, that is conduct.
If the qualities are complete, that is the result.

In general, for a being who has realized the view,
if there is nothing whatsoever to meditate on,
that great meditator is without a practice.
If there is no conduct to perform,
in the yoga free from conduct,
there is no result whatsoever to be pursued.

The supreme view has no view;
philosophical conclusions are not needed here.

སྒོམ་དུ་མེད་པ་བསྒོམ་པའི་མཆོག
སེམས་འཛིན་འདི་ལ་དགོས་པ་མེད།།

སྤྱོད་པ་མེད་པ་སྤྱོད་པའི་མཆོག
ཚུལ་འཆོས་འདི་ལ་དགོས་པ་མེད།།

འབྲས་བུ་མེད་པ་འབྲས་བུའི་མཆོག
རེ་དོགས་འདི་ལ་དགོས་པ་མེད།།

ལར་གནས་ལུགས་དོན་ལ་མཐོང་རྒྱུ་མེད།།
ད་ནི་ལྟ་ཡང་མི་ལྟའོ།།

གཉུག་མ་འདི་ལ་བསྒོམ་རྒྱུ་མེད།།
ད་ནི་བསྒོམ་ཡང་མི་བསྒོམ་མོ།།

དབྱིངས་ཀྱི་ངང་ལ་སྤྱོད་དུ་མེད།།
ད་ནི་སྤྱོད་ཀྱང་མི་སྤྱོད་དོ།།

ལྟ་བ་མཐའ་དབུས་མི་གདའ་ན།།
ནམ་མཁའ་ཡིན་པ་ཀ་སྐམ་བགྱིད།།

སྒོམ་ལ་གཡོ་འགུལ་མི་གདའ་ན།།
རི་བོ་ཡིན་པ་ཀ་སྐམ་བགྱིད།།

ཉམས་ལ་གསལ་འགྲིབ་མི་གདའ་ན།།
ཉི་ཟླ་ཡིན་པ་ཀ་སྐམ་བགྱིད།།

སྤྱོད་པ་བླང་དོར་མི་གདའ་ན།།
ས་གཞི་ཡིན་པ་ཀ་སྐམ་བགྱིད།།

འབྲས་བུ་རེ་དོགས་མི་གདའ་ན།།
ཞེན་ལོག་ཡིན་པ་ཀ་སྐམ་བགྱིད།།

The supreme meditation is without meditation;
concentrating mind is not needed here.

The supreme conduct is without conduct;
misconduct is not needed here.

The supreme result has no result;
hope and fear are not needed here.

Moreover, in reality there is no object to see;
now, also, the view is not viewed.

In the original nature, there is nothing to meditate on;
now, also, meditation is not meditation.

In the natural state, there is no conduct;
now, also, conduct is not conduct.

If the view has no center or limits,
one might surely think it is space.

If there is no movement or wavering in meditation,
one might surely think it is a mountain.

If there is no obscuration of the clarity of experience,
one might surely think it is the sun and moon.

If there is no accepting and rejecting in one's conduct,
one might surely think it is the ground of the earth.

If there is no hope or fear for the result,
one might surely think one has turned away from grasping.

ལྟ་ཐོག་ཏུ་སྒོམ་པ་ཁེལ་མ་ཁེལ།།
ལྟ་ཐོག་ཏུ་སྒོམ་པ་ཁེལ་ཙམ་ན།།
གཏུག་མའི་དོན་ལ་ཡེངས་པ་མེད།།

སྒོམ་ཐོག་ཏུ་ལྟ་བ་ཁེལ་མ་ཁེལ།།
སྒོམ་ཐོག་ཏུ་ལྟ་བ་ཁེལ་ཙམ་ན།།
བསམ་གཏན་གྱི་རོ་ལ་ཆགས་པ་མེད།།

སྤྱོད་ཐོག་ཏུ་ལྟ་སྒོམ་ཁེལ་མ་ཁེལ།།
སྤྱོད་ཐོག་ཏུ་ལྟ་སྒོམ་ཁེལ་ཙམ་ན།།
མཉམ་རྗེས་མེད་པའི་ཉམས་རྟོགས་འཆར།།

སེམས་ལ་རྟོགས་པ་མ་སྐྱེས་པའི།།
ལྟ་བ་མཐོ་བས་ཅི་ལ་ཕན།།

ཉོན་མོངས་གཉེན་པོར་མ་སོང་བས།།
སྒོམ་ལ་བཟང་བས་ཅི་ལ་ཕན།།

ཤེས་རབ་སྙིང་རྗེས་མ་ཟིན་པས།།
སྤྱོད་པ་ཞིབ་པས་ཅི་ལ་ཕན།།

རང་སྐྱོན་ཁ་ཡང་མ་འབྲི་བས།།
ཡི་སངས་རྒྱས་ཀྱིས་ཅི་ལ་ཕན།།

སྐྱེ་བ་མེད་པའི་དོན་རྟོགས་ན།།
ལྟ་བ་ཚད་དུ་སྐྱོལ་བ་ཡིན།།

མཉམ་གཞག་རྗེས་ཐོབ་གཉིས་མེད་ན།།
སྒོམ་པ་ཚད་དུ་སྐྱོལ་བ་ཡིན།།

ཚར་གཅད་རྗེས་གཟུང་སྙོམས་པ་ན།།
སྤྱོད་པ་ཚད་དུ་སྐྱོལ་པ་ཡིན།།

Meditation may or may not have been integrated into the view,
but when meditation is integrated into the view,
there is no distraction in the ultimate original nature.

View may or may not have been integrated into meditation,
but when the view is integrated into meditation,
there is no grasping to the taste of *dhyana*.

View and meditation may or may not have been integrated into conduct,
but when view and meditation are integrated into conduct,
the experiential realization of meditation and post-meditation arises.

Of what benefit is a high view,
if realization does not arise in the mind?

Of what benefit is good meditation,
if it does not become an antidote to the defilements?

Of what benefit is precise conduct,
if wisdom is not connected with compassion?

Of what benefit is primordial buddhahood,
if one's faults are undiminished even on the surface?

When the meaning of non-arising is realized,
one has arrived at the limit of the view.

When both meditation and post-meditation do not exist,
one has arrived at the limit of meditation.

When destruction and protection are neutralized,
one has arrived at the limit of conduct.

ཆོས་སྐུ་གཟུགས་སྐུ་གཉིས་ཐོབ་ན།།
འབྲས་བུ་ཚད་དུ་སྐྱོལ་བ་ཡིན།།

[5.]

ལྟ་བ་རང་གི་སེམས་ལ་དྲིས།།
རྟག་ཆད་འདུག་གམ་མི་འདུག་ལྟོས།།

སྒོམ་པ་རང་གི་སེམས་ལ་དྲིས།།
ཡིང་བ་འདུག་གམ་མི་འདུག་ལྟོས།།

སྤྱོད་པ་རང་གི་སེམས་ལ་དྲིས།།
ཐ་མལ་འདུག་གམ་མི་འདུག་ལྟོས།།

འབྲས་བུ་རང་གི་སེམས་ལ་དྲིས།།
དཀའ་ཐུབ་ནུས་སམ་མི་ནུས་ལྟོས།།

ལྟ་བ་སེམས་ཀྱི་སྐྱེལ་མ་ཡིན།།
སྒོམ་པ་སེམས་ཀྱི་འགྲོ་ལམ་ཡིན།།
སྤྱོད་པ་སེམས་ཀྱི་གྲོགས་པོ་ཡིན།།
འབྲས་བུ་སེམས་ཀྱི་སྲུན་མ་ཡིན།།

ལྟ་བའི་དགུང་སྔོན་མཐོ་ན་བཞེད།།
སྒོམ་པའི་རྒྱ་མཚོ་ཟབ་ན་བཞེད།།
སྤྱོད་པའི་ཞིང་ས་གཤིན་ན་བཞེད།།
འབྲས་བུའི་ལོ་ཏོག་སྨིན་ན་བཞེད།།

བདག་ཤེས་རབ་ཅན་ཡང་མ་ལགས་ཏེ།།
བླ་མ་མཁས་པ་བསྟེན་པ་དང་།།
ཐོས་བསམ་བྱས་པའི་ཡོན་ཏན་གྱིས།།
རྫོགས་པའི་གོ་ཚུལ་འདི་ལྟར་སྐྱེས།།

རྒྱ་མཚོའི་རུས་སྦལ་གཉའ་ཤིང་ལྟར།།
མི་ལུས་ཐོབ་པ་དཀའ་བར་གོ།།

When one has obtained both the dharmakaya and the rupakaya,
one has arrived at the limit of the result.

5. Examining the Mind

One should examine one's own mind for the view;
See if permanence and annihilation exist or don't exist.

One should examine one's own mind for meditation;
See if distraction exists or doesn't exist.

One should examine one's own mind for conduct;
See if vulgarity exists or doesn't exist.

One should examine one's own mind for the result;
See if the ability to endure hardship exists or doesn't exist.

View is the guide of the mind;
meditation is the path of the mind;
conduct is the friend of the mind;
the result is the host of the mind.

The sky of the view is considered to be high;
the ocean of meditation is considered to be deep;
the field of conduct is considered to be tilled;
the crop of the result is considered to be ripened.

Although I do not possess the best understanding,
yet by studying with learned gurus and
by accumulating the knowledge of hearing and contemplation,
my understanding of realization arose.

Understand that a human body is difficult to obtain,
like a sea turtle [surfacing through] a yoke.

འཛོག་ཕོའི་གཙུག་གི་ནོར་བུ་བཞིན།།
བླ་མ་རྙེད་པར་དཀའ་བར་ཤོག།

དུས་བཞི་ལུས་ཀྱི་འགྱུར་བ་འདི།།
འཆི་བའི་བྱ་གཏོང་ཡིན་པར་ཤོག།
སྐྱེས་བུ་དགྲ་ཡི་ཡུལ་བཏོན་བཞིན།།
ཐམས་ཅད་བཞག་ནས་འགྲོ་བར་ཤོག།

རྨ་བྱའི་མདོངས་ཀྱི་ཁ་དོག་བཞིན།།
ཐམས་ཅད་ལས་ལས་སྐྱེས་པར་ཤོག།
རང་བཞིན་སྟོང་པ་ཉིད་རྟོགས་ན།།
འཁོར་བར་སྐྱེ་བ་མེད་པར་ཤོག།

མེ་ལོང་ནང་གི་གཟུགས་བརྙན་བཞིན།།
སྣང་བའི་རང་བཞིན་སྟོང་པར་ཤོག།
རྨི་ལམ་ལྟད་མོ་མཐོང་བ་བཞིན།།
སྟོང་པའི་རང་བཞིན་སྣང་བར་ཤོག།

ཁ་ཆུ་དྭངས་པའི་གསེར་བཞིན་དུ།།
རང་བཞིན་རྣམ་པར་དག་པར་ཤོག།
སྤྲིན་དང་རྡོག་མ་གཡའ་བཞིན་དུ།།
རྣམ་རྟོག་གློ་བུར་ཡིན་པར་ཤོག།

རྣམ་རྟོག་འཁོར་བ་ཡིན་པར་ཤོག།
རྟོག་མེད་མྱང་འདས་ཡིན་པར་ཤོག།

འཁོར་བ་སྡུག་བསྔལ་ཡིན་པར་ཤོག།
ཐར་པ་བདེ་བ་ཡིན་པར་ཤོག།

བདེ་སྡུག་གཉིས་སུ་མེད་པར་ཤོག།
ཡེ་སྟོང་ཡེ་གྲོལ་ཡིན་པར་ཤོག།

Understand that it is difficult to find a guru,
like the jewel of Takshaka's crown.

These changes of the body with four seasons—
understand them as the secret sign of death.
Understand that everything is left behind when passing away,
like a person being exiled to an enemy country.

Understand that everything is born from karma,
like the colors of a peacock's feathers.
Understand that there is no birth in samsara
if emptiness by nature is realized,

Understand the nature of appearances as emptiness,
like a reflection in a mirror.
Understand the nature of emptiness as appearances,
like a display seen in a dream.

Understand the nature as completely pure,
like the golden luster of whey.
Understand conceptuality as adventitious,
like clouds, dirt, or rust.

Understand conceptuality as samsara;
understand nonconceptuality as nirvana.

Understand samsara as suffering;
understand liberation as bliss.

Understand that both happiness and suffering do not exist;
understand primordial emptiness as free from origin.

[6.]

ལར་སེམས་ལ་གོ་རྟོགས་ཤར་ན་བདེ།།
ལྟ་བ་རྟོགས་ན་ཡང་ཀྱང་བདེ།།

རྣམ་པར་སྨིན་པའི་སྐུ་ལུས་བདེ།།
ན་ཚ་མེད་ན་ཡང་ཀྱང་བདེ།།

རི་ཁྲོད་དགོན་པ་བརྟེན་ན་བདེ།།
བྱ་བ་བཏང་ན་ཡང་ཀྱང་བདེ།།

ཆོས་དང་མཐུན་པའི་འཚོ་བ་བདེ།།
ལོག་འཚོ་སྤངས་ན་ཡང་ཀྱང་བདེ།།

ལུས་སེམས་གཞོན་པའི་འདོད་ཡོན་བདེ།།
ཐབས་ཀྱིས་ཟིན་ན་ཡང་ཀྱང་བདེ།།

ལྟ་སྤྱོད་མཐུན་པའི་གྲོགས་པོ་བདེ།།
གཅིག་པུར་སྡོད་པའི་ཉམས་ལེན་བདེ།།
ཞེན་ཆགས་མེད་པའི་ཟས་ནོར་བདེ།།
ངེས་པ་མེད་པའི་སྡོད་ས་བདེ།།
ཛོ་སྲུང་བྲལ་བའི་མཐུན་འཇུག་བདེ།།
རང་དབང་རང་གིས་ཐོབ་ན་བདེ།།

[7.]

བདག་བསོད་ནམས་ཅན་ཅིག་མ་ལགས་ཏེ།།
མི་ལུས་གཙང་མ་ཐོབ་པ་དང་།།
སངས་རྒྱས་བསྟན་པ་དར་བ་གཉིས།།
དེ་གཉིས་དུས་མཉམ་གཅིག་ཏུ་བྱུང་།།

མི་ཆོས་ལ་ཞེན་པ་ལོག་པ་དང་།།
ལྷ་ཆོས་ལ་སྤྲོ་བ་སྐྱེས་པ་གཉིས།།
དེ་གཉིས་དུས་མཉམ་གཅིག་ཏུ་བྱུང་།།

6. Bliss Again

Generally, if comprehension arises in the mind, bliss;
if the view is realized, also bliss.

The ripened illusory body is bliss;
if there is no disease, again, bliss.

Relying on the seclusion of retreat is bliss;
if activities are abandoned, also bliss.

Livelihood agreeing with Dharma is bliss;
if wrong livelihood is abandoned, again, bliss.

The desire-objects of the youthful body and mind are bliss;
if one is connected with the method, also bliss.

Friends with agreeable view and conduct are bliss.
Practicing in solitude is bliss.
Food and wealth without grasping and attachment are bliss.
Having no definite residence is bliss.
Friendship free of obligation is bliss.
If one obtains freedom, bliss!

7. Both Have Occurred at the Same Time

I am not someone who possesses merit,
but both my obtaining a complete human birth,
and the spread of the Buddhadharma—
both of those occurred at the same time.

Both turning away from clinging to worldly dharma,
and the arising of enthusiasm for spiritual Dharma—
both of those occurred at the same time.

རང་ཡུལ་སྤངས་ནས་ཕྱིན་པ་དང་།།
ཁྲིས་སུ་བླ་མ་མཇལ་བ་གཉིས།།
དེ་གཉིས་དུས་མཉམ་གཅིག་ཏུ་བྱུང་།།

སྡེ་སྣོད་ལ་ཐོས་པ་བྱས་པ་དང་།།
ཚིག་དོན་གཉིས་ཀ་ཤེས་པ་གཉིས།།
དེ་གཉིས་དུས་མཉམ་གཅིག་ཏུ་བྱུང་།།

ཐུགས་ཀྱི་བླ་མ་རྙེད་པ་དང་།།
དབང་བཞི་རྫོགས་པར་ཐོབ་པ་གཉིས།།
དེ་གཉིས་དུས་མཉམ་གཅིག་ཏུ་བྱུང་།།

སྙན་བརྒྱུད་གདམས་ངག་གནང་བ་དང་།།
ངེས་ཤེས་གཏིང་ནས་སྐྱེས་པ་གཉིས།།
དེ་གཉིས་དུས་མཉམ་གཅིག་ཏུ་བྱུང་།།

རྗེ་ལ་མོས་པ་སྐྱེས་པ་དང་།།
ཁྲིད་ཐབས་རྒྱུད་ལ་ཞུགས་པ་གཉིས།།
དེ་གཉིས་དུས་མཉམ་གཅིག་ཏ་བྱུང་།།

ཕྱི་ཡུལ་སྒྲོ་འདོགས་ཆོད་པ་དང་།།
རང་བྱུང་ཡེ་ཤེས་ཤར་བ་གཉིས།།
དེ་གཉིས་དུས་མཉམ་གཅིག་ཏུ་བྱུང་།།

བསྐྱེད་རིམ་ལྷ་རུ་གསལ་བ་དང་།།
རྫོགས་རིམ་ཉམས་སུ་མྱོང་བ་གཉིས།།
དེ་གཉིས་དུས་མཉམ་གཅིག་ཏུ་བྱུང་།།

ལུས་ལ་བདེ་དྲོད་འབར་བ་དང་།།
སེམས་ལ་སྣང་སྟོང་སྐྱེས་པ་གཉིས།།
དེ་གཉིས་དུས་མཉམ་གཅིག་ཏུ་བྱུང་།།

ཀུན་རྫོབ་འཁྲུལ་པར་གོ་བ་དང་།།
དོན་དམ་སྟོང་པར་ཤེས་པ་གཉིས།།
དེ་གཉིས་དུས་མཉམ་གཅིག་ཏུ་བྱུང་།།

Both having left one's country abandoned,
and meeting the guru in exile—
both of those occurred at the same time.

Both hearing the scriptures,
and understanding their words and meanings—
both of those occurred at the same time.

Both finding a Vajrayana guru,
and obtaining the four *abhishekas* completely—
both of those occurred at the same time.

Both the bestowal of the oral transmission and instructions,
and the arising of profound certain knowledge—
both of those occurred at the same time.

Both arousing devotion for the master,
and the entry of blessings into the mindstream—
both of those occurred at the same time.

Both cutting doubts about the outer objects,
and the arising of spontaneous wisdom—
both of those occurred at the same time.

Both having clarity in the creation stage deity,
and experiencing the realization of the completion stage—
both of those occurred at the same time.

Both having the heat of bliss blazing in the body,
and the arising of appearance and emptiness in the mind—
both of those occurred at the same time.

Both understanding delusion as relative,
and understanding emptiness as ultimate—
both of those occurred at the same time.

ཤེས་པ་ཡུལ་ལ་ཤོར་བ་དང་།།
དྲན་པའི་ལྕགས་ཀྱུས་ཟིན་པ་གཉིས།།
དེ་གཉིས་དུས་མཉམ་གཅིག་ཏུ་བྱུང་།།

རྒྱན་ངན་ཟག་པ་བྱུང་བ་དང་།།
གཉེན་པོའི་ར་མདས་སླེབ་པ་གཉིས།།
དེ་གཉིས་དུས་མཉམ་གཅིག་ཏུ་བྱུང་།།

འདོད་པ་ཡུལ་ལ་ཤོར་བ་དང་།།
ཐབས་ལ་མཁས་པས་ཟིན་པ་གཉིས།།
དེ་གཉིས་དུས་མཉམ་གཅིག་ཏུ་བྱུང་།།

བདེ་སྡུག་ཉམས་སུ་སྨྱོང་བ་དང་།།
དེ་ཉིད་སྒྱུ་མར་ཤེས་པ་གཉིས།།
དེ་གཉིས་དུས་མཉམ་གཅིག་ཏུ་བྱུང་།།

སེམས་ཅན་སྡུག་བསྔལ་མཐོང་བ་དང་།།
སྙིང་རྗེ་གཏིང་ནས་སྐྱེས་པ་གཉིས།།
དེ་གཉིས་དུས་མཉམ་གཅིག་ཏུ་བྱུང་།།

རྒོལ་བའི་ཀླན་ཀ་བྱུང་བ་དང་།།
གཏན་ཚིགས་ཡོང་ནས་ཤར་བ་གཉིས།།
དེ་གཉིས་དུས་མཉམ་གཅིག་ཏུ་བྱུང་།།

བསོད་ནམས་ཆུ་མིག་རྫོལ་བ་དང་།།
ཟས་ནོར་ཞེན་པ་ལོག་པ་གཉིས།།
དེ་གཉིས་དུས་མཉམ་གཅིག་ཏུ་བྱུང་།།

ཚུལ་འཆོས་སྤྱོད་པ་དོར་བ་དང་།།
ཅི་དགའི་སྤྱོད་པ་བྱེད་པ་གཉིས།།
དེ་གཉིས་དུས་མཉམ་གཅིག་ཏུ་བྱུང་།།

ཐོས་དང་ཤེས་རབ་འཛོམ་ཡང་འཚལ།།
ལུང་དང་རིགས་པར་འཛོམ་ཡང་འཚལ།།

Both losing awareness of the object,
and being connected with the hook of recollection—
both of those occurred at the same time.

Both being robbed by misfortune,
and the arrival of friends, the antidotes—
both of those occurred at the same time.

Both losing desire in objects,
and being connected with skillful means—
both of those occurred at the same time.

Both experiencing happiness and suffering,
and understanding them as illusions—
both of those occurred at the same time.

Both seeing the suffering of sentient beings,
and the arising of profound compassion—
both of those occurred at the same time.

Both producing an argument with an opponent,
and the dawning of proof inside oneself—
both of those occurred at the same time.

Both revealing the spring of merit,
and turning away from attachment to food and wealth—
both of those occurred at the same time.

Both abandoning misconduct,
and doing whatever conduct is pleasing—
both of those occurred at the same time.

Please, may hearing and wisdom also meet;
please, may scripture and reason also meet;

བླ་མ་བརྒྱུད་པར་འཛོམ་ཡང་འཚོལ།།
གདམས་ངག་ཉམས་ལེན་འཛོམ་ཡང་འཚོལ།།
དད་པ་བརྩོན་འགྲུས་འཛོམ་ཡང་འཚོལ།།
ཡོན་ཏན་གྲགས་པར་འཛོམ་ཡང་འཚོལ།།

ཤེས་རབ་མེད་པའི་ཐོས་པ་དེས།།
གོ་རྟོགས་སྐྱེ་བར་མི་གདའ་ན།།
ལུང་གིས་མ་ཟིན་རིགས་པ་དེས།།
ངེས་ཤེས་སྐྱེ་བར་མི་གདའ་ན།།

བརྒྱུད་པ་མེད་པའི་བླ་མ་དེས།།
བྱིན་རླབས་འབྱུང་བར་མི་གདའ་ན།།
བརྩོན་འགྲུས་མེད་པའི་དད་པ་དེས།།
ལག་ཏུ་ལོན་པར་མི་གདའ་ན།།

ཉམས་ལེན་མེད་པའི་གདམས་ངག་དེས།།
རང་ལ་ཕན་པར་མི་གདའ་ན།།
གྲགས་པ་མེད་པའི་ཡོན་ཏན་དེས།།
གཞན་ལ་ཕན་པར་མི་གདའ་ན།།

[8.]

སྒོང་མེད་བྱ་དེ་གང་ནས་བྱུང་།།
བྱ་མེད་སྒོ་ང་ཅི་ལས་བྱུང་།།
བྱ་དང་སྒོ་ང་གང་སྔའོ།།

རང་བཞིན་སྐྱེ་བ་མེད་པ་ལ།།
རྐྱེན་གྱིས་བྱེད་པར་མི་འདུག་ན།།
རྒྱུ་དང་འབྲས་བུ་གང་སྔའོ།།

སེམས་ཉིད་གདོད་ནས་དག་པ་ལ།།
རྣམ་རྟོག་ཡེ་ཤེས་གཉིས་མེད་ན།།
སངས་རྒྱས་སེམས་ཅན་གང་སྔའོ།།

please, may the lineage and the guru also meet;
please, may practice and oral instruction also meet;
please, may diligence and faith also meet;
please, may fame and qualities also meet.

No comprehension will arise
from hearing without wisdom.
No certain knowledge will arise
from reason not connected with scripture.

No blessings will come
from the guru without a lineage.
There will be no achievement
with faith without diligence.

There is no benefit for oneself
from oral instruction without practice.
There is no benefit for others
from good qualities without fame.

8. Which Is First?

Without an egg, where does the chicken come from?
Without a chicken, where does the egg come from?
Which is first: chicken or egg?

In the non-arising nature,
if there is no creation by conditions,
which is first: cause or result?

In the original purity of mind itself,
if both conceptuality and wisdom do not exist,
which is first: the Buddha or sentient beings?

ཆོས་རྣམས་ཡེ་ནས་མེད་པ་ལ༎
འབྲས་བུ་སངས་རྒྱས་མི་འབྱུང་ན༎
ཆོས་དང་སངས་རྒྱས་གང་སྤྲོའོ༎

དོན་ལ་ཅི་ཡང་མེད་པ་ལ༎
འཁྲུལ་དང་མ་འཁྲུལ་གཉིས་མེད་ན༎
ཀུན་རྫོབ་དོན་དམ་གང་སྤྲོའོ༎

དོན་ལ་སངས་རྒྱས་མེད་པ་ལ༎
སྡེ་སྣོད་གསུམ་པོ་སུ་ཡིས་གསུངས༎
སྟོན་པས་ཆོས་འགའ་མ་གསུངས་ན༎
པུསྟི་གླེགས་བམ་ཇི་ལྟར་ཡིན༎

འགག་པ་དངོས་མེད་ཤི་བ་དང་༎
སྐྱེ་བར་འགྱུར་བ་གང་ཐམས་ཅད༎
བྱས་པ་དོན་མེད་ཅེས་གསུངས་ན༎
ལས་ལས་འབྲས་བུ་ཅང་འབྱུང་ངམ༎

རང་བཞིན་གདོད་ནས་མ་སྐྱེས་པ༎
འགག་པར་འགྱུར་བ་ཇི་ལྟར་ཡིན༎

ཆོས་ཀྱི་དབྱིངས་ལས་མ་གཏོགས་པའི༎
དངོས་པོ་གང་ཡང་ཡོད་པ་མིན༎
འགྱུར་བ་མེད་པའི་ཆོས་ཉིད་དེ༎
སྐྱེ་འགག་ཡོད་པ་ཇི་ལྟར་ཡིན༎

ཆོས་རྣམས་ཐམས་ཅད་བརྫུན་ཡིན་ན༎
ཀློ་སླུས་བྱེད་པ་ཇི་ལྟར་ཡིན༎
ཆོས་རྣམས་ཐམས་ཅད་བདེན་ཡིན་ན༎
ཐམས་ཅད་བསླུ་བ་ཇི་ལྟར་ཡིན༎

འཁོར་བ་སྡུག་བསྔལ་ཉིད་ཡིན་ན༎
སྡིག་པ་བྱེད་པ་ཤིན་ཏུ་འཁྲུལ༎
མཐོ་རིས་ཐར་པ་མེད་གསུངས་ན༎

Since dharmas do not exist from the beginning,
if the result, buddhahood, never occurs,
which is first: dharmas or the Buddha?

Since, ultimately, nothing whatsoever exists,
if both delusion and non-delusion do not exist,
which is first: relative or ultimate?

Since in the ultimate there is no Buddha,
by whom was the Tripitaka taught?
If no Dharma was taught by the teacher,
how are there volumes of scriptures?

If it is said, "Cessation is nonexistent;
all will die and be born;
the conditioned is ultimately nonexistent,"
how can it be that a result is produced from action?

If the nature does not arise from the beginning,
how will there be cessation?

Aside from the *dharmadhatu*,
nothing whatsoever actually exists.
In that immutable dharmata,
how can there be birth and death?

If all dharmas are false,
why do we think them reliable?
If all dharmas are true,
how is it that everything is deceptive?

If samsara is suffering itself,
performing nonvirtue is extremely deluded.
If it is said there is no liberation to higher realms,

དེ་རྒྱུ་དགེ་བ་བྱེད་པ་འཁྲུལ།།
ལས་འབྲས་བདེན་པ་ཉིད་ཡིན་ན།།
རང་བཞིན་སྟོང་པ་ཡིན་པ་འཁྲུལ།།

ཆུ་ཟླ་ནམ་མཁའི་ཟླ་བ་མིན།།
དེ་ལ་མ་ལྟོས་དེ་སྣང་མེད།།
དེ་བཞིན་དངོས་པོ་ཐམས་ཅད་ཀྱི།།
རང་བཞིན་བདེན་པ་གཉིས་སུ་གསུངས།།

བདེན་པ་གཉིས་ལས་མ་གཏོགས་པའི།།
ཆོས་དེ་འཐད་པར་མི་འགྱུར་ཏེ།།
རང་བཞིན་བདེན་མིན་བརྫུན་མིན་པས།།
བདེན་པ་གཉིས་སུ་འཛིན་པ་འཁྲུལ།།

[9.]

འདོད་ཡོན་སྲེད་པའི་ཚ་ཆུ་ལ།།
ཇོམས་པའི་དུས་གཅིག་མི་གདའ་ན།།
མཛེ་པོས་མེ་ལོང་བལྟས་པ་བཞིན།།
ཞེན་པ་ལོག་ན་ཇོམས་པ་ལགས།།

དུཿཁ་ཆུ་བོའི་གཉེར་མ་ལ།།
སངས་པའི་དུས་གཅིག་མི་གདའ་ན།།
ཐབས་ཀྱིས་མི་བསད་དུ་བ་བཞིན།།
སྡིག་ལས་ལོག་ན་སངས་པ་ཡིན།།

སྐྱེ་རྒ་ན་འཆིའི་ཆུ་བོ་ལས།།
ཐར་པའི་དུས་གཅིག་མི་གདའ་ན།།
ཆུ་ལ་ཟམ་པ་བཙུགས་པ་བཞིན།།
སྐྱེ་མེད་རྟོགས་ན་ཐར་པ་ལགས།།

འཁོར་བའི་རྒྱ་མཚོ་ཆེན་པོ་ལ།།
བསྐམ་པའི་དུས་གཅིག་མི་གདའ་ན།།

performing virtue to cause that is deluded.
If the result of karma itself is true,
the nature, emptiness, is deluded.

The moon in the water is not the moon in the sky,
but without depending on that [moon], that [reflection] does not appear.
Similarly, the nature of all things
is taught as the two truths.

There are no dharmas other than
those included in the two truths;
but because the nature is neither true nor false,
grasping to the two truths is deluded.

9. Never at Any Time

Desire-objects, the salt water of craving,
will never satiate [craving] at any time;
like a leper looking in a mirror,
if one turns away from attachment, one is sated.

The ripples of the river of *duhkha*
will never be removed at any time;
like the smoke of a methodically extinguished fire,
if one turns from nonvirtue [one's duhkha] is removed.

From the river of birth, aging, sickness, and death,
one will never be freed at any time;
like constructing a bridge over a river,
if one realizes non-arising, one is liberated.

The great ocean of samsara
will never dry up at any time;

སྲིད་པའི་ཉི་བདུན་ཤར་བ་བཞིན།།
འདོད་སྲིད་ཡོག་ན་སྐམ་པ་ཡིན།།

འདུས་བྱས་བྱ་བའི་ལས་དཀའ་ལ།།
ཟིན་པའི་དུས་གཅིག་མི་གདའ་ན།།
ཆུ་དག་འོལ་ཁ་བསྐྱུར་བ་བཞིན།།
ཅིག་གིས་བཞག་ན་ཟིན་པ་ལགས།།

གཏི་མུག་མུན་པ་ཐིབས་པོ་ལ།།
སངས་པའི་དུས་གཅིག་མི་གདའ་ན།།
མུན་ཁུང་ནང་དུ་སྒྲོན་མེ་བཞིན།།
ཡེ་ཤེས་ཉི་མ་ཤར་ན་སངས།།

བདག་མེད་ཡེ་ཤེས་ཉི་མ་ལ།།
འཆར་བའི་དུས་གཅིག་མི་གདའ་ན།།
ཉི་མ་འཆར་བའི་སྐྱ་རེངས་བཞིན།།
ཆོས་མཆོག་རྒྱུད་ལ་སྐྱེས་ན་འཆར།།

རྣམ་རྟོག་ཉོན་མོངས་ཟུག་རྔུ་ལ།།
འབྱིན་པའི་དུས་གཅིག་མི་གདའ་ན།།
སྨན་པ་མཁས་པས་མདེའུ་བཏོན་བཞིན།།
གཉེན་པོ་སྟོབས་དང་ལྡན་ན་འབྱིན།།

བདག་འཛིན་སེར་སྣའི་མདུད་པ་ལ།།
གྲོལ་བའི་དུས་གཅིག་མི་གདའ་ན།།
དར་གྱི་མདུད་པ་བཀྲོལ་བ་བཞིན།།
ཡོངས་སྤྱོད་སྒྱུ་མར་ཤེས་ན་གྲོལ།།

ཁམས་གསུམ་འཁོར་བའི་བཙོན་དོང་ནས།།
ཐར་པའི་དུས་གཅིག་མི་གདའ་ན།།
བཙོན་བུ་དོང་ནས་བཏོན་པ་བཞིན།།
གཟུང་འཛིན་ལྟུགས་སྒྲོག་གྲོལ་ན་ཐར།།

like the arising of the seven suns of existence,
if one turns away from craving desire-objects, [one's own samsara] is dried up.

The difficult conditioned activities of work
will never be completed at any time;
like changing canals for irrigation,
by leaving [the work] as it is, it is finished.

The dense darkness of ignorance
will never be removed at any time;
like a lamp in a dark room,
if the sun of wisdom arises, [ignorance] is removed.

The sun of the wisdom of selflessness
will never arise at any time;
like the dawning of the rising sun,
if the supreme dharmas arise in the mindstream, [wisdom] dawns.

The painful defilement of concepts
will never be extracted at any time;
like an experienced doctor extracting an arrowhead,
if one possesses the powerful antidotes, [defiled concepts] are extracted.

The knot of avaricious selfishness
will never be untied at any time;
like untying a knot of silk,
if one understands that possessions are illusory, it is untied.

From the prison of samsara's three realms
one will never be freed at any time;
like a prisoner being released from a cell,
if one is liberated from the iron chains of the grasper and grasped, one
is freed.

མྱ་ངན་འདས་པའི་གྲོང་ཁྱེར་དུ།།
ཕྱིན་པའི་དུས་གཅིག་མི་གདའ་ན།།
འགྲོན་པོ་ལམ་དུ་ཞུགས་པ་བཞིན།།
ཐར་པའི་ལམ་སྣ་ཟིན་ན་ཕྱིན།།

བླ་མ་དགེ་བའི་བཤེས་གཉེན་དང་།།
མཇལ་བའི་དུས་གཅིག་མི་གདའ་ན།།
རྟག་ཏུ་ངུ་དང་ཆོས་འཕགས་བཞིན།།
སྔོན་སྦྱངས་ལས་འཕྲོ་ཡོད་ན་མཇལ།།

གདམས་ངག་བདུད་རྩིའི་ཆུ་རྒྱུན་ལ།།
འཐུང་བའི་དུས་གཅིག་མི་གདའ་ན།།
སྐོམ་པས་བཏུང་བ་རྙེད་པ་བཞིན།།
སྙིང་ལྡན་བྱ་བ་བཏང་ན་འཐུང་།།

གཉིས་མེད་ཕྱག་རྒྱ་ཆེན་པོ་ལ།།
རྟོགས་པའི་དུས་གཅིག་མི་གདའ་ན།།
ཛ་མོ་བུ་དང་འཕྲད་པ་བཞིན།།
སེམས་ངོ་ཤེས་ན་རྟོགས་པ་ལགས།།

ཐ་སྙད་ཚིག་གི་ལོ་མ་ལ།།
འཇོད་པའི་དུས་གཅིག་མི་གདའ་ན།།
ཀ་ཆ་ཟད་པའི་ཡོ་ལང་བཞིན།།
རྣམ་རྟོག་ཟད་ན་འཇོད་པ་ལགས།།

རང་རྒྱུད་ཀོ་བ་སྒྲོང་པོ་ལ།།
ཐུལ་བའི་དུས་གཅིག་མི་གདའ་ན།།
ཆུ་སེར་ཅན་ལ་སྨན་ཆུ་བཞིན།།
ཆོས་བཞིན་བྱེད་ན་ཐུལ་བ་ལགས།།
སྐུ་གསུམ་ཡེ་ཤེས་ལྷུ་ལྡན་ལ།།
ཐོབ་པའི་དུས་གཅིག་མི་གདའ་ན།།
བསོད་ནམས་བསགས་པའི་རྒྱལ་སྲིད་བཞིན།།
ཚོགས་གཉིས་རྫོགས་ན་ཐོབ་པ་ལགས།།

The city of nirvana
will never be reached at any time;
like a guest entering onto a path,
if one is connected with the beginning of the path of liberation, one will arrive.

The guru, the spiritual friend
will never be met at any time;
like Dharmodgata and Sadaprarudita,
if a past accumulated karmic connection exists, [the guru] will be met.

The stream of nectar of oral instruction
will never be drunk at any time;
like finding a drink because of being thirsty,
if a suitable student abandons [mundane] activities, [that student] drinks.

Nondual mahamudra
will never be realized at any time;
like a camel meeting with her calf,
if the mind is recognized, [mahamudra] is realized.

The leaves of the words of conventions
will never be exhausted at any time;
like [closing up] business activities due to exhausting one's merchandise,
if conceptuality is exhausted, [words] are exhausted.

The rawhide of one's mindstream
will never be tamed at any time;
similar to medicine for one with disease,
if one practices according to Dharma, [the mindstream] becomes tamed.
Possession of the three kayas and the five wisdoms
will never be obtained at any time;
like a kingdom from gathered merit,
if the two accumulations are completed, those [kayas and wisdoms] are obtained.

[10.]

ཐོས་བསམ་བྱས་པའི་གྲྭ་པ་རྣམས།།
མདོ་རྒྱུད་དགོངས་པ་ལངས་ལགས་སམ།།
སྒྲོ་འདོགས་ཆོད་པ་མེད་ཉེན་ཆེའོ།།
ཐ་སྙད་ཕྱོགས་སུ་མི་བཏང་འཚལ།།

ཟིན་བཤད་མཛད་པའི་སྟོན་པ་ཀུན།།
རང་ལ་ངེས་ཤེས་བདོག་ལགས་སམ།།
དམ་པའི་གདམས་ངག་ཙུད་ཆོད་ཅིག།
མཁས་པ་ཐ་མལ་འཆི་ཉེན་གདའོ།།

ཉམས་ལེན་མཛད་པའི་སྒོམ་ཆེན་ཀུན།།
བྲེ་མོའི་ལས་ལ་མ་དགའ་མཛོད།།
ལྟོ་རྒྱབ་གཏུང་བ་མ་ཆེ་མཛོད།།
བསམ་གཏན་རོ་ལ་མ་ཆགས་མཛོད།།

སྡིག་ལས་ལོག་པའི་ཆོས་པ་ཀུན།།
མདོ་རྒྱུད་ལྟ་རྟོགས་བག་རེ་མཛོད།།
སྐབས་སུ་བླ་མའི་ཆགས་ཕྱིར་འབྲང་།།
རྟག་ཏུ་རང་གི་སེམས་ལ་ལྟོས།།

དགེ་བའི་ཕྱོགས་ལ་གཡེལ་བ་ན།།
འཆི་བའི་འགྱུར་བ་ཡིད་ལ་གྱིས།།

ཡུལ་ལ་ཆགས་སྣང་སྐྱེས་པ་ན།།
ཆོས་ཀྱི་ཆོས་ཉིད་ཡིད་ལ་གྱིས།།

འཁོར་དང་ཟང་ཟིང་འབྲེལ་པ་ན།།
བདུད་ཀྱི་བསླུ་བྲིད་ཤེས་པར་གྱིས།།

ཇི་ལྟར་བྱས་ཀྱང་མ་བདེ་ན།།
འཁོར་བའི་ཉེས་དམིགས་ཡིད་ལ་གྱིས།།

10. Always Practice Dharma

Do monks who have done hearing and contemplation
comprehend the intent of sutras and tantras?
It is dangerous not to cut doubts;
please do not spend [your time] in pursuit of conventional designations.

Do all teachers who write and teach,
have the benefit of definite knowledge?
Inquire into the sacred oral instruction;
there is a danger that scholars will die in an ordinary way.

All [you] great meditators who practice,
please do not enjoy engaging in idle talk;
please do not yearn greatly for food and clothing;
please do not become attached to the taste of dhyana.

All [you] Dharma practitioners who turn away from nonvirtue,
please comprehend the view of sutra and tantra a little;
occasionally follow the guru as an attendant;
always look into your own mind.

If there is laziness toward the side of virtue,
[keep] the impermanence of death in mind.

If desire and anger arise toward objects,
[keep] the dharmata of dharmas in mind.

If connected with a circle of people and things,
[keep] the deceptions of Mara in mind.

If, despite whatever you may do, there is no happiness,
[keep] the faults of samsara in mind.

ཆོས་ཀྱིས་འདི་དང་ཕྱི་མར་བདེ།།
སྲིད་པ་བར་དོར་བདེ་བ་སྟེ།།
སྐྱེ་བ་ཕྱི་མར་བདེ་བ་ཡིན།།
སྐྱེ་བ་མེད་པས་ཤིན་ཏུ་བདེ།།
རང་བདེ་གཞན་བདེ་གཉིས་ཀ་བདེ།།
དེ་བས་རྟག་ཏུ་ཆོས་མཛོད་ཅིག།

མི་ལུས་གཙང་མ་ཐོབ་དུས་སུ།།
ལྷ་ཆོས་མི་བགྱིད་ཇི་ལྟར་ལགས།།

བླ་མ་དམ་པ་བསྟེན་བསྟེན་ནས།།
མཉེས་པར་མི་བགྱིད་ཇི་ལྟར་ལགས།།

གདམས་ངག་ཟབ་མོ་ཞུ་ཞུ་ནས།།
ཉམས་སུ་མི་ལེན་ཇི་ལྟར་ལགས།།

ཆོས་ལ་ངེས་ཤེས་སྐྱེས་སྐྱེས་ནས།།
སླར་ལ་ལྡོག་པ་ཇི་ལྟར་ལགས།།

[11.]

ཡར་རང་ཡུལ་སྤྱོངས་ལ་བྱེས་སུ་སྤྱོད།།
ཡུལ་དང་བྲལ་ཡང་འགྱོད་པ་མེད།།

བློ་ཕུགས་དཀར་པོའི་ཆོས་ལ་གཏོད།།
དབུལ་བར་སྐྱེས་ཀྱང་འགྱོད་པ་མེད།།

ཡི་དམ་གཙོ་བོར་བླ་མ་བསྟེན།།
ཡོ་བྱད་ཟད་ཀྱང་འགྱོད་པ་མེད།།
བླ་མ་བསྟེན་བཀུར་གང་ཡིན་བྱ།།
ཐུགས་མི་འདོགས་ཀྱང་འགྱོད་པ་མེད།།

ལུང་དང་བསྟན་པའི་མན་ངག་ཞུ།།
ཉམས་ལེན་མ་བྱུང་འགྱོད་པ་མེད།།

With Dharma, this life and the next life are blissful,
the *bardo* existence is blissful,
rebirth is blissful;
[these are] very blissful because of birthlessness.
Oneself is blissful, others are blissful, both are blissful;
therefore, please always practice Dharma.

At the time of obtaining complete human birth,
why is it that one does not practice spiritual Dharma?

Having been with a sacred guru again and again,
why is it that one has not pleased him?

Having requested the profound oral instruction again and again,
why is it that one has not done any practice?

Having aroused definite knowledge in the Dharma again and again,
why is it that one goes back again?

11. Have No Regrets

Generally, leave your homeland and remain in exile;
even though one is separated from one's country, there is no regret.

Direct the mind always to positive dharmas;
even if one is born in hell, there is no regret.

Rely on the guru as the principal deity;
even if one's resources are exhausted, there is no regret.
Do any devotional service for the guru;
even if [the guru] shows no interest, there is no regret.

Request the upadeshas in accord with scripture;
even if one cannot practice, there is no regret.

དགེ་སྦྱོར་གཙོ་བོར་བྱ་བ་ཐོང་།།
དངོས་གྲུབ་མ་ཐོབ་འགྲོད་པ་མེད།།

སོ་ནམ་གཙོ་བོར་དམ་ཚིག་སྲུངས།།
གྲོགས་ཀྱིས་ཁྲེལ་ཡང་འགྲོད་པ་མེད།།

ཚོགས་སོགས་མི་ཚེ་ཆོས་ལ་སྐྱེལ།།
ཤི་བར་གྱུར་ཀྱང་འགྲོད་པ་མེད།།

རང་རེ་མི་འགྲོད་ཙམ་རེ་མཛོད།།
གཞན་གྱིས་འཕྱུས་ཀྱང་འགྲོད་པ་མེད།།

གྲོགས་ལ་མ་དགའ་གཅིག་པུར་སྡོད།།
ནད་གཡོག་མེད་ཀྱང་འགྲོད་པ་མེད།།

ལྷ་རྫོགས་གཙོ་བོར་སེམས་ལ་ལྷོས།།
ཀོ་རྫོགས་ཆུང་ཡང་འགྲོད་པ་མེད།།

ནད་དང་མཐུན་པའི་ཁ་ཟས་བསྟེན།།
ན་ཚ་བྱུང་ཡང་འགྲོད་པ་མེད།།

རྐྱེན་དང་མཐུན་པའི་སྤྱོད་པ་གྱིས།།
ཚུལ་འཆོས་སོང་ཡང་འགྲོད་པ་མེད།།

གཞན་སྐྱོན་མ་རྟོག་རང་སྐྱོན་རྟོག།
ཤ་ཚ་ཆུང་ཡང་འགྲོད་པ་མེད།།

བསམ་མནོའི་གཙོ་བོར་གཞན་ཕན་སེམས།།
རང་དོན་ཤོར་ཡང་འགྲོད་པ་མེད།།

ཉམས་དང་མཐུན་པའི་གླུ་ཆུང་ལོང་།།
ཐོ་ཅོར་ཤོར་ཡང་འགྲོད་པ་མེད།།

ཡོ་ལང་བསྲིས་ཀྱི་ཚོད་དང་སྦྱོར།།
སྟོན་མོ་ངན་ཡང་འགྲོད་པ་མེད།།

Abandon activities, as the principal virtuous conduct;
even if *siddhis* are not obtained, there is no regret.

Protect your promises as your principal concern;
even if one is ridiculed by friends, there is no regret.

Spend your life in the Dharma, gathering accumulations;
even if one dies, there is no regret.

Please do not create regret for yourself;
even if blamed by others, there is no regret.

Reside alone, without attachment to friends;
even if one is without attendants, there is no regret.

Look into the mind as the principal realization of view;
even if one's realization is small, there is no regret.

Rely on eating food to harmonize disease;
even when one is ill, there is no regret.

Perform conduct according to your vows;
even if it becomes misconduct, there is no regret.

Examine your own faults; do not examine others' faults;
even if there is little affection, there is no regret.

Make the benefit of others your principal consideration;
even if one's own benefit is lost, there is no regret.

Sing a small song agreeing with experience;
even though one may be lost to idle talk, there is no regret.

Apply the measure of thrift to possessions;
even if celebrations are poor, there is no regret.

རྒྱ་མཚོའི་ནང་དུ་རྡོ་བསྐྱུར་བཞིན།།
ཕྱིར་མི་ལྡོག་པའི་ཆོས་ཤིག་འཚལ།།

ཏྭ་ལའི་མགོ་བོ་བཅད་པ་བཞིན།།
སྐྱེ་བ་མེད་པའི་ཆོས་ཤིག་འཚལ།།

མུན་པའི་ཚོགས་ལ་སྣང་བ་བཞིན།།
གཉེན་པོར་འགྲོ་བའི་ཆོས་ཤིག་འཚལ།།

རིག་བྱེད་བྲམ་ཟེའི་སློབ་མ་བཞིན།།
ལུང་གིས་ཟིན་པའི་ཆོས་ཤིག་འཚལ།།

གསེར་ལ་ནག་ཚུར་བཏབ་པ་བཞིན།།
གྲོགས་སུ་འགྲོ་བའི་ཆོས་ཤིག་འཚལ།།

[12.]

ལྷ་ཁང་ནང་གི་སྒོ་སྲུང་དེ།།
བརྗིག་བརྗིག་འདྲ་ལ་མི་བརྗིག་གོ།

མངའ་ཐང་རྒྱས་པའི་ཁྱིམ་པ་དེ།།
སྐྱིད་སྐྱིད་འདྲ་ཡང་སྡུག་པ་ཡིན།།

དཀའ་ཐུབ་བྱེད་པའི་ཆོས་པ་དེ།།
སྡུག་སྡུག་འདྲ་ཡང་སྐྱིད་པ་ཡིན།།

སྦྱིན་པ་བཏང་བའི་ལོངས་སྤྱོད་དེ།།
འཛད་འཛད་འདྲ་ཡང་འཕེལ་བ་ཡིན།།

སངས་རྒྱས་སེམས་ཅན་མཉམ་པ་ལ།།
སྐྱིད་སྡུག་ཁྱད་རེ་ཆེ་ཞིག་བྱུང་།།

བདག་དང་གཞན་དུ་མཉམ་པ་ལ།།
ཚེད་འཛིན་ཁྱད་རེ་ཆེ་ཞིག་བྱུང་།།

Please seek an irreversible Dharma,
like a stone thrown into the ocean.

Please seek a non-arising Dharma,
like a banana tree with its top cut off.

Please seek an antidotal Dharma,
like a light in a mass of darkness.

Please seek a scripturally authorized Dharma,
like a disciple of a Vedic brahmin.

Please seek a conducive Dharma,
like applying vitriol to gold.

12. The Great Differences

Although those door protectors inside the temple
seem to be hitting, hitting, they do not hit.

Although those increasingly powerful laypersons
seem happy, happy, they are miserable.

Although those Dharma practitioners facing hardship
seem miserable, miserable, they are happy.

Although that wealth coming from generosity
seems to be dwindling, dwindling, it is increasing.

Sentient beings and buddhas are equal,
yet happiness and sadness create the great difference between them.

Self and others are equal,
yet the reason for grasping creates the great difference between them.

དགྲ་དང་བུ་ཏུ་མཉམ་པ་ལ།།
བྱམས་སྡང་ཁྱད་རེ་ཆེ་ཞིག་བྱུང་།།

མི་ལུས་ཐོབ་པར་མཉམ་པ་ལ།།
རྒྱལ་ཕམ་ཁྱད་རེ་ཆེ་ཞིག་བྱུང་།།

མི་ལུས་ཐོབ་པའི་སྐྱེས་བུ་ཀུན།།
སྡིག་པའི་ལས་ལ་མ་དགའ་མཛོད།།
ཚེ་འདིའི་དུཿཁ་སྨོས་ཅི་དགོས།།

དགེ་བ་བྱེད་པ་ཐམས་ཅད་ལ།།
ལྷ་བ་བསྔོ་བས་ཟིན་པར་མཛོད།།
ཟག་བཅས་དགེ་བར་མི་གཏང་འཚལ།།

འཁོར་བ་པ་ལ་བདེ་བ་མེད།།
རང་ལ་དེ་དོན་མི་གནས་པར།།
ཞལ་ཏ་བྱས་པའི་ཅི་ལ་ཕན།།

ཚེ་འདིའི་འདུ་ཤེས་མ་ལོག་པར།།
ཆོས་སྒོར་ཞུགས་པས་ཅི་ལ་ཕན།།
སྐྱེ་ཤིའི་འཇིགས་པ་མེད་པ་ལ།།
གདམས་ངག་བསྟན་པས་ཅི་ལ་ཕན།།

རྣམ་རྟོག་སྒྲ་ལོ་མ་བྲིགས་པའི།།
མགོ་སྐྱ་བྲེགས་པས་ཅི་ལ་ཕན།།
ཐ་མལ་འདུ་ཤེས་མ་བསྒྱུར་བར།།
གོས་མདོག་བསྒྱུར་བས་ཅི་ལ་ཕན།།

བླ་མ་དམ་པ་མ་བསྟེན་པར།།
རང་ཡུལ་སྤངས་པས་ཅི་ལ་ཕན།།
གདམས་ངག་ཉམས་སུ་མ་བླངས་པར།།
ཐོས་བསམ་བྱས་པས་ཅི་ལ་ཕན།།

Enemies and children are equal,
yet loving kindness and anger create the great difference between them.

Everyone obtaining a human body is equal,
yet victory and defeat create the great difference between them.

Beings who have obtained a human body,
do not rejoice in sinful activity;
since the duhkha of this life is unbearable, what need is there to mention [the duhkha of lower realms]?

All the virtue you perform,
perform connected with view and dedication;
please do not make it into defiled virtue.

"There is no happiness for samsaric beings";
if that meaning does not exist for oneself,
what is the benefit of giving teachings?

Without turning away from thoughts of this life,
what is the benefit of engaging with the Dharma?
Without fear of birth and death,
what is the benefit of teaching the oral instructions?

Without cutting the hairy leaves of conceptuality,
what is the benefit of shaving one's head?
Without bringing change to ordinary perception,
what is the benefit of changing the color of one's clothes?

Without relying on the sacred guru,
what is the benefit of abandoning one's country?
Without actually practicing the oral instructions,
what is the benefit of hearing and contemplation?

འཆི་བའི་དུས་ལ་བབས་པ་ན།།
ཆོས་མིན་ཕན་པར་མི་གདའོ།།

ལར་འདོད་ཅན་བླ་མ་གཡོ་སྒྱུ་ཅན།།
ཟབ་མོའི་གདམས་ངག་གནང་དུས་མེད།།
དྲང་དོན་བསླུ་བྲིད་བརྫུན་པོ་ཆེ།།
ངེས་པའི་དོན་དང་མཇལ་དུས་མེད།།

འཁོར་བའི་དུཿཁ་ཚན་པོ་ཆེ།།
མྱ་ངན་འདས་པ་ཐོབ་དུས་མེད།།
གཉི་མུག་མུན་ནག་ཚབས་པོ་ཆེ།།
ཡེ་ཤེས་ཉི་མ་འཆར་དུས་མེད།།

[13.]

སྒྱུ་མ་ལྟ་བུའི་དོན་རྟོགས་ན།།
བདེན་ཚིག་ཟད་ནས་ཆོད་པ་ལགས།།

སྐྱེ་བ་མེད་པའི་དོན་རྟོགས་ན།།
འཁྲུལ་པ་ཟད་ནས་ཆོད་པ་ལགས།།

རྒྱུ་དང་འབྲས་བུའི་དོན་རྟོགས་ན།།
དྲང་དོན་ཟད་ནས་ཆོད་པ་ལགས།།

ནམ་མཁའ་ལྟ་བུའི་དོན་རྟོགས་ན།།
ངེས་དོན་ཟད་ནས་ཆོད་པ་ལགས།།

སྟོང་པ་ཉིད་ཀྱི་དོན་རྟོགས་ན།།
རྣམ་རྟོག་ཟད་ནས་ཆོད་པ་ལགས།།

བླ་མ་དམ་པའི་ཐུགས་རྗེན་ན།།
གདམས་ངག་ཟད་ནས་ཆོད་པ་ལགས།།

When the time of death arrives,
nothing helps aside from Dharma.

Generally, a greedy and deceitful guru
has no time to bestow the profound oral instructions.
A big liar misleading others with provisional meanings
has no time to meet with the definitive meaning.

A great magnifier of samsara's duhkha
has no time to obtain nirvana.
One in the great black darkness of ignorance
has no time for the dawn of the sun of wisdom.

13. Searching and Uncovering

If the meaning of "illusion-like" is realized,
one's search has uncovered words of truth.

If the meaning of non-arising is realized,
one's search has uncovered delusion.

If the meaning of cause and result is realized,
one's search has uncovered provisional meaning.

If the meaning of "space-like" is realized,
one's search has uncovered definitive meaning.

If the meaning of emptiness is realized,
one's search has uncovered conceptuality.

If one is connected to the mind of the sacred guru,
one's search has uncovered the oral instructions.

ཇི་ཙམ་པ་ཡི་ཆོས་ཤེས་ཀྱང་།།
གདམས་པའི་སྤྱོད་དང་མི་ལྡན་ན།།
ལྟ་བ་རྟོགས་པར་མི་གདའོ།།

ཐ་སྙད་སྤྲོས་པ་མ་ཆོད་པའི།།
འཇིག་རྟེན་གཡེང་བས་མ་གཡེངས་ཤིང་།།
གཅིག་པུར་སྤྱོད་ཅིག་མ་ནུས་ན།།
དངོས་གྲུབ་ཐོབ་པར་མི་གདའོ།།
འཁོར་དང་ཟང་ཟིང་སྤྲོངས་ལ་ཐོང་།།

དོན་གྱི་བཙུད་ཐིགས་མ་རྟོགས་ན།།
ཐ་སྙད་སྤྲུན་ལ་སྙིང་པོ་མེད།།
ཆོས་བརྒྱུད་གཡེང་བས་མ་ཁྲེར་བར།།
བྱ་བ་ཐོང་ལ་ཉམས་སུ་ལོངས།།

[14.]

ལྟ་བ་སྒོམ་པ་འབྲེལ་ལམ་ལྟོས།།
སྤྱོད་པ་དུས་དང་འབྲེལ་ལམ་ལྟོས།།
གདམས་ངག་ལུང་དང་འབྲེལ་ལམ་ལྟོས།།
ཆོས་དང་གང་ཟག་འབྲེལ་ལམ་ལྟོས།།
མཉམ་གཞག་རྗེས་ཐོབ་འབྲེལ་ལམ་ལྟོས།།
བླ་མ་བརྒྱུད་པར་འབྲེལ་ལམ་ལྟོས།།

ལར་མདོ་རྒྱུད་ཚིག་ལ་ཐུག་པ་མེད།།
ད་ནི་ཚིག་འཕྲོ་གཅོད་ལས་ཆེ།།
དོན་ལ་སྒྲོ་འདོགས་ཆོད་ནས་གདའ།།
ད་ནི་ལྟ་འཕྲོ་གཅོད་ལས་ཆེ།།

འཇིག་རྟེན་བྱ་བས་དགོས་པ་མེད།།
ད་ནི་གཡེང་བ་སྤངས་ལས་ཆེ།།

འཆི་བདག་གཤིན་རྗེ་བློ་ལྟོས་མེད།།
ད་ནི་ཉམས་སུ་ལེན་ལས་ཆེ།།

Furthermore, however much of the Dharma is understood,
If one is not a suitable recipient of instructions,
the view will not be realized.

Do not be diverted by the worldly distractions
of not cutting off conventional proliferations.
If one is not able to live in solitude,
one will not obtain siddhis;
give up and leave your circle of people and things.

If the germ of the ultimate is not realized,
there is no essence in the husk of convention.
Not carried away by the distractions of the eight worldly dharmas,
abandon activities and take up practice.

14. See the Connections

See the connection between view and meditation;
see the connection between conduct and time;
see the connection between oral instruction and scripture;
see the connection between the person and Dharma practice;
see the connection between meditation and post-meditation;
see the connection between lineage and guru.

Generally, there is no end to the words of sutras and tantras;
right now, the important thing is to stop words.
Having cut doubt in the meaning,
now, the important thing is to stop looking.

[There is] no purpose in doing worldly activities;
now, the important thing is to abandon distractions.

One cannot depend on Yama, the lord of death;
now, the important thing is to practice.

ནམ་འཆི་ཆ་མེད་བརྩོན་འགྲུས་བསྐྱེད།།

སྐྱིད་ན་བླ་མའི་བཀའ་དྲིན་ཡིན།།
སྡུག་ན་སྔོན་གྱི་ལས་འཕྲོ་ཡིན།།
རྒྱུད་ན་ཞུམ་པར་མི་བགྱིད་ཅིང་།།
འབྱོར་ན་དྲེགས་པར་མི་བགྱིད་འཚལ།།

[15.]

ཆོས་སྒོ་བརྒྱད་ཁྲི་བཞི་སྟོང་ལས།།
དད་པ་ཅན་གྱི་གང་ཟག་གིས།།
སྡིག་ལས་ལྡོག་པ་དེ་ཡིན་མོད།།
དགེ་བའི་བྱ་བ་འཇུག་དགོས་ལ།།
བྱར་མེད་བློ་དང་ལྡན་དགོས་ཀྱིས།།
ཆོས་ཀྱི་བྱ་བའང་ཞིག་ལ་ཐོང་།།

ཆོས་ལ་སྨོད་པ་མ་ལགས་ཏེ།།
གང་ཟག་ལ་ཡང་གཤེ་མ་ལགས།།
ཆོས་དང་གང་ཟག་འཛོལ་བ་མཐོང་།།
དེ་ཡང་ཇི་ལྟར་མཐོང་ཞེ་ན།།
ཐོས་ཆུང་ཤེས་རབ་ཞན་པ་ཡིས།།
གང་ཟག་ཆོས་ཀྱིས་བསླུས་པ་མཐོང་།།
རྟོགས་པའི་དོན་དང་མི་ལྡན་པར།།
ཆོས་དང་གང་ཟག་སྒྲོ་སྐུར་ཆེ།།
རྣམ་རྟོག་སྲིན་བུའི་ཁ་ཆུས་གཏུམས།།
ང་བཟང་བདུད་ཀྱི་ལྕགས་ཀྱུས་ཟིན།།
དུ་མ་རོ་གཅིག་གནད་དང་བྲལ།།
བཀའ་གདམས་ཆོས་ཀྱང་ཞིག་ལ་ཐོང་།།

དགེ་སྡིག་བླང་དོར་མི་བྱེད་པས།།
མི་ཤེས་བཞིན་དུ་མཁས་པར་བརྫུ།།
ཧད་མེད་ཐོ་ཅོའི་སྤྱོད་པ་བྱེད།།
སྨྱུ་བྱེད་རྒྱལ་ཁམས་བརྫུན་གྱིས་འགེངས།།
རྣལ་འབྱོར་ཆོས་ཀྱང་ཞིག་ལ་ཐོང་།།

The time of death is uncertain; develop diligence.

If one is happy, it is the kindness of the guru;
if one is sad, it emanates from previous karma.
If you suffer loss, don't be discouraged;
if you experience gain, don't be arrogant.

15. Leave Dharma and Go!

The person of faith
in the eighty-four thousand gates of Dharma
may turn away from sinful actions.
One must engage in virtuous activity;
it is necessary to possess a mind without [mundane] activity.
Further, give up Dharma activities and go!

Do not slander the Dharma
and do not abuse the person.
Perceiving a confusion between Dharma and person,
one may then ask how that is perceived;
a person is perceived to be misled with Dharma
because of [their] inferior intelligence and small learning.
Without possessing the goal of realization,
greatly exaggerating and disparaging Dharma teachings and persons,
covered by the worm spittle of conceptuality,
grabbed by the hook of the Mara of conceit,
without the key point of many being of one taste;
leave also Kadampa dharma and go!

Not making a distinction between the acceptance and rejection of virtue and nonvirtue,
pretending to be knowledgeable without having understanding,
performing wild conduct without heat,
creating deceptions and filling the country with lies;
leave also yogin dharma and go!

གསང་སྔགས་ཆོས་སུ་ཁས་བླངས་ནས།།
སྨིན་ལམ་དབང་དང་མི་ལྡན་ཞིང་།།
གྲོལ་ལམ་ཐབས་ཀྱི་གནད་དང་བྲལ།།
གསང་སྔགས་རྗེ་བཙུན་མ་མཇལ་བས།།
ཕྱག་ཆེན་ཆོས་ཀྱང་ཞོག་ལ་ཐོང་།།

ཐེག་ཆེན་ཆོས་སུ་ཁས་བླངས་ནས།།
སྙིང་རྗེ་བྱང་ཆུབ་སེམས་དང་བྲལ།།
རྩོལ་མེད་གཞི་ཡི་ཆོས་སུ་ལས།།
ཆོས་དང་གང་ཟག་འབྲེལ་པ་མེད།།
རྫོགས་ཆེན་ཆོས་ཀྱང་ཞོག་ལ་ཐོང་།།

ཕུང་པོ་གཞི་མེད་རི་བོང་རྭས།།
ཁྱད་པར་ཁ་མིག་གཉེར་མ་བགྲང་།།
མཚན་གཞི་མེད་པར་མཚན་ཉིད་ཚོལ།།
མངོན་པའི་ཆོས་ཀྱང་ཞོག་ལ་ཐོང་།།

འཁྲུལ་སྣང་དངོས་མེད་བསླུ་བ་ལ།།
དོན་མེད་འགལ་འགལ་འབྲེལ་རྩིས་བྱེད།།
སེམས་ལ་མི་ཕན་འཆི་ཁར་བསླུ།།
ཚད་མའི་ཆོས་ཀྱང་ཞོག་ལ་ཐོང་།།

འཁྲུལ་སྣང་བདེན་འཛིན་ཡོང་སྐྲན་ཅན།།
སྟོང་ཉིད་ཁས་ལེན་སྙིང་པོར་འཛིན།།
ཁྱབ་པ་ཕྱོགས་ཆོས་རྩོལ་སྒྲུབ་ཅན།།
དབུ་མའི་ཆོས་ཀྱང་ཞོག་ལ་ཐོང་།།

ཐ་སྙད་ཚིག་ལ་མི་ཚེ་བསྐྱལ།།
མཁས་ཀྱང་སེམས་ཀྱི་དོན་མི་ཤེས།།
འཆི་ཁར་སྦྱོངས་པའི་ལུས་སུ་འཆི།།
མཚན་ཉིད་ཆོས་ཀྱང་ཞོག་ལ་ཐོང་།།

སློབ་དཔོན་མཚན་ཉིད་མི་ལྡན་པར།།
གསུམ་ལྡན་ཆོས་ཀྱིས་འབྲེལ་པར་བྱེད།།

Having accepted secret mantra as Dharma
without possessing the ripening path of abhisheka,
separated from the key points of the method of the path of liberation
because of not having met a lord of secret mantra;
leave also Mahamudra dharma and go!

Having accepted Mahayana as Dharma,
separated from compassion and bodhichitta,
action, dharma, and person are not connected
in the dharma of the effortless basis;
leave also Dzogchen dharma and go!

Like a rabbit with horns, the aggregates are without a basis—
in particular, counting mouths, eyes, and wrinkles,
searching for a characteristic without a basis of a characteristic;
leave also Abhidharma and go!

A reckoning that connects contradiction with contradiction
to deceptive, unreal, deluded appearances is meaningless
and, not benefiting the mind, one is deceived at the time of death;
leave also logic dharma and go!

Possessing an internal tumor of grasping truth in deluded appearances,
holding the acceptance of emptiness as the essence;
with the effort of establishing the pervasion of the minor premise;
leave also Madhyamaka dharma and go!

Spending life pursuing conventional words,
having no understanding of the meaning of mind, however knowledgeable,
when death comes, one dies in a body of delusion;
leave also dialectical dharma and go!

The master, not possessing qualifications,
makes dharma connections with the following three:

འདོད་ཆེན་ཆོས་ལ་རིན་ཐང་འདེབས།།
དམ་མེད་བླ་མའི་ཇོ་མོ་སྐྱུད།།
ཐབས་མེད་སྦྱོར་སྒྲོལ་གཉིས་ལ་ཞེན།།
སྔགས་པའི་ཆོས་ཀྱང་ཞོག་ལ་ཐོང་།།

ཚུལ་འཆོས་ལུས་ངག་བཙོན་དུ་འཛིན།།
སེམས་ཉིད་ལྷ་སྒོམ་དོན་དང་བྲལ།།
དོན་མེད་དཀའ་ཐུབ་ངོ་སྐྱིག་ཅན།།
བཙུན་པའི་ཆོས་ཀྱང་ཞོག་ལ་ཐོང་།།

ཐོས་བསམ་མ་བྱས་སླིན་སྒོམ་བྱེད།།
སྡོད་ན་ཚེམས་དུབས་མཁར་ལེན་བྱེད།།
གྲོང་དུ་འགྲོ་ན་ཚུལ་འཆོས་བྱེད།།
ཐུན་ཞབས་བྱིང་རྨུགས་གཉིད་དུ་གཏོང་།།
ལྷ་ན་ཁུར་གྱི་འོག་ཏུ་ལྷ།།
ཁུར་ཅན་མཚམས་ཀྱི་ནང་དུ་གཏོང་།།
ཁུར་མེད་སྒོ་ཡི་ཕྱི་རུ་སྡོམ།།
དད་ཟས་ནོར་གྱིས་ཚ་སྲིང་གསོ།།
སྒོམ་ཆེན་ཆོས་ཀྱང་ཞོག་ལ་ཐོང་།།

ཆོས་ཟབ་བཤད་ན་གོ་བ་མེད།།
འབྲེལ་མེད་ཡོང་གཏམ་བཞད་གད་དང་།།
སྙུ་བྱེད་བྲོ་དང་གླུ་ལ་དགའ།།
ཁ་ཆོས་ཁ་ལྷ་གཡོ་སྒྱུ་ཅན།།
ཡ་མ་ཁ་མཆུ་ཕྲ་མ་སྐྱེལ།།
ཐབ་ན་ཁྱིམ་མཆོས་ནང་ནོར་བརྐུ།།
བྱར་མེད་ཁྱིམ་སོ་རླུང་ལ་བསྐུར།།
ཉ་མའི་ཆོས་ཀྱང་ཞོག་ལ་ཐོང་།།

ཁེ་གྲགས་འཐབ་རྩོད་འཚོ་སྐྱོང་དང་།།
ཚོལ་ཁྲོ་དུ༔ ཁ་བྱུར་གྱི་ཚང་།།
དགེ་བའི་ཆོས་ལ་རྒྱབ་ཀྱིས་ཕྱོགས།།
དོན་མེད་མི་ཚེ་སྟུག་ལ་སྐྱེལ།།

greedily charging prices for Dharma,
enjoying the consort of the guru without samaya,
and being attached to both union and liberation without the method;
leave also Vajrayana dharma and go!

Held in the prison of misconduct of body and speech,
mind itself is without the view and meaning of meditation.
Duplicitous hardship is purposeless;
leave also ordained dharma and go!

Ignorantly meditating without hearing and contemplation,
doing construction or sewing when sitting,
behaving with misconduct if one goes to the village,
ending meditation sessions in foggy and sluggish sleep;
if one looks, one looks for gifts,
permitting those with gifts into the retreat boundary
and leaving those without gifts outside;
supporting their relatives by feeding them with devotional offerings;
leave also great meditator's dharma and go!

Not understanding if the profound Dharma is explained;
enjoying jokes, pointless idle talk,
seductive dances, and song;
the dharma and view of these deceitful ones is merely "in the mouth."
Creating calumny and disputes here and there;
if they can, robbing wealth from the neighbor's home;
disregarding family responsibilities and remaining idle;
leave also housewife dharma and go!

Profit, fame, conflicts, arguments,
livelihood, frustration, dissatisfaction:
a source of misfortune and suffering opposed to virtuous dharmas;
spending life in misery without any purpose,

འགྲོ་ས་ངན་སོང་གསུམ་ལས་མེད།།
ཁྱིམ་པའི་ཆོས་ཀྱང་ཞོག་ལ་ཐོང་།།

དང་པོ་སྡིག་གི་བྱ་བ་ཐོང་།།
བར་དུ་འཇིག་རྟེན་བྱ་བ་ཐོང་།།
ཐ་མ་ཆོས་ཀྱི་བྱ་བ་ཐོང་།།

བྱ་བཏང་རྣལ་འབྱོར་བློ་རེ་བདེ།།
ནོར་སོགས་སྒོམ་ཆེན་ཁྱིམ་པ་ཡིན།།
མཚན་བཅས་སྒོམ་པ་རྣམ་རྟོག་ཡིན།།
ལུས་ངག་དགེ་སྦྱོར་ཚུལ་འཆོས་ཡིན།།

བྱར་མེད་ཚོགས་དྲུག་ལྷུག་པར་ཞོག།

ཆགས་ན་ལྷ་ལ་ཆགས་ཀྱང་འཆིང་།།
འདོད་ན་སངས་རྒྱས་འདོད་ཀྱང་འཁྲུལ།།
ཞེན་ན་ཆོས་ལ་ཞེན་ཀྱང་བསླུ།།
རིག་པ་དབྱིངས་ཀྱི་ངང་ལ་ཐིམ།།

[16.]

གོ་བ་རྣམས་ལ་གདམས་ངག་ཡིན།།

སེམས་སྐྱོང་པའི་ནང་ན་རིག་པ་འགྱུ།།
གཟུང་འཛིན་མཚན་མ་རང་སར་གྲོལ།།
ཕྱུགས་རིས་ཞེ་འདོད་མིང་ཡང་མེད།།
ལྟ་བ་ཐག་ཆོད་བློ་རེ་བདེ།།

སྒོམ་མེད་ནང་ན་ཡེངས་མེད་འགྱུ།།
རྣམ་རྟོག་མཚན་མ་རང་སར་གྲོལ།།
བྱིང་རྒོད་གཉིས་ཀྱི་མིང་ཡང་མེད།།
སྒོམ་པ་ཐག་ཆོད་བློ་རེ་བདེ།།

there is nowhere to go but down into the three lower realms;
leave also householder dharma and go!

First, leave nonvirtuous activities;
in the middle, leave mundane activities;
finally, leave Dharma activities.

The mind of the yogin who has relinquished activities is happy;
the great meditator who gathers wealth is a layperson;
meditating with characteristics is conceptuality;
the virtuous actions of body and speech are misconduct.

Without activity, leave the six consciousnesses relaxed.

If attached, even attachment to the deity is bondage.
If desirous, even desire for buddhahood is deluded.
If grasping, even grasping at Dharma is deceived.
Dissolve awareness into the natural state.

16. The Oral Instruction for Those Who Understand

This is the oral instruction for those who understand:

Awareness flows into the emptiness of mind;
characteristics of grasping and grasper are liberated at their own place;
even the term "biased opinion" does not exist;
the mind realized in the view is blissful.

Non-distraction flows into non-meditation;
the characteristics of conceptuality are liberated at their own place;
even the terms "sluggishness" and "agitation" do not exist;
the mind realized in meditation is blissful.

འགག་མེད་ནང་ན་ཤུགས་འབྱུང་འཁྱོ།།
ཚུལ་འཆོས་མཚན་མ་རང་སར་གྲོལ།།
སྣང་དོར་བྱ་བའི་མིང་ཡང་མེད།།
སྤྱོད་པ་ཐག་ཆོད་བློ་རེ་བདེ།།

སྐྱེ་མེད་ངང་ནས་འཆི་མེད་འཁྱོ།།
རེ་དོགས་མཚན་མ་རང་སར་གྲོལ།།
འདི་དང་ཕྱི་མ་མིང་ཡང་མེད།།
འབྲས་བུ་ཐག་ཆོད་བློ་རེ་བདེ།།

ལྟ་བ་གཟའ་གཏད་མེད་པ་འབྱུང་།།
འཁྲུལ་པ་འཇིག་ན་འདི་ཡིས་འཇིག།
ཞེ་འདོད་ཕྱོགས་རིས་མི་བདོག་པས།།
གཟུང་འཛིན་མི་གནོད་ངོ་མཚར་ཆེ།།

སྒོམ་དུ་མ་བཅོས་ཤུགས་བྱུང་འབྱུང་།།
ལམ་ས་ཆོད་ན་འདི་ཡིས་ཆོད།།
དམིགས་པ་གཏད་རྒྱུ་མི་བདོག་པས།།
བྱིང་རྒོད་མི་གནོད་ངོ་མཚར་ཆེ།།

སྤྱོད་པ་འགག་མེད་ཤུགས་བྱུང་འབྱུང་།།
ཞེན་པ་བཟློག་ན་འདི་ཡིས་བཟློག།
དགག་སྒྲུབ་འདུ་ཤེས་མི་བདོག་པས།།
སྣང་དོར་མི་གནོད་ངོ་མཚར་ཆེ།།

འབྲས་བུ་མ་བཅལ་ལྷུན་གྲུབ་འབྱུང་།།
ཐ་སྙད་ཆོས་སྐུ་འདི་ཡིས་ཐོབ།།
སྤངས་ཐོབ་འདུ་ཤེས་མི་བདོག་པས།།
རེ་དོགས་མེད་པ་ངོ་མཚར་ཆེ།།

རེས་འགའ་ནམ་མཁའི་མཐོངས་ན་བདེ།།
མཐའ་དབུས་མེད་པའི་ངང་ལ་བདེ།།

རེས་འགའ་རྒྱ་མཚོའི་གཏིང་ན་བདེ།།
གཡོ་འགྱུལ་མེད་པའི་ངང་ལ་བདེ།།

Naturally occurring [conduct] flows into ceaselessness;
the characteristics of misconduct are liberated at their own place;
even the terms "acceptance" and "rejection" do not exist;
the mind realized in conduct is blissful.

Deathlessness flows into the state of non-arising,
the characteristics of hope and fear are liberated at their own place,
even the terms "present" and "future" do not exist;
the mind realized in the result is blissful.

The view is produced without being eclipsed;
if delusion is destroyed, it is destroyed by this;
having no opinionated bias,
the absence of the harm of grasper and grasped is amazing!

Unfabricated meditation occurs naturally;
if the paths and stages are reached, they are reached by this;
not having the cause of focusing on objects,
the absence of the harm of sluggishness and agitation is amazing!

Ceaseless conduct naturally occurs;
if grasping is turned away, it is turned away by this;
not having the thought of refutation and establishment,
the absence of the harm of acceptance and rejection is amazing!

Not seeking the effortlessly produced result,
conventionally, dharmakaya is obtained by this;
not having the thought of abandonment and achievement,
the absence of the harm of hope and fear is amazing!

Sometimes there is bliss in the space of the sky;
there is bliss in the state without extremes or center.

Sometimes there is bliss in the depths of the ocean;
there is bliss in the state without movement or agitation.

རེས་འགའ་ཉི་ཟླའི་སྟེང་ན་བདེ།།
གསལ་འགྲིབ་མེད་པའི་ངང་ལ་བདེ།།

རེས་འགའ་ཆུ་བོའི་གཞུང་ན་བདེ།།
རྒྱུན་ཆད་མེད་པའི་ངང་ལ་བདེ།།

རེས་འགའ་བླ་མའི་དྲུང་ན་བདེ།།
གདམས་ངག་སྒྲོས་པ་གཅོད་ཅིང་བདེ།།

རེས་འགའ་རི་ཁྲོད་གནས་ན་བདེ།།
གཅིག་པུར་ཉམས་ལེན་བྱེད་ཅིང་བདེ།།

རེས་འགའ་ཚོང་འདུས་དབུས་ན་བདེ།།
སྣང་བ་ལམ་དུ་ཁྱེར་ཞིང་བདེ།།

རེས་འགའ་རྣལ་འབྱོར་གྲལ་ན་བདེ།།
ཉམས་མྱོང་རྟོགས་པ་བསྡུར་ཞིང་བདེ།།

རེས་འགའ་མཛེ་སྦྲང་གསེབ་ན་བདེ།།
རོ་སྙོམས་སྤྱོད་པ་བྱེད་ཅིང་བདེ།།

རེས་འགའ་རྒྱལ་ཁམས་ཡངས་ན་བདེ།།
ཕྱོགས་མེད་གཅིག་ཧྲོམ་བྱེད་ཅིང་བདེ།།
རྟག་ཏུ་གནས་ལུགས་སྟེང་ན་བདེ།།
ཕྱོགས་རིས་མེད་པའི་ངང་ལ་བདེ།།

དང་པོ་གྲོས་རེ་ལེགས་ཤིག་བྱུང་།།
བར་དུ་སེ་རེ་བསོད་ཅིག་བྱུང་།།
ཐ་མ་སློ་རེ་བདེ་ཞིག་བྱུང་།།

བྱ་བ་བཏང་བས་ལམ་སྣ་ཟིན།།
ཅོག་གེ་བསྡད་པས་ལམ་ས་ཆོད།།
མགོ་བོ་གཏུམས་པས་རྒྱང་མིག་གསལ།།

Sometimes there is bliss in the sun and moon;
there is bliss in the state of unobscured clarity.

Sometimes there is bliss in the middle of a river;
there is bliss in the unceasing state.

Sometimes there is bliss in the presence of the guru;
there is bliss in the oral instructions for cutting proliferation.

Sometimes there is bliss residing in retreat;
there is bliss in practicing in solitude.

Sometimes there is bliss in the middle of the market;
there is bliss in carrying appearances into the path.

Sometimes there is bliss in a row of yogins;
there is bliss in comparing experiential realization.

Sometimes there is bliss in the midst of begging lepers;
there is bliss in performing the conduct of equal taste.

Sometimes there is bliss in the wide-open country;
there is bliss in wandering aimless and alone.
There is bliss when permanently abiding in reality;
there is bliss in the state without bias or partiality.

In the beginning, a good consultation arose;
in the middle, enjoyment arose;
finally, mental bliss arose.

By leaving activities, one is connected to the beginning of the path;
by relaxing, the paths and stages are reached;
by covering the head, the distance is clearly seen.

སེམས་ཅན་དམྱལ་བའི་གཡང་ས་ཡང་།།
འོག་མིན་ཆོས་ཀྱི་ཕོ་བྲང་ཡིན།།
ཚ་གྲང་གཉིས་ཀྱི་སྡུག་བསྔལ་ཡང་།།
སྤྲོས་དང་བྲལ་བའི་ཆོས་སྐུ་ཡིན།།

ཕྱི་པ་མུ་སྟེགས་གྲུབ་མཐའ་ཡང་།།
སྙིང་པོ་དོན་གྱི་དབུ་མ་ཡིན།།
བླ་མ་དམ་པའི་གདམས་ངག་ཀྱང་།།
སྒྱུ་མས་སྒྱུ་མ་བསླུ་བ་ཡིན།།

རང་གི་རྟོགས་པ་ཉམས་སྐྱོང་ཡང་།།
ཆུ་ལ་རི་མོ་བྲིས་པ་ཡིན།།
ལམ་ལྷ་ས་བཙུ་ཤར་བ་ཡང་།།
རི་བོང་རྭ་གཉེར་བགྲང་བ་བཞིན།།

ཕུན་སུམ་ཚོགས་པའི་སངས་རྒྱས་ཀྱང་།།
དོན་ལ་མེད་པའི་མིང་ཙམ་ཡིན།།
རིག་པས་གྲུབ་པའི་ཆོས་ཉིད་ཀྱང་།།
སྙིང་པོ་མེད་པའི་ཆུ་སྦོང་ཡིན།།

ཕྱུར་མེད་གནས་ལུགས་རྟོགས་པ་དང་།།
ངེས་ཤེས་མེད་པའི་ཁ་ལྷ་གཉིས།།
འདྲ་ནི་འདྲ་སྟེ་ནོར་དོགས་ཡོད།།

དབང་པོ་རྒྱ་ཡན་གདམས་ངག་དང་།།
ཚོགས་དྲུག་ཡན་པར་ཤོར་བ་གཉིས།།
འདྲ་ནི་འདྲ་སྟེ་ནོར་དོགས་ཡོད།།

ཞེན་ལོག་ཤུགས་ཀྱིས་བྱུང་བ་དང་།།
ཕྱོ་ཚེ་སྨྱོན་པའི་སྤྱོད་པ་གཉིས།།
འདྲ་ནི་འདྲ་སྟེ་ནོར་དོགས་ཡོད།།

རེ་དོགས་གཏིང་ནས་ཟད་པ་དང་།།
ཁོང་སྐྱན་ཅན་གྱི་འདོད་མེད་གཉིས།།
འདྲ་ནི་འདྲ་སྟེ་ནོར་དོགས་ཡོད།།

Even the deepest hell of sentient beings
is the Dharma palace of Akanishtha.
Even the suffering of both hot and cold [hells]
is the dharmakaya free from proliferation.

Even philosophical conclusions of non-Buddhists
are the essential meaning of Madhyamaka.
Even the oral instructions of the holy gurus
are illusions deceived by illusions.

Even one's own experience of realization
is a picture drawn on water.
Even the arising of the five paths and ten stages
is like counting the number of horns on a rabbit.

Even the accomplished Buddha
is just a name without ultimate existence.
Even dharmata established by awareness
is a banana tree without a heartwood.

Because the realization of reality without activities
and the verbal view without certain knowledge
resemble one another, there is a danger of error.

Because the oral instruction of relaxing the sense organs
and losing the six sense consciousnesses to distraction
resemble one another, there is a danger of error.

Because intensely produced renunciation
and the coarse behavior of a madman
resemble one another, there is a danger of error.

Because the complete exhaustion of hope and fear
and the aversion of one who has an inner grudge
resemble one another, there is a danger of error.

[Authorship Statement]

དགེ་བསྙེན་གྲགས་པ་རྒྱལ་མཚན་གྱིས།།
ཉམས་མྱོང་ཀླུ་ཙུ་གླངས་པ་ཡིན།།
མདོ་རྒྱུད་གཉིས་ལ་བརྟེན་པ་ཡིན།།
ཚིག་གི་སྦྱིབ་སྦྱོར་བྱས་པ་ཡིན།།
སྙན་ངག་རྒྱན་གྱིས་སྤྲས་པ་ཡིན།།
མཁས་པའི་ང་རྒྱལ་གཙོག་པ་ཡིན།།
དད་ཅན་སྤྲོ་བ་བསྐྱེད་པ་ཡིན།།
ཞེས་མགུར་དུ་གསུངས་པ་རྫོགས་སོ།།

Authorship Statement

The upasaka Dragpa Gyaltsen
sang this song of experience
in reliance upon both sutra and tantra,
the words composed in verse
and beautified by poetic ornamentation
to decrease the arrogance of scholars
and increase the enthusiasm of the faithful.
Thus, the teaching of the song is complete.

༄། །རྗེ་བཙུན་རིན་པོ་ཆེ་
གྲགས་པ་རྒྱལ་མཚན་གྱི་
བསྟོད་པ་བཞུགས་སོ།།

བླ་མ་དང་འཇམ་པའི་དབྱངས་ལ་གུས་པས་ཕྱག་འཚལ་ལོ།།

སྲིད་པའི་འཁྲི་ཤིང་དྲྭ་བ་དྲལ་མཛད་དེ།།
ཡོན་ཏན་རྒྱ་མཚོ་ཞི་ལམ་མཆོག་སྒྲོགས་པ།།
རྐང་གཉིས་དབང་པོ་ཉེ་བར་བརྙེས་པ་ཡི།།
གོ་འཕང་དམ་པ་ཐོབ་པར་མཛད་པ་རྒྱལ།།

བློ་གྲོས་དཔག་ཡས་ཆོག་གི་གཏེར་མངའ་བ།།
འགྲོ་བའི་བླ་མའི་ཞབས་ལ་ཕྱག་འཚལ་ནས།།

APPENDIX 2

Complete Translation of Sakya Pandita Kunga Gyaltsen's *Praise to Jetsun Rinpoche Dragpa Gyaltsen*

I pay homage with devotion to the guru and Manjughosha.

[To] the one who is free from the entangling vines of existence,
an ocean of qualities, the proclaimer of the supreme path of peace,
the victorious one who has obtained the sublime stage
that approaches the king of humans;

to the feet of the guru of migrating beings—
the master of a treasure of words with infinite wisdom—I prostrate.

ཆོས་རྗེ་དཔལ་ལྡན་ཆོས་ཀྱི་རྒྱ་མཚོ་ཡི།།
རྣམ་ཐར་མེ་ཏོག་གུས་པས་བརྒྱུ་བར་བྱ།།

ཁྱོད་ནི་སྦྱངས་པའི་ཤེས་བྱ་ལ།།
རྣམ་པར་མཁས་པ་ལྷུ་ཙི་སྨྲོས།།
ཡང་དག་ཚིག་འབྲུ་དོན་བཅས་གཞན།།
འཐད་བཅས་མཁྱེན་པ་ངོ་མཚར་ཆེ།།

གང་ཞིག་ཕུན་ཚོགས་མི་ཟད་མངའ།།
དེ་ལའང་འཇིག་རྟེན་སྤྱོད་མི་འཇུག།
དེ་གཅིག་ཁོ་ནར་མ་ཟད་དེ།།
སྲིད་ཁྲལ་ཁྱོད་ལ་ཕྱག་འཚལ་ལོ།།

ཁྱོད་ཀྱི་ཚིག་དོན་འདི་ལ་རྒྱུ།།
ཐ་དད་ཡོད་ཅེས་གང་གསུངས་པ།།
དེ་ལ་མཁས་པ་བྱེ་བས་ཀྱང་།།
ཆོས་དང་མཐུན་པར་བརྒལ་མི་ནུས།།

མནལ་ཚེ་ཆོས་རྣམས་གླེགས་བམ་གྱི།།
ཚལ་གྱི་ཁོང་དུ་ཚུད་གྱུར་པ།།
དེ་ཡི་མོད་ལ་ཆོས་ཀུན་གྱི།།
དེ་ཉིད་གཟིགས་པ་ཁྱོད་ལ་འདུད།།

ཡེ་ཤེས་སེམས་དཔའི་མཚན་བརྗོད་ལ།།
ཡང་སྲིད་རྣམ་པ་བདུན་དག་ཏུ།།
ལེགས་པར་སྦྱངས་པས་སྐྱེ་བ་འདིར།།
རང་བྱུང་ཉིད་དུ་མངོན་རྟོགས་གྱུར།།

དེ་ལ་རྟོག་གེ་བདག་འདྲ་ཡི།།
བློ་ཡང་ཐེ་ཚོམ་མི་འཇུག་སྟེ།།
གཏན་ཚིགས་བཟང་པོ་དང་ལྡན་པ།།
དེ་བས་ཁྱོད་ལ་བསྟོད་ཕྱག་འཚལ།།

And now, with devotion, I shall string together the flowers of the
hagiography
of the glorious lord of Dharma, an ocean of Dharma.

There is no need to mention your scholarship
in the subjects of knowledge.
The wisdom of your meaningful true words,
being validated by others, is amazing!

Homage to you,
one endowed with inexhaustible abundance,
who never engaged in worldly behavior,
and not only that, was free from affectations.

You are the one who said that in these words and meanings,
there are different reasons;
however, ten million scholars
were unable to find a contradiction according to the Dharma for that.

I bow to you, the one who properly comprehended
a volume of Dharma while sleeping,
and saw the nature of all phenomena
at the same time.

Having thoroughly learned
the *Manjushrinamasamgiti*
for seven lifetimes, in this life,
your realization arose automatically.

That realization prevented doubts from entering
into the minds of intellectuals like me.
Moreover, those with excellent reasoning
praise and pay homage to you.

གང་ཕྱིར་རྟོག་གེ་ལ་སྦྱངས་ཤིང་།།
སྒྲ་ལ་རྣམ་པར་མཁས་པས་ཀྱང་།།
ཁྱོད་ཀྱི་གསུང་ལ་སྐྱོན་འདི་ཞེས།།
ཆོས་བཞིན་བརྒལ་དུ་མ་མཆིས་པ།།

དེ་ཉིད་ཕྱིར་ན་ཁྱོད་ཀྱི་ཐུགས།།
རྣམ་པར་དག་པར་ཁོ་བོས་འཚལ།།
མཁས་པ་རྣམས་ཀྱིས་རྣམ་ཀུན་ཏུ།།
བསྔགས་པ་ཁྱོད་ལ་ཕྱག་འཚལ་ལོ།།

གཏིང་དཔག་དཀའ་བའི་ཆོས་ལ་ཡང་།།
ཁྱོད་ཀྱིས་འདི་ལས་མི་འདའ་ཞེས།།
ངེས་པར་གསུང་པ་དེ་ལས་གཞན།།
མདོ་སྡེ་རྣམས་ལས་དེ་བཞིན་འབྱུང་།།

དེ་འདྲ་ཁོ་ན་ལེགས་གསུངས་པས།།
ཁྱོད་གསུང་ཐུབ་པ་ཁོ་ན་འདྲ།།
བསྐལ་པའི་དོན་ཡང་ལེགས་གཟིགས་པས།།
དབང་ཕྱུར་ཁྱོད་ལ་ཕྱག་འཚལ་ལོ།།

ཡི་གེས་འདུལ་ལ་ཡི་གེ་དང་།།
རྩིས་པ་རྣམས་ལ་རྩིས་དང་ནི།།
འཚོ་བྱེད་རྣམས་ལ་འཚོ་བྱེད་གཞུང་།།
ཆོས་འདོད་རྣམས་ལ་ཆོས་ཀྱང་སྟོན།།

གང་གི་ཕན་དགོངས་ཐུགས་རྗེ་ཡིས།།
ཉེ་བར་ཕན་ལ་དེ་སྟོན་པ།།
སྟོན་མཆོག་ཁྱོད་འདྲ་མ་མཐོང་སྟེ།།
ཀུན་མཁྱེན་ཁྱོད་ལ་ཕྱག་འཚལ་ལོ།།

ཁྱོད་ཀྱི་ལེགས་བཤད་སེང་གེའི་སྒྲ།།
ལྷ་དང་གྲུབ་པར་རིག་འཛིན་གཙོ།།

Therefore, those who have trained in dialectics
and have become learned in grammar
could not find a contradiction according to the Dharma
nor point to any error in what you have said.

Therefore, I pay homage
to your pure mind,
and I prostrate to you,
the one who is praised by the learned in all ways.

You stated with certainty that
those Dharma teachings that are difficult to fathom
"Do not go beyond this"—
which is similarly mentioned in the sutras.

Since it was eloquently stated exactly like that,
your speech is the same as the Sage's.
Because you perfectly perceived what would benefit this *kalpa*,[47]
I pay homage to you, the powerful one.

You teach texts on grammar for those to be trained in grammar,
astrology for astrologers,
medicine for healers,
and also Dharma for those who are interested in Dharma.

Teaching what is beneficial,
with a compassionate motivation to benefit,
a supreme teacher like you has never been seen;
I pay homage to the omniscient one.

Your eloquent explanations are a lion's roar.
You are the chief of the vidyadharas of gods and siddhas,

47. *Kalpa* (Tib. *bskal pa*) is a unit of cosmological age, similar to "eon."

ཏྱོ་འཕྱེའི་དབང་པོས་ཉེར་བསྟེན་ཅིང་།།
རྒྱལ་བ་ཡིས་ཀྱང་མཐུན་པར་བསྔགས།།

དེ་སྐད་ཁྱོད་ཀྱི་རྣམ་ཐར་ལ།།
དད་པས་འཇུག་པ་སྨོས་ཅི་འཚལ།།
ཁྱམས་པ་དེ་དག་དགེ་དཔྱད་ན།།
ཀུན་ནས་དོན་ལྡན་ཁྱོད་ཕྱག་འཚལ།།

སྡོམ་བརྩོན་ཁྱོད་ནི་ཐོས་པ་དང་།།
དོན་ཡོད་མཐོང་ན་ཉམས་སུ་འཕེལ།།
བསྟེན་ན་དགེ་ལེགས་རིན་ཆེན་གཏེར།།
སྤྱོལ་མཛད་གཅིག་པུར་གྱུར་པ་ལགས།།

ཡོན་ཏན་མེད་ལ་སྒྲོ་བཏགས་ནས།།
སྐྱེ་བོ་ངན་རྣམས་ཡོན་ཏན་སྒྲོགས།།
ཡོན་ཏན་ཅན་ཁྱོད་མཁས་རྣམས་ཀྱིས།།
ཡོན་ཏན་བསྒྲགས་པ་ཁྱོད་ལ་འདུད།།

མང་དུ་ཐོས་པས་བློ་གསལ་བ།།
གྲགས་ལྡན་སྡོམ་བརྩོན་དབང་རྣམས་ཀྱི།།
བློ་གྲོས་མཐོང་བས་ཁྱོད་ལ་སྨར།།
དད་པའི་མེ་ཏོག་རྒྱས་པར་འགྱུར།།

ཇི་བཞིན་གཟིགས་པས་ཐུགས་དག་པ།།
བློ་མཆོག་ཁྱོད་ལ་ཕྱག་འཚལ་ལོ།།
འགྲོ་རྣམས་ཐུགས་རྗེས་མི་གཏོང་བ།།
བརྩེ་ཆེན་ཁྱོད་ལ་སྐྱབས་སུ་མཆི།།

ཇི་ལྟར་འབད་ཀྱང་ཁྱོད་ཀྱི་དྲིན།།
ལན་པར་འགྱུར་སྙམ་མི་བགྱིད་དེ།།
གང་གིས་ཁྱོད་དྲིན་འདི་འདྲ་ཞེས།།
རྣམ་ཐར་བསམས་ན་མཆི་མ་དཀྲུ།།

attended by powerful nagas
and similarly praised by the Victor.

Therefore, what need is there to mention
when faith arises in your hagiography?
Homage to you, meaningful one in all aspects
when what is to be comprehended has been well examined.

Diligent in discipline and learned;
when you saw the meaning, your experience increased.
When relied upon, you alone bestow
a precious treasure of virtue.

Ignorant people praise the qualities
of those lacking good qualities,
but the learned ones proclaim your qualities.
I bow to you, the one endowed with qualities.

Having seen your wisdom,
the faith of famous scholars endowed with ethical conduct,
mental clarity, and extensive learning
blossoms once again.

Your mind is pure, seeing things just as they are.
I pay homage to you, the one with supreme wisdom.
With compassion that does not leave migrating beings behind,
I go for refuge to you, the one with great kindness.

Any effort made to repay
your kindness is insufficient.
Whoever reflects on your kindness
in the hagiography will shed tears.

བཀྲལ་བར་འོས་མིན་ནོངས་མི་མངའ།།
དྲི་མ་མེད་ལ་འཐད་པ་ཅན།།
རྣམ་པར་དག་ལ་མཚན་བཟང་བ།།
ཁྱོད་ལ་གང་གིས་ལན་ཡོན་འགྱུར།།
འབྲེལ་པའི་སྒོ་ནས་མི་བསྟོད་དོ།།
བཀའ་དྲིན་སྒོ་ནས་ཅིས་མ་བསྟོད།།
གལ་ཏེ་ཕྱོགས་སུ་ལྷུང་ཉིད་ན།།
བསྟོད་པར་གྱུར་ཀྱང་སྨད་པའི་གནས།།

དུ་བས་མེ་བཞིན་རྣམ་ཐར་ལས།།
ནང་གི་ཡོན་ཏན་ལེགས་བརྟགས་ཏེ།།
གྲགས་པ་རྒྱལ་མཚན་ལ་བསྟོད་པ།།
འདི་འདྲ་ཁོ་ནས་བསྟོད་ལགས་གྲང་།།

དད་པའི་སྒོ་ནས་རྟབས་ཚུལ་གྱིས།།
ཚིག་གི་སྤེལ་སྦྱོར་བཏང་སྙོམས་གྱུར།།
ཚིག་ལ་དགྱེས་པའི་མཁས་རྣམས་དང་།།
ཚིག་གི་མངའ་བདག་བཟོད་པར་གསོལ།།

བདག་ཉིད་ཆེན་པོ་བློ་གྲོས་རྒྱ་མཚོ་ཡི།།
ཡོན་ཏན་མེ་ཏོག་གུས་པས་སྤེལ་བ་ལས།།
བསོད་ནམས་གྲུབ་པ་གང་ཡིན་དེ་ཡིས་བདག།
སྲིད་གསུམ་བླ་མའི་གོ་འཕང་ཐོབ་པར་ཤོག།

དེ་ལྟར་བསྟོད་འདི་དཔལ་ལྡན་ཀུན་དགའ་ཡི།།
རྒྱལ་མཚན་གྱིས་སྤེལ་འདི་ལ་གང་དགྱེས་པ།།
བློ་གསལ་དེ་ལ་བླ་མའི་ཐུགས་རྗེ་ཡི།།
ཡེ་ཤེས་གཟིགས་པའི་བྱིན་རླབས་འཇུག་པར་གྱུར།།

འཕགས་པ་འཇམ་པའི་དབྱངས་ཀྱི་ཞབས་ཀྱི་ཟེའུ་འབྲུ་ལ་སྤྱི་བོས་རེག་པས་ཤེས་བྱའི་དཀྱིལ་འཁོར་ལ་མངའ་བརྙེས་ཤིང་། གདུང་རྒྱུད་རྣམ་པར་དག་པའི་དགེ་བསྙེན་གྲགས་པ་རྒྱལ་མཚན་ལ་བསྟོད་པ་བཟང་སྤྲོད་པ། ཀུན་དགའ་རྒྱལ་མཚན་གྱིས་སྦྱར་བ་རེ་ཞིག་རྫོགས་སོ།།།

Without violations, possessing no fault,
immaculate, reasonable,
pure, and with excellent signs,
who can question you?
I am praising [Jetsun Dragpa Gyalsten] neither because we are related
nor because of his kindness;
if there is bias,
even praising can become degrading.

Like inferring fire from smoke,
this praise to Dragpa Gyaltsen
is praise composed solely by
investigating the inner qualities found in his hagiography.

As this was rendered hurriedly with faith
and ignoring elements of proper composition,
I beseech scholars who enjoy words
and the masters of words to be patient.

Whatever merit is accomplished
from spreading the qualities
of the ocean of the great being's wisdom with the flowers of devotion,
may I attain the stage of the guru of the three realms.

May the blessings of the guru's compassionately
gnostic vision enter those intelligent ones
who rejoice in promulgating this praise
by Palden Kunga Gyaltsen.

This praise to Upasaka Dragpa Gyaltsen—one from the pure family lineage, who realized the wisdom of all subjects of knowledge and touched the anthers of the feet of Arya Manjushri with his crown—composed by linguist Kunga Gyaltsen, is complete.

Index

L

M

W

About the Author

Khenpo Migmar Tseten has served as Buddhist chaplain at Harvard University since 1997. He received both a traditional and a contemporary education in India, graduating with an *acharya* degree from the Central Institute of Higher Tibetan Studies at Sanskrit University in Varanasi. His Holiness the Dalai Lama awarded him medals for achieving first positions consecutively every nine years among his class of students from the Nyingma, Sakya, Kagyu, and Geluk schools, and His Holiness the Sakya Trichen awarded him with the title of *khenpo*. He served as the head of the Sakya Center in Rajpur, India, and the Sakya Monastery in Puruwalla. Khenpo Migmar has supervised the editing and publication of more than fifty rare volumes of Sakya literature and is the author of many books, including *The Play of Mahamudra*. Since 1989, Khenpo has regularly led many group and solitary retreats, including weekend ngöndro practices, the three-month Vajrapani Bhutadamara practice, and three-year Hevajra Lamdre retreats at the 160-acre Sakya Choekhor Yangtse Retreat Center in Barre, Massachusetts until its closing. As a faculty member of the internationally renowned yoga center of Kripalu in the Berkshires, Massachusetts, Khenpo led retreats and workshops on Buddhist yantra and different yogas, including lucid dream yoga, for many years. Since 2020, Khenpo has led several one-year retreats of Chakrasamvara from the three traditions of Ghantapada, Krishnapada, and Luipada, and several one-year Vajrayogini retreats for accumulating the *drubum* (100,000 repetitions per syllable) of Vajrayogini's mantra at the Sakya Institute for Buddhist Studies in Cambridge, Massachusetts. Learn more at lamamigmar.net.

About the Author

What to Read Next from Wisdom Publications

Reality and Wisdom
Exploring the Buddha's Four Noble Truths and the Heart Sutra
Lama Migmar

"In *Reality and Wisdom*, Khenpo Migmar Tseten explains important sutras clearly for students who wish to understand them more deeply. Careful study and practice of these important teachings will bring great blessings in one's daily life and Dharma practice."
—His Holiness the Sakya Trichen

The Play of Mahamudra
Spontaneous Teachings on Virupa's Mystical Songs
Lama Migmar Tseten

"This new collected edition of Khenpo Migmar Tseten's *Play of Mahamudra* volumes constitutes a veritable treasure for all who are deeply engaged on the path to enlightenment. Khenpo Migmar's translation of Mahasiddha Virupa's *Treasury of Dohas* and of Sachen Kunga Nyingpo's *Praise to Virupa* makes us intimately familiar with the essence of these root texts, and his elucidation of the *Dohas* offers us a deep and clear understanding of their core meaning. Anyone who truly contemplates on Mahasiddha Virupa's words is certain to attain realization."
—His Holiness the Sakya Trichen

Luminous Melodies
Essential Dohās of Indian Mahāmudrā
Karl Brunnhölzl

"These beautiful songs of experience offer glimpses into the awakened minds of the Mahāmudrā masters of India. Karl Brunnhölzl's masterful translations are a joy to read for how they express what is so often inexpressible."
—His Eminence the Twelfth Zurmang Gharwang Rinpoche

Sounds of Innate Freedom
The Indian Texts of Mahamudra
Karl Brunnhölzl

"With these vivid renditions of the songs of the Indian mahasiddhas, Karl Brunnhölzl brilliantly launches what is certain to be one of the great Buddhist scholarly projects of our time: a complete six-volume English translation of the Indian works foundational to the theory and practice of mahamudra, the great sealing of the nature of mind, which is one of the most significant and widespread of all Tibetan meditation systems. These volumes—which will be a landmark in our quest to comprehend Indian tantric Buddhism and the Tibetan great-seal practice—are sure to captivate scholars and practitioners alike."
—Roger R. Jackson, author of *Mind Seeing Mind: Mahamudra and the Geluk Tradition of Tibetan Buddhism*

Wisdom

About Wisdom Publications

Wisdom Publications is the leading publisher of classic and contemporary Buddhist books and practical works on mindfulness. To learn more about us or to explore our other books, please visit our website at wisdomexperience.org or contact us at the address below.

Wisdom Publications
132 Perry Street
New York, NY 10014 USA

We are a 501(c)(3) organization, and donations in support of our mission are tax deductible.

Wisdom Publications is affiliated with the Foundation for the Preservation of the Mahayana Tradition (FPMT).